Tide *and*
Continuities

Tide and *Continuities*

LAST AND FIRST POEMS
1995–1938

Peter Viereck

THE UNIVERSITY OF ARKANSAS PRESS
Fayetteville 1995

99   98   97   96   95   5   4   3   2   1

Designed by Gail Carter

⊖ The paper used in this publication meets the minimum
requirements of the American National Standard for Perma-
nence of Paper for Printed Library Materials Z39.48-1984.

Library of Congress Cataloging-in-Publication Data

Viereck, Peter Robert Edwin, 1916–
    Tide and continuities : last and first poems, 1995–1938 /
Peter Viereck.
        p.   cm.
    Includes bibliographical references.
    ISBN 1-55728-313-3 (alk. paper). —
    ISBN 1-55728-314-1 (pbk. alk. paper)
    I. Title.
PS3543.I325T53   1995   95-6773
811'.54—dc20   CIP

All's flux? Yet continuities! Ring by ring
Through generations, through all-too-human wrong,
Continuities are the human way of flowering.
They're linking the cycles; they're consecrating
The beads of pair we string on strands of pang.
Short is our circle but the spiral long.

—from "Antistrophe to 'The Planted Poet,'" p. 187

Acknowledgments

Unrevised magazine versions of these poems appeared in the following periodicals: *Agni, American Letters* (Charleston, South Carolina), *American Poetry Review, The Atlantic Monthly, Bostonia, Botteghe Oscure* (Rome, Italy), *Boulevard, Chimera, Confrontation, Cronos, Decade* (anthology chosen by *New Letters* magazine), *Essays in Criticism* (Oxford University, England), *Hamden-Sydney Poetry Review, Harpers, Harvard Advocate, Hopkins Review, Horizon* (London, England), *Humanitas, International Quarterly, Literary Review, Michigan Quarterly Review, The Nation, Negative Capability, New Letters, New Mexico Quarterly Review, The New Republic, The New Yorker, New York Times Op/Ed, Parnassus, Partisan Review, Ploughshares, Poetry, Poetry Now, Prairie Schooner, Salmagundi, Shenandoah, Tomorrow, University of Kansas City Review, Webster Review.*

Here are some of the institutions as well as individuals to whom I owe thanks for making this book possible.

INSTITUTIONS: Mt. Holyoke College, American Academy in Rome, MacDowell Colony, Virginia Center for the Creative Arts, Millay Colony for the Arts. Prize awards from poetry contests, notably those of the New England Poetry Club. The generosity of the publishers W. W. Norton, New York: for letting me reprint (here often in greatly revised form) several poems from my earlier book, *Archer in the Marrow: The Applewood Cycles,* 1987, a companion volume to *Tide and Continuities.* Greenwood Press of Westport, Connecticut: for reprinting my out-of-print Scribner books (selections included here), the Pulitzer-Prize–winning *Terror and Decorum; Strike through the Mask; The First Morning;* and *The Tree Witch.* University Microfilms International of Ann Arbor, Michigan: for reprinting in hard copy as well as microfilm my out-of-print Bobbs-Merrill book of 1967, *New and Selected Poems,* and my out-of-print Scribner book of 1956, *The Persimmon Tree.* Library of Congress: for recording my 1992 readings from this book and for making the tapes available to the public.

INDIVIDUALS. Debbie Bowen Self and Miller Williams of the University of Arkansas Press, my editor and publisher respectively, the latter a first-rate poet in his own right. My agent and literary executor, Thomas D'Evelyn: for wise advice and encouragement. Betty Falkenberg: for her intelligent criticisms. Cynthia Morrell: for ingenuity and patience in getting the manuscript onto the required computer disk. Rita Weill Byxbe, the author and musician: for ably helping re-organize some of the longer poems. Julia Older, likewise a first-rate poet: for perceptive suggestions and for my use of her "let" concept.

Thanks to Prof. Jack Beeson of the Columbia University Music Department for setting many of this volume's poems so gracefully to music—too many to list here. Each has been published as a pamphlet by the New York firm of Boosey and Hawkes, from whom they may be obtained. Thanks to Prof. Bruce Trinkley of Penn. State College for setting six other poems of mine to music and for having them performed as choral dances by the State College orchestra and choir, 1992.

Contents

PART I

Mostly Hospital and Old Age

(New Long Poems, Mostly 1990–1995)

PART II

Ore

(Shorter Poems, Both New and Old)

Section One

PART III
The Planted Poet
(Old Long Poems, 1944–1966)

PART VI
Tide and Completions

Foreword

to Peter Viereck's Tide and Continuities: Last and First Poems

An introduction to a book
of poetry must have a look
of poetry. I thought a lyric
befits this work by Peter Viereck,
perhaps the greatest rhymer of
the modern period, a prof
of history at Mount Holyoke College,
famed for its feminists and foliage.

He's in his seventies. He saw
more of humanity's seesaw
than you who will peruse these pages,
heart-rending, gorgeous, outrageous,
thus spanning roughly five decades
—the Nazis, the Cold War, and AIDS,
the ogres turning mediogres—
such is the nature of our progress.

Quite full of morsels and of grits
as well as of old favorites,
this is his new "New and Selected"
(now out of print). And to neglect it
is to neglect that feast of rhyme
in which the upper hand of time
is forced, amid the paper rustle,
down by your mother tongue's strong muscle.

Detachment and serenity
are not this old man's cup of tea.
Past seventy, his blood runs quicker
on vehemence—this timely liquor
from which he plainly won't abstain:
his poems are returning pain
to life with interest: two gallons
of vehemence may boost your balance.

Thick and ubiquitous like grass,
sharp as a scalpel, piercing as
a syringe, Viereck's verses gorge on
his very flesh: he's his own surgeon,
his own malaise, his own morphine;
he's prone to lose himself to win
himself by couplets, plainly driven
by joy and terror breaking even.

For all this passage and its rites,
his hand stops trembling when it writes,
his heart craves that iambic measure
which makes its agony a pleasure.
The job of art is to outsmart
mortality. And Viereck's art
is therapeutic. But apart from
the cure, it is a brand new art form.

For all his talk of going bust
I've seldom read lines so robust
as his on "Hospital." Their shrillness
is both a metaphor for illness
and cure. Both desperate and brash
his verse would make his bedpan blush,
for tests might show his sense of humor
grown here into the sense of tumor.

Unlike the bulk of current stuff,
rough-hewn, minimalist, and tough,
this book, left to its own devices,
is an *hommage* to Dionysus:
it is a growth. In its design,
by turns malignant and benign,
it tends to leap, digress, meander;
in short, its target is its grandeur.

A dendrophil whose similes
burst with the images of trees
(due not to those that shade his college,
but echoing the tree of knowledge,

whose apple he consumed in spite
of finding that it had inside
a worm that bores through every segment,
but took it for a shrunken serpent).

He is a solitary tree
himself, both immobile and free
to ponder what's above and rake it
with naked branches and the naked
eye; he essentially is
finality that clearly sees
infinity: his own comeuppance.
He's presence that observes his absence.

It is indeed a monument
to an intelligence hellbent
on ruling not just undergrads
by pulling habits out of rats
of history and all its odds,
but on conversing with the gods
on matters abstract and empiric,
though in the company of Viereck,
so grand on questions and retorts,
the gods may feel quite lost for words.

Joseph Brodsky
May 1993

Preface

All is rhythm.

　　—Hölderlin

This book (my last because of age and illness) is really two manuscripts. Both are so overlapping, so cross-referenced, that they belong in the same book.

Manuscript one is here called "Part I," the newest and also the longest part. It contains the long poems of 1987–1995, mostly begun in hospitals in my seventies. Their theme: old age and its coming to terms with the archetypal trio: Persephone, Dionysus, Pluto (here the farmer's daughter, the traveling salesman, the basement janitor).

Manuscript two is Parts II, III, IV, and V. These four middle parts are my lifetime's selected poems (1933–95) and mostly short. An earlier *New and Selected Poems* did appear in 1967, some three decades ago. It is not only out of print (except as "micro" reprint with University Microfilms of Ann Arbor, Michigan); it is also outdated, the majority of my present selected poems having been written later. Many are revised excerpts from my seven previous poetry books, as listed in the bibliography.

The concluding Part VI, called "Tide and Completions," 1992–95, has three long poems that unify the diverse threads of new manuscript one and old manuscript two. The occasional repetition of certain leitmotif phrases is serving this unifying function. Often the "I" in the newer poems is not me but a goofy dying Everyman, trying to ululate past doc and nurse.

To date every item would be pedantry. But dates of basic completion (not start) follow the very latest poems and the very earliest: because of the changes of style and subject.

· · ·

As an argument for free verse, critics correctly point out that English, an uninflected language, has relatively few rhymes.[1] I'd go even further and say: today masculine rhyme (one syllable) seems almost as exhausted as love-dove (except for conscious contrast or as unfalse *faux-naïf*). The solution is not abandoned rhyme but new kinds of rhyme. My later poetry keeps using newly coined feminine rhymes (two syllables) whenever the ear needs their sub-surface resonance: tortoise, rigor mortis, aortas in "Dionysus." Not rhyme for its own sake, of course, (mechanic formalism) but to link the unlinkable, to build living bridges of mood, meaning, sound. Obsessive rhyme plus mood-compelling meter: not as formal ornament but as orchestration of form.

For masculine rhymes, my later work inclines toward those of Wilfrid Owen: slant rhymes, consonance with alliteration, "Celtic consonance": gauze, gaze, cargoes, etc., in "Hospital Window." Also my own eccentric invention of "crisscross" (as defined on page 124).

More basic than mere technique ("Dost thou think because thou art virtuoso," to misquote Sir Toby, "there shall be no more cakes and ale?") is a good ear: an ear eavesdropping on the biology of poetry, the body language of Duke Ellington's "It don't mean a thing / If it ain't got that swing." Imagine you're drowning. The water swallows you. Suddenly an arm tugs you to shore. A lifeguard revives your heart and your lungs, breathing into your mouth once for every five heart massages, as he or she has been taught. Five ta-TUMs per line of breath. Your life has just been saved by an old "outdated" iambic pentameter. How Elizabethan of nature! Both life and poetry depend on such body rhythms. Would you trust your life to a free-verse lifeguard?

Until recently, I considered the formless variety of free verse the main danger to American poetry. After all, the literary revolt of 1912 had ossified into a new Academy, a once refreshing nonconformity that became a stodgy new one. In Frost's familiar words: "tennis without the net." Such was the theme of my 1979 essay (in the magazine *Critical Inquiry*) "Strict Form in Poetry: Would Jacob Wrestle with a Flabby Angel?" The essay grew into the prose appendix of my 1987 poetry book, *Archer in the Marrow* (Norton, New York).

Subsequent developments have evolved an equal menace to creativity in much (not all) of the new formalism. The menace occurs when form's living metronome of walking, breathing, feeling is replaced by a dead mechanical metronome—call it the net without the tennis. Result: instead of full-throated song, a bloodless correctness, a thin-lipped disapproval. The new formalism does what all guilds, all academies do: takes the passion out of art and substitutes rules. What true form does is take the frigidity out of traditional rules and substitute passion, passion inside the rules and re-animating them. Why is it today urgent to say something so seemingly obvious? The cult of how-to manuals? The replacement of art by technique? Most free verse (not all) is the artlessness that conceals artlessness. Most neoformalism (not all) is tame finger exercise. True metric form, being Time in leotards, is strict wildness.

Form, yes; formalism, no. Political reactionairies discredit an ethical conservatism by provoking the revolution they seek to prevent. Analogously, neoformalism will provoke (I give it ten years) a pendulum swing back to (alas) the most formless of free verse.

• • •

Re this book's title: the great throbs of "tide"—lives, seasons, the swell of clay—are spiraling through fixed "continuities." So are the human-scale sub-continuities of our conserving core (otherwise "no foundation all along the line"). Yet these indispensable value-codes must be outrageously counter-balanced (lest decent rigor become rigor mortis) by human messiness, rash exploration, ornery skepticism, "gypsy laughter in the bushes," the wise clowning of caprice. Thereby the conserving core, ever enduring yet ever shifting its center, is ever taking away conservatism from the "conservatives"— and is often better conserved under anticonservative labels. Here a good ear (in this case for the rhythms of history) plays the same key role as in poetry.

Inhuman abstract isms (the nobler, the worse) violate human-scale rhythms; we've seen—in history, in literature—what happens when Procrustes is bedding either Clio or Melpomene. Both muses prefer Antæus. Few statesmen and few writers know the roles they actually play. Sometimes opposites need each other to fulfill—unwittingly—a third role.

L'esprit d'escalier: after a lifetime alternating between poetry books and books of history, have I at seventy-nine any departing comment on both disciplines? Yes, and with words not my own. Vachel Lindsay: "Courage and sleep are the principal things." Ralph Ellison: "Humanity is won by continuing to play in the face of certain defeat." And (as isms become wasms) William Morris: "Men fight and lose the battle, and the thing they fought for comes about in spite of their defeat; and when it comes, turns out to be not what they meant; and other men have to fight for what they meant under another name."

P. V.

(1995)

NOTE

1. Italian, for example, has only one-eighth the number of distinct vowel sounds that English does, making eight times as many masculine rhymes possible. Far more than eight times is the number of feminine rhymes possible in inflected languages, like Italian, German, Spanish, Russian, because of so many more two-syllable endings.

Mostly Hospital and Old Age

(new long poems, mostly 1990–1995)

(Dionysus is) a drive towards unity, reaching beyond person-
ality, the quotidian, society, reality, across the chasm of transi-
toriness: an impassioned and painful overflowing into a darker,
fuller, more buoyant state: an ecstatic affirmation of the totality
of life as what remains constant—not less potent, not less
ecstatic—throughout all fluctuation: . . . the eternal will for
regeneration, fruitfulness, recurrence; the awareness that
creation and destruction are inseparable.

—notebook jotting by Nietzsche,
1888, just before going mad

At the spread-eagled arch of my gateways,
The millennia curtsy and pass.
I glaze old treadmill-relays
With my inexhaustible grass.

—Persephone in "Goat Ode in Mid-Dive," p. 45

At My Hospital Window
(for Joseph Brodsky)

This poem first appeared in the magazine *New Letters,* Awards issue, spring 1991, vol. 57, #2, and in the anthology *Life on the Line,* 1992, published by Negative Capability Press, Mobile, Alabama.

> *Sick people . . . need a literature of their own. . . . A critical illness is one of our momentous experiences; yet I haven't seen a single nonfiction book that does it justice.*
>
> —Anatole Broyard, *New York Times Books,* April 1, 1990

> *The sublime as the artistic conquest of the horrible.*
>
> —Nietzsche

Part One	Part Two
1. Sacred Wood	7. Sacred Code
2. Sacroiliac	8. Unsacrosanct
3. Sacre de Printemps	9. Safe Inland
4. Sacrilege	10. Sacerdotal
5. Sanctuary	11. Sacrament
6. Sacred Ode	

Part One

1. *Sacred Wood*
Land of shy kindnesses and embarrassing stains.
Land of appraising stares and starched white stance.
Like cameras that reverse their glance
To photograph their cameraman's
Own face, own disgrace,
These thousand hungry hospital windows graze
On us as if our nerves were grass.
Hospital; flesh-eater; sarco-phagus.
Here the Boojum Snark of the childhood to which we regress
Is the Conqueror Germ. Its hunters, face muffled with gauze,
Are the surgeons. You'd never guess
They're really white blood cells in surgeon-white togas.
With gaze of Argus,
These phagocyte cops—in their bogus

Biped disguise—
Are gumshoeing after our cargoes
Of germ in blood's archipelagoes.
As sunlessly pale as a fungus,
We breathe the air-conditioned poison gas
Of progress. In such Freudian vertigoes,
Disinfectants are stern superegos.
     And our ids? They're the rats, down where the garbage goes.

              •   •   •

Land—no, cocoon—where butterflies unhinge
(Regressing into caterpillars) wings.
Land of droll metaphors: doc says of gut,
"You've got a garden hose I've got to cut."
Snip snip—he solves me like a Gordian knot.
When he claims I look young, is gut's inmost decay
My Picture of Dorian Grey?
Come praise—more than "the dignity of man"—
The faced indignity; go clear-eyed down.
When even charm and status face the deadpan
Smirk of the bedpan, indignity
Is the great leveler.
Outside our lair,
That surreal clown, Mr. Reality,
Taunts "loss"—the word's my leitmotif today.
I've seen lost beauty; the patina went away
Not altogether.
I've seen lost awe; the wonder went astray
Not too far to regather.
In the sacred wood of losers, still some tatter
Of loved-enough loss must stay.
"All's illusion"—still some there is really there.
. . . And yet what's there, no matter what its form,
Crashes. "So be it." Share
Leftovers; dregs matter, ashes
     Warm.

2. *Sacroiliac*
Must we blubber at death (what a dowdy gaffe)
Or counterclown instead?
Uneasy (it only hurts when we laugh)

4   MOSTLY HOSPITAL AND OLD AGE   •   PART I

Lies the clown that wears a head.
All patients have jitters—O isn't that why
Our cocktails are bitters, our whiskey is wry?
"O.R." (I looked it up) means "owner's risk" and/or
"Operation room": court of last appeal
("Doc, what odds I'll live till April?")
When odds appal.
Hospital: a nation. Where the buildings inhabit the people.
Where tender-loving-Medi-care reigns papal.
Where, when I sleep, my nurse-spy-pal
Wakes me to give me my sleeping pill.
Hospital: a campus the fund raisers propel.
Where Pain is dean in regal purple
And Angst his flunky prof and I their flunking pupil.
I complain? Yet I scorn—all the more when the lines are mine—
    Confessional verse's professional moan.

       · · ·

Enough fluff. Only elementals hone
Simultaneously brow and sacroiliac zone.
Elementals hurl the elements;
Flesh is the beach their hone-waves drench
With sea's—with bloodstream's—undulance.
Waves and moonrays, back and forth.
Rays work waves as tongue works tooth.
Armor for continuities:
Rays as frail as gold-thread gowns,
Stored in old trunks for granddaughters by crones:
Stored powers, veiled as frailties.
Far voice (seeping through from worlds more unreal, more true):
"Don't tease elementals—nobody paws
Buzzsaws. Tide can't be shushed."
Oh yes it can: my tideproof window-screen
As earplug. Here I'm stashed
Soundproof inside when the hone-waves pound.
Sick, safely sick, in walls a gut-length thick
And fever-tall, by anesthesias guarded,
I'd "bet my life" (a harmless cliché I don't really mean)
That I'll never again hear tide.
    Far voice: "Bet recorded."

3. *Sacre de Printemps*
Just once
To be one with the dew on the leaf, with the sun's
Autograph on the dew.
—No! Too "nature" simper. Too
Poesie. Outside my window's
Real-world prose,
What arsenic-colored plague resumes its tour,
What verdant saboteur?
The blithe metastasis of May
Is spreading the recidivist gangrene
Called "spring," its tumors flowering.
Their sweet pus lures, they bud and preen;
Wing'd pimps reel round the brew.
Bees poke each flower, as they're gened to do.
But bees can't hump my sickroom's rose bouquet
(Its chastity belt is the window screen)
Sent by true friends too Important to come.
I'm a vase for a poppy of rosier bloom,
My blood its sap, my meat its loam.
A shot of morphine its opium,
     Its garden the surgery room.

4. *Sacrilege*
Above the border that's the neck's,
Senility stages less bloody a bout:
An optic test. *Fiat lux* or *fiat nox?*
My eye scans fadeless CAT-scans of my eye;
Says fader to fadeless, "Do I flunk or sneak by?"
Says metal to jelly, "Prognosis: lights out.
Cataracts gone amok."
Comes nurse; one hand holds my water mug,
The other a vacuum cleaner *de luxe*
To vacuum the mess on my rug
From the "previous tenant," now cinders in morgue;
Fiat Electrolux.
Nurse—water—to toast my friend who got toasted. No, stop!
Those dentures he'd lost and got furnaced without,
They're bobbing—stop pouring—like crabs down and up

(Clack clack) in the water jug.
At once I recognize Grim Jack
The Reaper's style of joke,
Half merry jig, half crying jag,
With *humeur noire* his pet gag.
Straight down like the sun at the equinox,
His scythe gleams overhead. My neck's
Already feeling the first teasing nicks.
"Judge Reaper," I shout, "when your gavel knocks,
Why is your verdict on plea bargains 'nix'?
From hospitals to hospices, Old Nick's
Scythe connects.
Yet gentle sorceries—found in no almanacs,
Rhyme's whispering web, mild garden nooks,
The on-target quip, the just gibe, the human-scale knacks,
Shapeliness (in thought or in carved onyx)—
Defuse your nukes.
I've hide-and-seek burrows you'll never annex,
A poise that no longer panics."
—"Your exorcist-spells of slant-rhyme knickknacks
Are duds," death cackles. "To hide from my *nox*
(Since Thanatos' mother is night-goddess Nyx)
Is SACRILEGE. Here I come. Ready or—
Not."
I need help quick—I invoke on the spot
My anti-death "her":
"You life-core of ocean, creatrix long hidden,
Half soother of storm, half stormy harridan,
    Don't let your clown-priest down."

5. *Sanctuary*
Enter (what price sanctuary?) a new kind of showdown.
Invoking my her, I've unleashed from history's den
Surf's very first hone-hug of dune.
Just when I'd fled from tragedy into farce
(And wanted to bask there like fops in cafés)
What's this unwanted tidal fuss?
Though I fear it, I trust her; I can't refuse;
Elementals return and claim their sacrifice.

She's all the world's seas, I'm suddenly all the world's surface.
Out of control; my lines not mine; all's cleft *or* cliff, her fierce
Full emptiness *or* peninsula's counterforce.
Revise that; not "or" but "and"; in my new cycle's phase,
Her seas *and* my shores—O nothing less—suffice.
Polarities: sparring face to face
Without bodies—till lusts fuse foes.
Are we pipe dreams of opposite fictions, embodied only as pairs?
Ta-TUM-ing—into existence—each other, my iambs and hers?
Whole continents, pounded by seesawing pistons,
Their mist—in the distance—a fading oasis,
Are crumbling between us. Only the spray's
Shapeliness stays.
Strength isn't hard lone rocks that surf erases
But fragile intertwining laces,
These sand-probed bays, these salt-probed beaches:
Both reshaped by what they're shaping,
Each the player and the plaything,
Neither wholly sea or land.
Fleshed mutualness, each reached by what it reaches,
Shares Holy Land.
These my shards and these my riches
    Till the third Fate's fatal shears.

6. *Sacred Ode*
Right now as I talk, are her seas, are my shores
Straitjackets we burst when we sleepwalk?
Straitjackets? The hospital really a looney
Bin for the love-curs'd?
We inmates acting out hang-ups as "therapy theater"?
Asleep, let's escape—let's clamber toward Luna—
Let's eke real-life theater from farce
By love's sheer force.
Done! Like champagne corks our souls pop up with a fizz.
Safe till we wake into prose, right now do we teeter
On tightropes of moon-pull as if they were stairs?
No! No to such a romantical saga.
Once more my fantasies totter
Toward poesie-mush unawares.

And I must resist. Neither godly nor gaga,
We lovers, we seas and shores,
We're down-to-earth matter, true poetry's meter:
The resonance of my odes, the undulance of her doze,
Oneness from twos.
Ashamed—O they cloy—of woe-is-me hospital blues,
I'm starting an ode of stark joy
To her whose cavernous darkness lights my dark:
"Life-code of surf-sob, hear your landlocked landfish;
Will you shield me from the Reaper till I finish?"
    Sea's voice (or is it my echo?) answers, "Finish!"

                 • • •

And when my ode ripens, when my reap-time is due,
What then?
Then it's you, you-my-her, I'll be reaped back into.
Beached mapless from sea lap and panting for water,
I'll then be scythed home to the foam
Your famous giddy daughter blossomed from.
Sea older than Venus, you grandma of algae,
You globe's first fecundity:
Midwifed by silver
Forceps of Luna.[1]
Then I, a twitch of that primal shiver,
Will join all your flotsam, all bobbing in chorus,
My ode your metronome's sonorous quiver.
(Wheel of Fortuna, spin slow till I end my rhyme.)
Then I'll "step twice in the same river,"
Ebbing my time-wheel backward in time
From my lungfish-ancestor's beachhead to birth's first arena.
    Then, vulva of Unda Marina, sway me the tide of the dead.

Part Two

7. *Sacred Code*
All my life is a search: to hear—to decipher—her source.
I track her Morse through the inland lurch
Of sea in seed's underground bells.
"Depth" and "death" sound alike; how infer
Which undertow counter-tracks me from afar?

(Near is the morgue's crematorium-belch, getting rid
Of its diet in hiccups of red.)
No message emergent; I've eavesdropped in vain
On the musical migraine of shells,
Gull's cryptic cacophony, salmon's steep road
To *Liebestod.*—Suddenly
I hear her. I hear her far breakers, resurgent
(Or is it the morgue belching nearer?).
She's throbbing throb-throbbing a message most urgent
    In a code I cannot read.

8. *Unsacrosanct*

Can Abstract set up shop behind shingles
Announcing, "I'm really concrete"?
Can ideas dance on physical sandals
With metaphysical feet?
Though your seas pulse a touchable sonance,
They can be deconstructed by savants
As tropes my need carved from air.
Though waves tinkle cymbals, they're really tide's symbols,
Not meat but metaphor.
Your vitality has no resemblance
To vita. Your there is un-there.
—And yet (refuting what I've said so far)
My carved need comes alive when I speak the right sentence.
Your pheromone-thereness then sends the old signals,
Those brine-stings of senses in gene-mingle seasons,
    That nose-eye-touch tangle, the musk of brute fur.

      .   .   .

Land can't escape waves, you their breath, you their broth.
Stealing your froth, I too brew a spell;
My waves are sound waves; they too can compel.
    (Compel? There's an Eden earliness,
    An electric gooseflesh-eeriness,
    As if song were invented this morning,
    When kindred sounds of unkindred meaning
    Meet in rhyme's assignation motel.
    They sing a balcony-scene duet
    Of three. The third the poet.)

Ignore my parenthetic ego trip—
But not our complicity: flesh-tuners both, dear sea trope.
I tuning with ink, you with bath;
I micro—you macro—musician.
You scan me with brine tweak; with rhyme beep I scan
You right back.—Or reversed? Which first?
Who whom? And did "will be" or "was"
Make creation's first skyrocket zoom?
We earth bums, we flukes of a rogue gene's birth,
It's we who hatched Big Bang.[2]
The bang was a hearerless boom, the world a scam,
Not even a trickster to blame,
Till nested in conscious "I am."
Creation? Brow's spasms outwomb
All merely cosmic merely immortal loins.
Parental world-sea, you're my oversized
Baby, anthropomorphized by these very lines.
And now that you're lessened, unsacrosanct, down from *"l'amor*
Che move il sole" to sunny wee loans
Of warmth on my windowpane lens,
I love you not less but touchably-humanly more—
　　　While on his scythe my waiting Reaper leans.

9. *Safe Inland*
Hospital. Back from my sea trip (*if* that's where I've been).
Spring's rampage is back at my window screen.
Last night some kind of solitary reaper
(That phrase, a quaint Wordsworthian sound)
Haunted my trip, my dream scene.
It's good to reap grain. Why did I scream
At the word "Reaper"?
It's good I woke up, safe inland and undrowned—
Except that there's no inland and there's seaweed in my hair.
The breakers the breakers, they're far off, not here—
Except that some arms reach far.
More about ocean—it's one big briny tear,
Fed by the tears our tightwad eye-banks owe
The dead and are slow to shed.
Will finny bill collectors gouge from our dunned sockets
Our salt debts?

Unda Marina, rocked by moon's penumbra,
    Cradle my slumber when breakers break over my head.

            •   •   •

Now brine (or more illusion, mere rain?)
Pelts me as if in a land-sea quarrel,
Floods me as if no glass to my chamber,
And floats me like driftwood lumber.
Bard crowned with seaweed, not laurel,
I'm summoned by seas crowned with treacherous coral. Who
Crossed the bleak tundra of my windowpane?
I'm a pond-skimming pebble no brakes can encumber.
I'm ringed by Marina's rotunda; pelt harder.
I'm nearing—to drown or reach haven?—her harbor.
No answer? I'm hurtling too headlong to hamper.
    Unda, where to, where to?

10. *Sacerdotal*
Overheard next day from a goodhearted underpaid nurse's aide:
"Wet again. Like he vanishes somewheres for secret swims.
Between you and I, he got them so vexed
They morphined him to stop his—can geezers that old have wet dreams?
It figures the drugs are what grew
Sea guck on his scalp—that's science for you.
    I declare, what'll they think of next?"

            •   •   •

After another morphine needle jabbed my hide,
I levitated from the operating slab to confide,
"Don't tell the spies of tide, but I invented the moon;
I'd all that green cheddar, and cows need exercise.
In case your cures don't kill me, my next book's the three:
Dionysus, Pluto, Persephone,
Smuggling the seasons my hospital window banned."
Then my floating head prophesied like a Delphic balloon,
"Gadgets have wronged the elementals—beware.
You all are retractable breaths of salt air.
The gills of the sea, they'll re-inhale the soul of the land,
Leaving it blank-eyed. Mind will end."
. . . Puffed up with this Cassandra venture,
I hear—clack clack—a new tormentor,

My cindered predecessor's missing denture,
Chortling, "I nip your heels when your hubris tugs.
The moths are at your sacerdotal togs.
Gold was brow's goal, gut's rot has made it dross."
      Watch me shape shapely silver from gold's loss.

                 • • •

Nothing shaped. Once a bore came to abort
(*Flagrante delicto*) doped Coleridge's hug of the muse.
Pain-killer-drugged, I, too, have Xanadus,
My promised ode being daily cut short
By some goody-bore's "HAVE A GOOD DAY."
Well, back to work; now I'll finish—
What was it I promised her I'd finish?
And who was "her"? And why of the sea? And where did I lay
My glasses? Memories shed.
(We differently-abled golden agers
Are mnemonically-challenged underachievers.)
      Tomorrow I'll shape, not shed. The best is ahead.

11. *Sacrament*

Days passed. Nothing shaped. Am sealed from the plans I've forgot.
I now indeed "have a good day." But:
Where never-born futures are kept, where "almost" is stowed,
There's some one I owe an ode. Blurred belovéd, accept—
As an inept lover's caress—
Unfinishedness. Invent
For lovers a new Sacrament,
The sharing of leftovers.
The unholy Communion of the unfulfilled.
. . . Once I willed to go down clear-eyed.
Now my blurring eyes are glued
To spring's window. Have a good
Bye. Where's sea? My only tide
Is my catheter bag and my I.V. pouch:
My two ebb-flow machines.
Plugged into gimmicks of expensive ouch,
      I squint gray cataracts at what regreens.

                                          (1988–95)

NOTES

1. "Life could start only in aqueous solutions of certain chemical compounds. . . . The frequent but gentle mixing produced by the tidal ebb and flow, caused by the moon, hastened the protobiogenesis in these solutions."—S. Lem.

2. "The universe needs us in order to exist . . . Has the universe required the future observer to empower past genesis? . . . The observer is as essential to the creation of the universe as the universe is to the creation of the observer."—John Archibald Wheeler.

"John Archibald Wheeler, the greatest living expositor of quantum physics, . . . means that we shape the properties of the universe by our very observation of it."—Alan Lightman in *New York Review of Books*, February 13, 1992, p. 38.

Dionysus in Old Age

The character of the "mysterious smiling heartless Stranger" (in Euripides, The Bacchae) *who came out of the east, disquiets the mind: divine in some manifestations . . . and the shadow of imposture falls upon some. Pentheus called him "a foreign wizard," he may have been nothing more, but he sent the women of Thebes to rave and dance upon the hills, and he had the still more perilous gift of self-intoxication.*

—E. M. Butler, *The Myth of the Magus*

Dionysus-Bacchus was the vine which is always pruned as nothing else that bears fruit; every branch cut away. . . . Like Persephone . . . who also rose from the dead . . . Dionysus died with the coming of the cold. Unlike her, his death was horrible; he was torn to pieces. He was the tragic god.

—Edith Hamilton, *Mythology*

As god of earth Dionysus belongs like Persephone to the world below as well as above. . . . In connection with the death of vege-tation in winter . . . he was called Zagreus ("Torn-in-pieces").

—*Dictionary of Classical Antiquities*

I. Hacked (To My Gatherer)

BACKGROUND: The most familiar parallels of seasonal sacrifice and regrowth in-clude Persephone (Proserpina, Kora, Kore) re-ascending from Pluto's Hades, Isis regathering the fourteen strewn pieces of Osiris, and the grapes renewing the hacked vine-limbs of Dionysus (Bacchus, Iacchus, Zagreus). Persephone's mother is the crops-and-fertility goddess Demeter-Ceres ("cereals"). Isis becomes pregnant with renewed sun when her hips straddle the posthumous erection of the murdered Osiris: in Egypt, god of inseminating waters; in Greece, equated with the "torn-in-pieces" vine god. Both countries knew both gods as "the many-faced," the tricky shape-juggler. In what follows, his masks include plant, seagull, wino, con man, Asian prince with leopards.

Not theological nor supernatural in its myth-echoes, the poem treats Dionysus and Persephone as partly the old folklore humor of traveling salesman and farmer's daughter. But gradually the speaker also becomes the voice of the scribbler, addressing his "belle dame sans merci" muse.

SCENE: vineyard. Time: autumn. Sole speaker: Asian stranger, addressing farm girl.

They're deft, Frost's hit-men, but I've foiled his prowess
Six months—not bad—with scarves of foliage. Even

When his red sports-hearse zaps me—fall's his season—
Your warmth outflanks his morgue's Plutonian powers.

His half-time moll, you sulk in dead soil's innards,
Beauty queen of his winter-carnival pageant.
Betray his underground; dear double agent,
Trigger the annual comeback of the vineyards.

But don't demean us; don't, Cereal's daughter, mete us
Her pep-talk crackle, the waked year's breakfast cornflake.
Pop us a crocus, March's first green mandrake,
Kicking soil's belly like a furious fetus.

Tough midwife Ceres, that belly underfoot,
Rips forth no pastoral of doves and loves,
No dainty-gauzy primavera fête;
This sweaty murderess treads red screaming leaves.

Are we daubed with "life" by mortician-crayons
Of seasonal frostbite and seasonal blazons?
Tombed daughter, save us from such salvations;
Once flout your cycle, *reverse* the play once:

Carve pine from mast, eke juicy grapes from raisins.

     • • •

Not leaf's—a loftier treading—grape's renascence,
That's what your prunings promised my impatience.
When maenad groupies snatched me from the Asians,
I risked the terrible jump of all creations:—

Wine's jump from its own skin into the . . . where?
Into abysses? These honor—they raise back up—
Art that outleaps its artist. O spill-and-gather
Me in soused future's cup.

Self-soused you call me? Test my bard-bravado.
Riding the same ill wind by which I'm riven,
I'm the one spore to make your fallow meadow
Hum with the humus of remembered rhythm.

And anyway, who cares how much frost shuffled
My ripped-off wrappers—fanning forth from man
To worm and back, through spore's accordion span—
So long as rogue-gene smirks within, unruffled.

Don't you smirk too; I know I'm all awry.
I'm fluff, I stick to every whim like lint.
I'm dandelion fuzz; my gold spikes dry
And silver off with every aimless wind.

I wear whatever glistens—birch or trout.
My motes traipse far—I gawk from every spark.
I smoke from smokestacks, intersect with soot,
And stun noon's sauna with my sunnier dark.

My quicksilver (I'll grant) is hard to fathom.
Agreed, my hashed-up selves have hushed my thunder.
My words—these leaves that pelt your downstairs slumber—
Pall. To your frost-numbed ears I seem a phantom.

Seem. Yet made flesh by touching. Must I pinch you
(Already I've sloughed a hand back) to convince you?
When I laugh back a leg or two, I'll lurch
Back as spring's springboard. Watch my dead bones launch

Your mulch's liveliest crocus-fling next March.

· · ·

Once more the wheel advances
Us back to fall's last parch.
Come twine—before these branches
Shed whiter avalanches—

Our brief uncolorfast dances under fall's last daubed arch.

Stroll to the ducklings' pond we once found peaceful.
Kick off your sandals, wade among toy ships.
Lend me the trust I'll forfeit. Fear no evil.
For the first hour we'll just touch fingertips.

Fall's afterglow and mine can't help but forfeit,
Tomorrow's wind being chill, the trust you covet.
Then glean from loss (feel pond's foreboding ripple?)
One day that's larger than the year is little.

Clouds blown but not yet jostling and contentious;
Some wings not yet pushed south; some plums still clinging;
While there's one sun-warmed seat on these cool benches,
Lean back—inhale the last bloom's lingering.

Lean open today to the day I've wrested from winter.
Green skirts get stained white anyhow tomorrow,
No procreant flow of plow but barren snow.
Fruit needs us needing each other; today I'm your kindler—

—and trickster,
                    and tricked: the chore of getting me torn
Hurts worse each round. To pry your hips from ice,
Must I play corpse? O then play Isis on
My impudent thighs.

My Bacchus credentials, these leopards I lure,
You see them tugging my cart?
Unnatural? More tricks? All the truer
(Ask Pentheus) my art.

Shrubs taunt me: "Gnarled old stump, lopped bare and limbless,
Where's now the grape-wreathed dandy of Olympus?"
Doze a solstice too long when patching my fourteen shapes,
And no more grapes.

                    •   •   •

Across the acres and eras we slough like husk,
I hurtle through mask after mask to your pheromone musk;
Not scorched but phoenixed by that moist flame, I press
Vulgar hands beneath whatever your era's dress.

Without antiphonal vulgarities,
No tide. From when the buds enfold the bees

Till the last closing of the plowshare's furrow,
Your furlow ebbs; then back to Pluto's burrow.

Your tide? Who'll bridge its lace and its typhoon,
The fragile moonbeam and the frenzied moon?
I, human-scale god, not God, it's I who've cut
The veil between soul-in-love and flesh-in-rut.

I'm a god who's also a plant with fruit,
A hybrid hyphen between earth and air,
My crest tickling clouds with my foreplay, my root
Spelunking a lap-cave ajar for both coffin and spore.

       •   •   •

(Stage direction: the Christian Son of Man enters briefly as silent listener.)
A Son of Man—he's listening—once my brother—
Went slumming as decoy for a slumlord father.
Men throng to stroke—in father shepherd's shed—
A lamb. They'll find a bull with lowered head.

If—one son torn, One nailed—our brotherly war ends,
Unsnarling burrs of dogma from our garlands,
If east and East reverse west's icy rout,
Father watch out.

We whelps of God: we trigger spring's
Jack-in-the-box. We're ladderlessly chained
Below. But what when we two, blending, bend
Chains into rungs?

Then writhe, old worm of the star ditch,
In the Milky Way slime of your skin,
Trailing your vast white vacuum. Vast in vain:
Small earth, being dense, bursts your clutch.

They said, "We must duel near water"—"water," the earthlings called.
They said, "We feel salt stinging"—the brine in them yanked by the salt.
The showdown with the Showman must end where the show began:
Land's End again.

Beach; I, spying as sea bird; when the scions
Of lungfish duel with God, they'll need a god's alliance.
That hour I'll be my brother—no, he'll be me, my heathen
Gull wings bursting dovecotes Galilean.

. . .

Or am I nothing but bones from urns Aegean?
Or puppet of some homesick modern's paean?
But whether you're goddess of farms or farmer's daughter,
Hear what I, wine-dream's traveling salesman, offer:—

Flesh being gene-scrawled for neither music nor justice,
Let's improvise them, no matter what the script is.
Parching on Scylla or drowning on Charybdis,
We're Proteus dodging blueprints of Procrustes.

I'm flow; you can't step twice in the same me.
You're grow; a thousand winters freeze in vain.
Towns rinse their stinking dentures in our holy
Shared tide; we couldn't care less; we bloom from stain.

Your globe-size bell of clay (the sun your sexton,
Ringing your seasons) tolls my vintage home;
Could I but voice the clangor of a claxon,
I'd fell whole cities on your quaking loam.

You, gentler, salvage what Octobers topple,
A plum twig or a storm-plucked mallard plume.
Enfold me in the corduroys I rumple,
Your robe of corrugated sag and zoom.

Fused by brine's aphrodisiac aroma,
We—time's *noyades*[1]—drown with a warm defiance,
The way the beached momentum of a comber
Once tossed a fish[2] whose lung would dent sky's silence.

Enough of grandeurs. It's mud baths now I'll mimic.
I'm a wallow of toads; I'm a gamboling wart-hog, preening
Garbage-crowned bristles. When gods go demoning,
When self-demeaning

Skies stoop deep, depth has no limit.

                    •   •   •

From gross abyss, I'll then climb lace cascades,
Whatever's wisped or pendant,
Ear lobes or dew, a trellis of ivies or braids,
A comet-mane ascendant

Above grief's cypress . . . till I'm an air-vine named
"Flowering Nostalgia"; planted firm in cloud,
My petals droop their pity on earth's maimed
Sky-hopes as shroud.

I'll tell you what "life" is: water compressed by form.
Four billion years of cooped-up soup ago,
A first cell joined a second. But we earth-warm
Sprouters reap frost. In fall the glue lets go.

Too much sugar in these grapes, too gorged their ripeness:
My green seeps off in blue balloons of ferment.
So filled with fullness, doom swells predetermined
Between the August warming and the winepress:—

So deep in summer is not far from fall.

                    •   •   •

I used to get reborn from fall.
Not rind—the core's outworn this fall.
Rainfall's forlorn refrain:
"The torn stays torn this fall."

Having touched you where I've touched you in my spring and summer life
(Am now watching spring and summer pass me by)
And recalling where you've touched me, is it hard to figure why
I'm not dancing to the tabor and the fife?

Your months below were sometimes slow. But you came back.
Was last time longer? Pluto stronger? But you came back.
This time delayed? Your yawns of late? But you'll come back.
My foliage? Red. My crest? Half dead. (She not quite back?)

Are vine limbs (yearly hacked for next year's wine)
Me when you patch them, or is vine but vine?
If it's no error to Easter a flower, what shame
In doing as much for me? And whether your nickname

Is Isis or Magdalen or Persephone
And mine Osiris or Bacchus, let's feel flattered,
Not bored. Why are you snoring? Don't dare shed me;
We'll either be two phantoms or one body;—

I'm just as real as you are . . . merely scattered.

(1987–93)

NOTES

1. Noyades: nude couples, bound face to face and drowned in the French reign of terror of 1794.

2. This lungfish—our land-invading ancestor—sets us on our road of "selfsurpass." From lungs comes also that sky-invading weapon known as human song. Cf. the later poem "Rogue" in Part I.

II. Courage and Sleep

SPEAKER: Mr. Dionysus Jones, an ageing shabby wine salesman and magician, feeling vine's autumn.

1.

When the violins of the leaf-plucking winds
Play three-note chords of seed-bloom-corpse,
Fiddling my vine leaves into rotting sheaves;
When a shivering lark is the tuning fork
Of shook-up wilds;
When it's Pluto my half-year bedmate weds,
My sacred wolds now weeds;
When (chilblained gods being duds) no priestess woos
What was;
When the kooks—no, the wise—
Leap off the unmerry-go-round of global whirls;
When I'm chained to the treadmill-cadence that daily rewinds
Circadian woes;
When my solstice-day is a race night wins
As day wanes;
When I'm daubed with the leafy confetti of woods,
Strewing the year's wounds;—

    Then the diapasons of paling seasons
    Teach frozen vines the friskiness of the dead.
    Vines vines my wine-glow's arteries
    Now pump hot sap through their restored aortas.
    Alive, they budged less lively than a tortoise,
    But now they're galvanized from rigor mortis
    Into a capering row of spastic corpses
    In a fortress called Ago.
    Stem sagging from gallows of branches,
    Rebounding on springboards of breeze:
    Replayed by reverse-ticking watches,
    Can I grave-rob my own decease?
No, only if my eyes drink back their *lacrimae rerum*
From grief's playroom. Skies
Haul back no tear's no sparrow's no leaf's
Fall. . . .
And my counterclock twigs? Too convulsive a twitch

For leaves crawling up like red crabs from a ditch,
Clawing in vain for connection.
Leaf in my dooryard, you're sharing a fate
With a grape I once shed, both mulched underfoot:
Tortured for others' perfection.
Leaf god, soldier-spears[1] of seed
Shred your side.
Ordured, you resurrect a dead
Orchard. Yourself you can't unshed.

    Tweaked by a choreographic twinge
    Of wind's balletomane violins,
    Vine's stalks of nerves (hysteria's limbs,
    Stretched to the snapping-point of strings)
    Splice one taut double-thread.

November spliced with remembered June:
How tune such morose arpeggios
With chords that reconcile?
I'll sift one snowflake from the snows
And nestle it within June's whitest rose,
Two ivory keys, here merged from the year's two rival pianos,
Composing—lest my passion for oneness parch—
A counterpoint of half-year counterparts.
. . . It takes—to sweeten music—
Sour notes. Why did I sic
Those maenad groupies through that Theban arch?
To warn mere power:[2] don't monkey around with art's
Tiny autonomy of holy dread,
Terra's Andorra.

    Fading: my grip on my era, the autumn my Kora[3] fled.
    Poignant: this autumn aura, this afterglow half-shed,
    No matter which orphaned flora (youth, lust, or primavera)
    I hoard. And the end hard.
    —But harder this poignance, whittled by my rhymes,
    Song's stake through time's vampire heart. . . .
    If the ledger of flora must end "in the red,"
    If spring's a hoax of cardboard haloes,
    How come I once made masts in Hellas
    Open and sprout like green umbrellas?[4]
    Doesn't it show my clout with Mother Tellus?[5]

Come back, Aegean formcraft, and compel us
To groom Her parks again, to green what yellows.
Fall is the heartbreak Her Niobe-heart can't bear.
Halt—can you hear me?—you falling leaf up there;
Halt in mid-air.

2.

A butterfly, stamping its foot, may shift the cosmos;
Find the right rhythm and tilt the whole year's compass
South with the magnet of lilt.
Right rhythm: my spear between the ribs of Chronos.
I mean my spike of vine (what made me say "spear"?)
Between spokes of the juggernaut year.
    The year-wheel, I've stopped it. Come running, Persephone,
    A green flash of skirt, a white flash of knee,
    Sprinting against the tousling wind to stall
    Leaf's mid-air fall.
    (Outburst: mess up, mussed goddess,
    Each exquisite non-empathizer;
    An urbane poet is unforgivable;
    Gauche outrage at wrongs can right hell;
    No, it can't but is *de rigueur*.)
    No time for more outburst—we've wheel-spin to tilt
    With your warmth, with my lilt—both are one.
    The leaf-strumming winds play their violins
    In vain with their icicle bow.
    For the winds, the winds know I've touched you—they know
    Who's touched you touches sun.
    Right rhythm, right rhythm! Archaic singsong, swell
    My season-reversal spell:—
        (offstage music, crudely overstressed)
    Grapes, still unfreezing, are mobiles for breezes,
    Each cluster a chandelier, chimed by the gust.
    Foliage sonorously rustles in chorus,
    Each color a thawing caress.
    All's drunk not on drink but on drunkenness,
    Aether of attar.
And then? When my hour of wheel-spell ends?
Then vineyard-vertigo's delirium tremens

Resumes. Stems
Are berserk censers, hurling incense
From flowers with biped's nectars, men's and women's,
The smirking pistil-mouths, the slobbering stamens,
Both musks now venoms.
Grape pits, appalled at bearing acrid lemons;
Wasp-riddled apples, squishy as persimmons;
No greens, only toadstools, death-pale omens,
Ballooning immense.
With a speed-cop summons
Rot nabs the sprints of sprout. Mold kidnaps humans:
Dankly alluring in pelts it flayed from handsome
Dreams, it co-opts young dreamers (soul the ransom)
Into mildewed messiahs outdemoning demons.
    Who'll help? Where's mid-air's cliffhanger,
    My *Doppelgänger,*
    The leaf that's almost me and won't let go?
    Hang on! Trust patterns.—But straitjackets throw
    Fits. Masks drop. A suspiciously lush
    Land mine of puffballs comes popping from ambush.
    What vaults my hedge and lopes without a leash?
    A sabbath of tree-broomsticked witches?
    A daymare of witch-crotch'd trees?
    Landmarks amok; groomed parks awry and random;
    My guardian auras—laurel myrtle resin—
    Arisen too late; grape wizened into raisin;
    Moon baying at dogs, and sane asylums raving;
    My compass pointing not true but toward ravine;
    My landscaping of landscapes riven
    By frantic twisters, air's romantic
    Terrorists, simpering as they raven.
    Formcraft, where art thou? Wind's violins whimper,
    "Yours was wrong rhythm."

3.
My tall tale turned out much too true: the myth
I meddled with, the song-and-dance I peddled
Performing Zagreus the Hacked.[6]
Racked on the wheeling seasons,
Am I the nailed one's brother, we two the high one's sons,

Speared long since?
Was I sowed by lie or sky? Either way, the high one reaps
Me. All my leaf-lives sense
Their waiting compost heaps—but first the farm knives,
Fine-tuning the rack of ripe, the fondling that ends by pruning.
O get it over with fast, the hacking, the harvest phase.
    Who'll harvest me by treading on my face?
    "Who are these coming to the sacrifice?"
    No artifice here, no-arty farce;
    Nor noble-browed cant. They're just a trudging work-force,
    Too grimed by Fact for Grecian urn's décor
    Or for truth-beauty fuss.
    My rot-prone leaves know well what compost-sod
    Gives ardor to rose arbor;
    As a vulgar brass-tacks body-prone god,
    I celebrate not the rose but the trudgers' chore.
    The grape-stomp is their one-day exit-door
    From dreary rounds of sty and stable floor.
    This day no rites but vine's recur:—
    Grain's
    Joy-pangs of sprout, spore fruitful once more;
    Green's
    Saint Vitus dance, bounced on grape's trampoline floor;
    Chagrin's
    Grape-brook, flayed shoreless of peel before
    Glass becomes shore.
Aurora of juice, brow's corona,
Fauna and flora fuse;
    Then a piston-revel of grape-splashed knees
    Blurs into trees whose roots unravel,
    Whole groves pried free of clay and gravel,
    Each runaway trunk a hammering gavel,
    Bop-bobbing up-down—they can't stop.
This is the moment when sweltering meat stomps forth
A lively souse-god from a dead fruit's froth.
The armpit stink of shirtless farm-boy churls,
The sweaty crotch of aproned farmyard girls,
The calloused heels the purple bloodbaths drench,
The earth-globe thirst my grape-globes quench:
I (god they lynched or trickster) I decree

All of them beautiful, drunk with the drink of me.
     What are these god and goddess shapes?
     From vats of fumes of ooze of trampled grapes,
     What lava, sighed by what volcanic gorge?
     Or are they vapor, plague, mirage?
     Pouring time's sandglass-past in a wineglass
     Of future, suddenly the winepress
     Releases (*in vero vinitas*) the pair.
The hoarse-voiced sforzando, invoking, increases:
"Look, it's the bridegroom Dionysus,
Vine-tangled with his bride, look high, they're there."
Persephone: underground tide, whose circlings cover
Both sprout and parch. And I: her overground lover,
Dark-laughing elegist of betrayed roots.
The overflow of immemorial rites,
The boom of the drums of the spooks in the fumes,
Make treaders tread faster. The knives are now wands
Of harvest's magic paradox,
Renewer cut free by slasher, Eros
     By Jack-the-Ripper-Thanatos.
     A *pas de deux* of gods in heat unwinds
     Crescent moon into scabbard, stalactite into pharos:
     The wound that heals wounds
     And the self-untombed Jack-in-box:
     The pair, Cunnus, Phallus.

4.
That's long ago. Now violins of winter
Shatter love's wineglass with the shrill of frost.
No birds? Where's she, the crocus-bringer?
I'll sing the warmer for the warmth I lost.
Have I, a god defrocked in June's surrender,
Run out of worlds?
I've long (delirium never raved serener)
Made do with words.
No wines? Then binge of words; a bender
With rhetoric hangovers. But when as classic
Bartender of Pierian brew, I'm vendor
Of vintage true to my Aegean nest,
Then sunrise rises in the west. The West!

June in November.
　. . . But she?
Below for keeps, no Junes, no refills for grape juice.
She's now hooked on wines of entropy booze;
She brews them from poppies, not vines.
Her boutonnière: poppy's opiate-wafting stamen,
Where cyclamen once wafted spring.
The wriggle I once based my metronome on
Now squats in unpneumatic dignity
On a throne: with King Snowman, the necrophile deity.
Munching pomegranates, she feels at home in
His no-man's-land. "Pluto" his Roman
Cognomen: foeman to music and muse
Ever since seed first woke clay's snooze.
Friends, burn your corpses or the pigs will eat them
When graves cough up their half-digested pablum
Like gullets clogged with phlegm.
When a vineless loam on a Juneless terra
Becomes bitumen[7] and barren scoria,
What's my new role? All chosen models illumine
The chooser. Baleful omen:
As a has-been god, I mime the sleaziest human,—
The has-been showman who's stroking
(As if they were blurbs or tits)
Some fading press-clip token of faded hits.
That's just how I dream of my fans at Eleusis,[8]
Adrip with seaweed and sea,
Again chanting "Iacchus, Iacchus"—
To damn well remind her of me.
　. . . Or else—why mime bad models?—I'll switch
To the tact of good exits:
Alone, the timing my own.

5.

Poured forth from *chambré* flask to iced decanter,
My spirit—my spirits—flow north from pasts I can't re-enter.
Chilled by the sky-orb's cooling languor,
My vegetable day grows shorter and forlorner,
Though each faint ray incites me like a lancer
To linger longer.

Longer? What for when age has cindered
A scruffy *commis voyageur,* a scrubby vineyard?
Hindered, forced inward, why not hunker
Down with self-pity's "insulted and injured"?
Or go down yelping, lout in bunker?
Ressentiment—or lone-wolf rant?
No, neither; better can't than cant.
Instead I'll blossom (having lost to winter)
Loss into music. Losses: heart mere tinder,
Hope a splinter, I no laureled Pindar.
My life's-work? All remaindered by the printer.
If thine "I" offend thee, pluck it out.
No wine god: all too banally mortal, doubt
My only mentor.
Now that my circle shrinks into a dot,
I've nothing nothing nothing at my center.
Word-games in vain indict
(Quick, surgeon: fetch me something sharper, faster)
My festering *timor mortis* canker.
My mid-air leaf, the one that won't surrender
To Pluto's rancor,
Was plastic. Stripped pretender
In a hearse to the compost heap,
I spit at the blessings with which old age is cursed
And face—there are no spells, there's only courage and sleep—
Head-on the worst.
    I'm whistling in the dark? At least the whistle scans.
Sloughing my inward-facing masks like skins,
I hear (is it gloating or pitying?)
A vesper whisper of violins:
"Right rhythm and wrong—same string."
    Last blink. My two shrinking windows see
    Boughs swaying; different tempos; same tree.
When dust becomes conscious, there's trouble in reap-time.
I'm ready then.
    Stealing the ecstasy-prop made stale by verse
    And returning it fresh, despair its re-inventor,
    I feel the calm phrensy achieved by aware dust
    Just before dust is
                        dispersed.

I feel my tendrils flail intenser,
My grapes and grape-words swelling denser,
From green's shy first
Bud to the blood-red flabbergasting burst.

(1989–95)

NOTES

1. Soldier-spears: Gospel of St. John, 19:31, "But one of the soldiers pierced his side with a spear."

2. Power: Dionysus and his maenads destroying the powerful King Pentheus of Thebes.

3. Kora (Kore, Greek for maiden): another name for Persephone, wintering underground with Pluto in Hades and rising overground with the flowers of spring.

4. One of Dionysus' alleged miracles: making dead masts re-sprout.

5. Tellus: earth.

6. Zagreus (Greek for "torn in pieces"): name for Dionysus as the vine whose limbs were annually pruned off in Mediterranean vineyards. Earlier role (esp. in Crete): the bull god whose flesh was piously eaten, a worship later appearing in Orphism, Mithraism, and religions nearer home. The fastidious Greek scholar J. E. Harrison frowned on both roles: "Zagreus appears little in literature; a cult so primitive, so savage that a civilized literature instinctively passed him by."

7. Bitumen was used to seal the mouths of mummies.

8. In the Eleusian mystery religion, the Persephone worshipers bathed in the sea before chanting "Iacchus, Iacchus" (still another name for Dionysus) and carrying his image to Eleusis.

Goat Ode in Mid-Dive

SPEAKERS: wine god Dionysus and season shuttler Persephone.
TIME: today in America. The indented lines in italics and double quotes are
Persephone's.

I.

I faced a well when I raised your hood.
Yanked by the deeps your eyelids hide,
The moon of my reflected head
Dived in your well of gaze.
No glass now shows the face I had.
Out of the well-pit where it's hid,
It'll never snap back in place.
'You frog down there,' I ask my face,
'Is spring on the lam where you're underground,
Where loam's drums pound?
Up here, where old-age grays abound,
Green left no trace. Where's the lost month I chase?'
My hoppity face croaks back (deep bass,
With a tattle-tale grimace):
'Persephone dunnit! The half-year-she you're loaned!
She snuck March into her basement hideaways.'

. . .

Enter my she. You she-tide, season-taking
And season-bringing, now it's you who's talking,
Invading—barge right in—this solo ode
I thought I owned.
  "How can we two stay solo, we branding each other so?
  We're a duet of three; that snide third sound
  Is hourglass sand.
  With a robin on my wrist and pollen in a vase,
  With a wand of maize in my suitcase,
  I'll crocus back our March embrace,
  November at my heels, a blaze-tongued hound."
You've reined November's disarrays
In your relentless round.
And I, relentless, rhyme the word 'embrace'
In ever more obsessive ways—

Till sound's recurrent pairs (replayed)
Charade our re-embrace.
    "Your desperate loneness makes you rhyme 'embrace.'"
Your bigamous circlings make you fool
Around with rhymes for 'round.'
Those vowel-rich rhymes, they're flesh-talk, they're charade
Performed by sound. Now warm, now cool,
They shimmy like a belly-dancer 'stoned,'
Winding—unwinding—your landscapes like a spool,
All hills your breasts (Diane of the Ephesians),[1]
All sky your brow (Athena of the Grecians),
Seasons outswirling a dervish merry-go-round,
Regions of Möbius highways, *trompe l'oeil* byways,
Ambushing the shrinks who'd map your underground.
    "Don't map me as femme-fatale-ing all over the place.
    I'm too solid for fluffy romantic props.
    Not many a belle-dame-sans is also a nanny.
    With my glamorless chore of baby-sitting the crops,
    I'm hard-core no-nonsense ore.
    Yet my iron whim melts tenderly
    Whenever I feel like it. NO TRUDGED CONSISTENCY.
    I'm slapdash life, not school. No guild
    Can build on my quicksilver quicksand base,
    I dodging your x-ray's paraphrase."
You crystal of color-shifting glaze,
Kaleidoscope of living glass:
Whirled grass my famines graze.
    "I'm whirls of myth and science
    Through wheels of songs and silence."
You hub for skirts and seasons.
You ring that rings surround.
    "Pluto can't keep his mitts off me; he's conned
    By all that's round."
Would you stay topside all year round
(Forever spring) if I compound
Your selves, your changing musics, into one
Intimately-squeezed accordion?
    "I'm fractals. How predict how I'd respond?
    ... Won't Pluto win every last round?"

Not while we're earth-gone-self-aware. Dust unbound!
Observers change the observed as batons change a concert;
We, conscious, create the big bang and the now, both combined.
    "What, in your post-amoeba mess,
    Infected you with consciousness?"
The mischief began when life's onset
Grew spoilsport antennae called 'mind.'
That sunrise, discovering sunset,
Left innocence behind.

                    • • •

    "Enough meta. Gimme what's soothing and sure.
    Softsoap me with rhyme, make like a masseur,
    As tendrils of vine might stroke grapes gone sour
    (Strained similes being my pleasure).
    Flatter me when my nerves are sore,
    Provided it's banter and insincere.
    In turn, I'll be the calyx where your sear
    Octobers inhale new Mays."
So listen to my half-ironic praise.
You moon whose leash the wave obeys.
In the snifter of noon, you cognac bouquets.
You green against whom red inveighs. You tune
No discords faze.
    "I batten on discords. You confound
    My leaf-game wrong way round.
    Red mulch plays phoenix to my green rebound.
    I'm schizo double; chords and discords bond.
    They, not just you, are embracers. It follows
    All absolute bumps are relative hollows.
    Each player interplays.
    While zebra'd with black and white absolutes,
    I'm in furtive cahoots with grays."
Eros and Thanatos: same clown, recloned?
    "The fatal western gate awaits beyond
    East's fetal pond.
    'Are' soon must 'were.' And even 'always'
    Must 'was.'
    All. gods. were. immortal. 'Stays'
    Is your other doomed rhyme-pet, as mayfly-brief as 'embrace.'

No out from clay's maze."
Not out, not through. Up!
The way the grape-globes swell when roots refuel,
The way the globe's globe basks in noon renewal,
So does loam's pulsing catapult
Lob up our interlace.
So up that even the Milky Way's
Rays exult.
     "Why up? Why some grand cosmos cult?
     Give upness up. Your uplift-grandeurs
     (Earth is nest's place) debase."
I feel genes shove me (from today's
Nest) worm-deep downstairs.
     "Genies can be rebottled; not so genes.
     Speedinq the guest (that's you) who overstays,
     Genes are your bouncers: whether from
     Your first warm nine-month waiting room
     Or now your 'living' room.
     The winter theater-season plays
     Corpse-prance ballets."
Then I half-hate your half-year green-thumb ways,
Withholding ice's antidote till March.
Your loveliness: too loveless for gypped hearts.
And even the bronze your winter sunset glows,
The window arabesques your paintbrush froze,
The dreams that frisk when loam lolls comatose,
The icicles that bandy back the blows
Of sun as rainbows:
           all scream 'Thanatos!'
Blown oak leaves flutter their angst across my ears:
'Give back our chlorophyl.'—Give back my years.

II.
     "Are we slumming Olympians, earth our importer?
     Or, second choice, each a sleazy imposter,
     The 'traveling salesman' (of firewater)
     With the porn-joke 'farmer's daughter'?
     Or third, Viereck's puppets, his strings our halter?
     Check one of three."

All of above.

"*Puppets. But not numb wood in the place where friction*
Feels good, my Punch and Judy love:
Rolling on bedsprings over and over,
We come alive bouncing,—stripping each other
Free of the strings of the script we alter.
It's we who'll puppet our author.
We're fiction, he's fiction's fiction."

He lives us so deep into life, you, me, and Pluto,
That in far-off days, at some fireplace,
We'll be gabbed about, the earth-wheel trio,
As Helen is and Cleo.

"*And this, not our god scam, makes fadeless us three.*"

Fadeless or humanly fading, which are we?

"*Mixed bag. You less lasting. I more.*
The renewed can't outlast the renewer."

Already my shaggy brother
Mistah Pan—he dead.[2] Gods were
More human once, and humans godlier.
Byebye Greece. I'm the last recorder
Of that blurred halfgod border.

"*I, mediatrix of that mix,*
Teach crocus bulbs the arts—
Pop, pop—of how sun jump-starts March.
I, leaf-bringer, take away leaves. Into sproutable mulch.
A life-bringing slaughter."

Who needs a revolving-door cult?
We mortals (I'm often mortal) can't get un-killed.
Leaves—*we* leaves—are culled
From noon, and all we need when cold
Is sun and water.

"*I love you both, you and Pluto.*
You most, my topside boarder.
But death-rattle-deep below,
From a season's throat of ice,
Rise tones of primordial disorder
Against your ode-structured tunes.
I hate you both, you and Pluto."

Then why entice us with lies?

"The wheel's what entices. It programs me still
By dangling (to keep you both treading its mill)
The bait of my perjured thighs. Against my will."
Shut your eyes and think of England.
"I think of Enna, land
Of my pre-kidnap maidenhood:
No shuttle—then—between beds except of flowers;
No wheel but the spinning wheel of seemly maiden prowess."
How touching—not a dry eye in the house—
That a petal of hymen sealed off a bud.
But now the bud blossoms. In Pluto's Gehenna, not Enna.
"Now, because no ebb, no flow abide,
My shifting untruth keeps me true to tide.
The world's not just odd; it acts odder
Than any world possibly could.
What can't happen happens. All am is an other,[3]
A body-language code.
The erogenous zone of tide, that's what I'm listening to,
The Esperanto of spawn's undertow.
Spawnings are meat-grind contraptions where life gets ground,
Forever rebirthed and remurdered, round and round."
More like a sewage-treatment hutch?
"Well, aren't you recycled sludge?"

•   •   •

The ode I've mentioned takes time. Load
My beggar cup with your spare hours,
Just enough to finish my death song, outliving your evergreen powers.
"Not a dry eye in the house—are you an onion?—
When you sing swannishly.
Yet final songs are whistlings in the—"
Don't say it. 'Dark' was always art's companion.
"You'll die of an art attack. Brinked on the boneyard canyon,
What have you left to clutch?"
Terra. My brow enfolds her autumn gulch
That enfolds my foliage's yellow.
My small dust-heart is hotter
Than her red pump—and broader
Than pump's green aorta.
Dust swallows dust's own graveyard.

"Vineyard, it's time to let go of your last meadow,
Time to say ciao to the planet that's been your burrow."
Good to have known you, you planet of sparrows and hayricks,
Where not all flamingoes are plastics, not all rainbows tricks.
Where . . . on bruised bitter cheekbones . . . the battered petals flow
Mellow, the way snow settles soft on snow.
And even your volcano-tantrums hallow
Our too dim air with Impressionist-school shimmer.
    "An old guy exulting in earth makes earth-graves snigger.
    Sentenced to hang in an hour, would you start long odes to rope?"
I'd anyhow start what can't finish. Obsession in place of hope.
Who needs hope? 'Don't be morbid' rings hollow.
    "Unripe old age rings shallow."
As child, I dreamed with joy of a blue heron;
Not all dreams are grist for reductive dissection.
Hands I have cupped made ticktock slacken.
Breasts I have cupped made me forget I'll be forgotten.
I have seen wilt; grass paled away to hay,
The patient field below more richly fallow.
Dawnduskspringfall: one seamless tremolo.
And the smells! Sawdust. Grape-burst. Resin. Dung.
They don't make planets like you any more. So long.

      • • •

    "Transvestite impersonation of ape by grape:
    Is your ology zo or botany?"
I forgot how long since last I was a tree.
From marriage with fall undivorced,
I'm rooted in dust either way: as vine or as ape.
Shifting, you're mobile. I, when bit by frost,
Can't escape.
    "In my shuttle game, am gambling not for money
    But to win jackpot-earth. Which player is Gaia's true child,
    My spring force or deadly Jack Frost?"
Grim Jack Reaper?
              "Jack who rips.
    Cardsharp for Pluto when we come to grips."
Jack in whose box? Stacked deck. With Jack—not deuces—wild.
    "I'm betting a fecund Easter bunny
    Against his November chips.

But then I'll play all four seasons. To get them reconciled.
I'm a safe-house for none, a bridge for the many."
Am confused. Are you treason or harmony?

· · ·

Engodded, you've shed our mortal murk as dross.
Now nothing about you is finite. Hey, are you happy?
　"Makes sense to be. Goofy not to be. I've got to be.
　Yes, happy forever.
　Except when I get—like a night-sweat fever—
　A feel of—um—infinite loss."

III.
　"I've just two bedmates. What a brace
　Of duds! With opposite hang-ups. Yours erase
　Dear Pluto's necrophile kinks. Which in turn efface
　A flaky fetish of your own,
　A lust that strokes—from tone-deaf life—a tune,
　Making all matter metric, caressing it into music,
　As if bard's lyre were my pelvic bone.
　The bone deserves love for its own sake, not as ode's metronome."
My rhythms strum the petals of new Mays;
You, too, love love on beds of bloom's new lace;
But love, unless it lasts in odes, decays.
　"When I lean back, my nightie above my knee,
　Guess who 'responds' by . . . talking an ode at me?"
Six months who leaned *at* me across May's tombstone?
As moll of Pluto's gang, his topless barmaid,
You've leaned me mickey finns of pheromone,
Death's aphrodisiac: brewing from belladonna
(Ah, bedroom-eyed bella donna) deadly nightshade.[4]
　"Jack made me do it, that pimp."
What yawnful office grind comes next?
Am I a business memo faxed
From ice to crocus when the year reverses,
Filed by some weather-bureau wimp?
Hell no, I'm not your hibernating ursus
Who must dance thanks for thaw when trained by rods.
I'd rather dance on swords but call the tune
Than gambol for the baksheesh of your June.

"Yet my glorious double rites of spring,
Art's lilacs and utility's oats,—"
Tough on crushed toads.
Spring always ground a lot into the ground.
To rise takes lots of falling: wronged leaves your footfall goads.
I've had it with resurrections, incurable trauma of gods.
Am I vine's Dionysus, resprouting again,
Or that unresurrectable dust-heap called man?
(Tell me. Don't tell me. Dust or regreened?)
On crocus day, what howled from every orchard?
It wasn't for fun each tortured fruit-birth groaned
Creation's hoarse anathema:
'Easter's not Easter but new Golgotha.'
From night—through graveyard labia—to searing light:
I can't endure (O not again) these birth throes.
Ice, snuff out sun. Let me doze.

> • • •

Yet just one ray's enough and I've disowned
Doom. Don't be bound
To year-wheel's plodding pace.
With yoyo's hyped-up roundelays
Spin up the spring you downed. Replace
The crows of frost with jays.
Though calendars caw 'November,' let chirps of March resound.
You holy grove whose resin allays what slays:
You high-throned pistil to whom stamen prays.

> *"Too hifalutin. I straddle not thrones but bidets,*
> *And nothing wows me but the commonplace.*
> *Only the humdrum drudge of daily chore*
> *Renews sweet daily dawn, makes thaw recur.*
> *As a god with a human core,*
> *Godly because so human, not an altar,*
> *I'm drudging: gardening green ricochets*
> *Your chilbains nag me for.*
> *My sweat—it's no eau de cologne—is what waters your noon.*
> *Sky magic goes when down-to-earth is gone;*
> *When starved of earthworms, skylarks falter;*
> *When truly-true love turns me on,*
> *The lubrication isn't holy water."*

A queen of spades calling a spade a spade?
        "To honor Venus, I'm calling a spayed a spayed.
        Bard, woo me plain-toned; prose is no disgrace."
You want plain? I'm a sock in your laundromat, lost
In cycles your spinning seasons tossed
(Fish out what meteorology mislays).
But I won't don the faux-naïf berets
Of folk art. And I scorn the hearty-fake okays
A plain-toned donkey brays.
My odes serve loftiest high talk as canapés
On very colloquial trays.
Eon-old baby, my short seven decades
Are older than you: their long reach incarnates
The ageless westciv show biz.
Your magic isn't magic, my music is.

                •   •   •

        "Half-amused by such insolent music, I'll half-forsake
        Prosaic Pluto and hug away your ache.
        Though (in year's sinking phase) I'm still red-gowned
        With strays of tree-tossed autumn-blaze,
        I sprout green fingers clawing you awake."
Stretch out those . . . fondling fingers. Reach. Unparch
The leafy revenants of March
From their long coma's daze.
        "The recharged batteries of roots astound
        The popping crocus and amaze
        Returning robins when my thaw replays
        Grave's frozen mound."
Only your warmth can shape a flowering wound.
But only 'trag-oidia,' 'goat ode,' grants the grace
To shape—from heartbreak—systoles of praise.
Whether with cap-and-bells or cap of bays,
With formcraft clowned or crowned
I edit earth. With proofreader's renowned
White wipe-out ink, I blot snow's white clichés
        "Again you're granding. Seed-ink sprays
        A procreant third white (not some arty phrase)
        To grow my crops. Grand barren form won't raise
        Live maize."

Is it ebb, is it flow? Will you, won't you let me in?
　　"I'm as open to you as a wishbone's grin,
　　As closed as a zipped briefcase.
　　Kinglet Canute, your sceptered mace
　　Can't gain what tide gainsays."
Have raised your skirt, have raised your hood.
Have humped all selves you ever had.
Have probed their lips at hip and head.
But never reached clay's hoard.
Nothing is hid, and all is hid;
I can't decode you till I heed
A tide that can't be heard.
　　"Raise bets, raise hell, raise pigs—what's left to raise?
　　Tide zigzags; no straight code conveys
　　You through the maze of my unmerry-go-round."
Round, round—you've rounds. But I—I lose what frays.
Or can love's bonding make my lost get found?
　　"'Bonding': bland uplift-jargon that portrays
　　Venus depilatoried,—birth-cave's brand-mark
　　Prettied into a valentine from Hallmark.
　　. . . Yet our duet, grown lightning-prone, is our one landmark."
Don't bet on duets; the heat our black sun parlays
Isn't hearth's but auto-da-fé's.
　　"You opted for odes; your tragoidia backpack weighs
　　Heavy, weighs dark.
　　Or are we Goody-good's valets?
　　Rouged corpses? Funeral-home displays?
　　Perfumed against stink, and with well-groomed toupés?"
I taste your wound, you smell my brand-scorched carcase.
　　"When love is two hot irons, when predators are preys,
　　Our solos can't stay solo, we being branded so."
And is this bond or bondage? Cure or craze?
　　"Try me and find out. Like any genuine god,
　　I'm kooky magic that . . . works. A genuinely healing fraud.
　　My eyes!—growth dawns wherever I splash their gaze.
　　All castaways, all runaways,
　　Love and toad and March and face,
　　Creep huddling to my well like beasts around
　　A water-hole's haven-ground."
Haven? Where each of us stays and stays?

"Antæan⁵ searcher through Absurds of space,
Touch me—clay opens—touch me quick—NONE STAYS."

IV.
The pre-old grows, the post-young pays.
Narcissa, ever-young old hag,
Whose age-old dugs will never sag,
What do you know of that which never stays,
The mulch-fate of red fallers, trod
By risers new leaves tread?
　　"My dead are living, my living already dead.
　　Each renews when I damn well choose."

　　　　　•　•　•

'Damn well' sounds too high-horse. Your pride-steed neighs
Its condescension at flawed mortal ways.
I've no hoorays for these unearned cachets;
Their god-perfection is unlovable
Because invulnerable.
Like driftwood weathered by combers on Cape Cod,
Our vulnerable clay and clod get honed
By stormy inner weather into grace.
　　"That very clay to which that grace is owed
　　Is me the way you ARE your ode.
　　Clay is the pelt I wear
　　And moult and again wear,
　　Shaped to my contours."
　　　　　　　　　—Stop! You make clay sound
Like the panty-hose you once draped on my bedside chair.
　　"That was March. Then came winter and Pluto's round."
This polyandry of Persephone
Is the running-gag gossip of flower and tree.
In March the croci snigger,
'Still oozy from Pluto, she sprints toward hubby-two,
Their tryst the trigger to pop our bulbs anew.'
　　"I never lie to you (except when I do);
　　I thought (except when I didn't) only of you
　　Each night in Pluto's fridge.
　　We'll bridge grave's gap when noon-bloom melts my heart.
　　Under Niagaras of anèmonè,

Where fern-beds bob like waterbeds below me,
While whole Saharas bloom in sympathy,
We'll meet again—and this time never part
(Well, hardly ever)—while a waitress named Sun sashays
Back, serving grape and grain entrées."
Waitress? The tip you'll toss her (life's a scrape
None gets out of alive) is me.
"And I, to keep the flower-show on the road,
Can't brake for every wheel-trapped toad."
Green blinkers block your empathy for all that never stays.
That's why I can't quite love you, belovèd Persephone.
"Lean on the wind, you sea gull lost in a squall.
Lean on the wind, you leaf that dreamed toward sky.
Glide, not fly—glide, not fall—glide, glide to your she."
I'm darkness probing dark in darkening days.
Faster than show-off school-brats on their sleighs,
Down hills of ice my berserk winters race.
But when momentum spins me into space—?
"Then ride—I can't keep—why pretend?—my high-horse high—
Then ride—oh shit, I love ya like crazy—my tide."

• • •

I'd rather cup the breasts that aging flays,
The face that tears deface, the lap moon's pause waylays,
Than brows no Reaper-scythe dismays,
Nipples no clock surveys.
The flesh I sink my flesh in, let it fray together with me.
Together! Frayed faster than your dirndl sways.
"You know first-hand I'm the god (at toil or in heat)
Who prides herself on her very human sweat."
Only when hard-earned wrinkles mar
Your too smooth ass and forehead will you be
As earthly-human as you think you are,
My silly god, Persephone.

• • •

"And yet and yet we're 'we':
Two incompatible threads of DNAs
That love's hook crochets."
So be it. Then the terrible brand-mark stays.

Then go for broke. Then this time don't un-grand me;—
  ("I see what's coming, he's going cosmic on me")—
Then let me rave that if the seismic wave
Called 'we-ness' didn't brand you, didn't brand me
With its—yes—cosmos-warming scar,
Then ice would snuff the Milky Way's
Rays, mugging every star.
  "So it's ambi this and ambi that,
  Ambiv, ambig, now twine, now spat:
  Halves of the same iambic, your tick my tock.
  Without this ambidextrous clock,
  My seasons won't twirl round."
Lives aren't seasons. Your procreant lap-word 'round'
Won't rotate those who can't twirl round,
The ones (me too? me too?) with one-way ways.
  "I love your hate-spiced moriturus[6] ways
  From the bottomless of my heart. Which still betrays.
  Dare follow your one-way fate, your diving face.
  At the spread-eagled arch of my gateways,
  The millennia curtsy and pass.
  I glaze old treadmill-relays
  With my inexhaustible grass."

V.

Co-god me. I'll build you still comelier planets as solace,
Where gauche and wistful don't shatter, where nays become yeas,
Where workaholic Time takes holidays.
  "If I could, I'd re-June you. Just for you, I'd raze
  The forts of shiver. But even I am bound
  By Jack Frost to the murder-word, 'round.'
  While we shacked up, when Jack the Reaper phoned,
  I'd say you're out. Now ice can't be postponed.
  For those—you too?—infected with a case
  Of tomb-prone (life's malaise),
  What's left? Not much but enough. The mulch-you'll-be purveys
  Boomerangs underground."
You god amid mulchers, permanence amid flux,
O blaze, blaze, blaze amid the dark of nox:
Soar and fall feel alike. No diff. Except (why pretend?)

The end.

> "Days fall like acorns, centuries fall like days
> In my bottomless well, its walls all clay. Trust clay's
> Cornucopian rebound."

Ah me, who trusts a well gets drowned.

But diving I make trust true.

Mid-dive is forever: slow slow slow

(It's the years before that race).

I'm changing! Mid-dive vertigo

Sways me a comelier planet's air.

Can't you see—are you blind—my soaring? (Or

Am I seeing pit as sky?)

I leave all weight behind in hurtling haze.

Unbound from calendar's carapace,

Unwound from year-wheel's ticking,

I shed all ballast but light and sound

And with a goat ode send November packing.

(1992–93)

NOTES

1. The best-known statue of Diana (Artemis) in ancient Ephesus portrays her with multitudinous mammae.

2. Twilight of the Greek gods in early A.D.: that famous wail (according to Plutarch in the reign of Tiberius), "Great Pan is dead!"

3. Cf. Rimbaud, letter of May 13, 1871: *"Je est un autre."*

4. By a folk-etymology confusion with the poison bladina, "bella donna" (beautiful lady)—when written as one word—became the name of the poison (and beauty-enhancing eye dilator) called deadly nightshade.

5. The giant Antæus needed to touch earth to regain his strength.

6. Abbreviating in singular the famed salutation of Rome's "about to die" gladiators.

Pluto Incognito

SOLE SPEAKER: Pluto. Why the (literally) hell shouldn't he be Pluto? Isn't the universe surreal enough for this? Or is he instead—or in *addition*—the basement janitor of an American apartment house? Has a brain tumor made him think he is brother of Zeus and god of the Greek underworld?

TIME: Spring. His girlfriend has just deserted him for Dion, a wine-salesman poet on top floor of same building.

PLACE: A hospital dissection table, where—in a tumor autopsy—dead brain cells are galvanized awake for an instant by the surgeon-scalpel. Though the whole resultant Pluto monologue flashes by in that instant, the instant seems a million-year reign to the knife-sparked cells.

MYTHOS: Found in hospital libraries and read there by speaker, Bulfinch's *Mythology* has somewhat crudely popularized the familiar legend of Pluto and Persephone. After being kidnapped while gathering flowers at Enna, she forfeits any permanent return by her forbidden pomegranate nibble. Thereafter she shuttles. In spring: regreener of earth and of the wine god Dionysus-Bacchus-"Zagreus" (Greek for "the hacked"). In winter: Pluto's queen. Their watchdog: three-headed Cerberus. Their flower: asphodel. Their rivers: the Lethe of forgetfulness and the Styx of Charon, the obol-fee ferryman.

INDENTATION: Whenever speaker becomes aware of his human janitorial self.

I.

I.D. card: Greek and Roman made Hades my cognomen,
A.k.a. Dis or Pluto.
I'm act five, sparing no man. At Enna of ill omen,
I dragged me a bobby-sox goddess below,
A flower child then. She's a swinger now
As emcee of my foeman.
Before they swing too heated on vineyard's fertile seedbed,
Tell wine tout and his woman: if they commit the seed-spread
Perversion called life, with obscene plant or human,
They'll catch the plague called green.
Man's chromosomes know if death hadn't weeded
Hug's garden, they'd still (ask Darwin) be bugs.

· · ·

But octopoding upward through my freeze,
What sinister green tentacles are these,
Strangling the fields I'd freed from the life disease?
Sleazy rouged roses have turned on the spigots

Of spring propaganda for anti-death bigots.
What right have the bigots to get so polemical?
Am I accountable to some biodegradable chemical?
Mortality isn't popular with mortals.
They curse, they pray—I answer both with chortles.
They spurn (are they sick or mad?) a wholesome
Necrophilia. I'm broad-minded, but my portals
Allow no vitaphiles. They're just too loathsome.
The erotic being their most addictive narcotic,
Birth is their itchiest venereal infection,
Cured (over the counter, you need no prescription)
By a dose of antibiotic named Thanatos.
Call life—bed being where it's relayed—
A bedbug. A dandy cure is: squash it.
Or feed it prussic acid. Or just gas it.
I purify. Pure means BLANK SLATE.
Even for sky. My net's entropic strands
Scoop up all stars, these falling sandglass sands.

· · ·

Alcoholic of diabolic, I can't stop swigging doom.
Yet for beauty I'll always stop, panting with joy:
A sleek hearse, a cute shark, an intense bomb,
A well-crafted torture toy.
My tombs have panache worth dying for:
A user-friendly sepulcher.
Nineteenth-century deaths had style, two gems my best:
1821, the writ-in-water jest;
1865, the slow train west.
Why do the dying wrong me so,
As if I'm some feelingless juggernaut plow?
Tearing off wings or as urn's decorator,
I, not they, am the sensitive creator.
A bad press on funerals gets under my skin.
Humph, every one but me's a philistine.
I wish tamed wilds would spawn one untamed faun,
Even a mangy louse-nipped one,
To sigh my ugh at what apes uglify.
Hohum, I've outlasted so many eternities;
Each time, when nothing's left, not even zero,

This 'nothing' barfs a new big bang and—presto—
New galaxies.

. . .

> Or am I a corpse hallucinating all this?
> Dead brain re-sparked by my dissector's gashes?
> Waking a cell's last ember? Tickled ashes?
> A recharged battery's accidental sputter?
> My Pluto years only one second as true time is reckoned?
> (My only Greek the myth book on my cot?)
> No, no; the lies apes mutter
> Can't break my royal rod.
> Nor can the tricks of her upstart grape-shill god.
> Let him go back to Asia and take back
> The grotesque alcohol-berries he tries to hawk.
> (Name him? I wouldn't condescend.)
> Dissectors can shred me to bits; what they can't do is kill me
> So long as I say—no, screech—as the blades descend,
> "I'm not human. You're slashing quicksand."
> Me die? As death's boss, how *can* I? Reality
> Is what I tell it to be. As number-one god,
> I'm at peace with my lot.—O why am I really not?

O why? Too proud to admit it near my throne,
Even a night god needs personal noon:
HER homecoming footsteps traipsing down,
Hair still half-bleached from sun.
Here come my courtiers (boneyard, basalt, fossils)
To polish apples—I mean asphodels.
Ah, how they bore me when she's gone.
Here come my harems (lamias, lemurs, snow
Maidens). How I miss my one no-show.
Go-to-hell is the prettiest banner ever unfurled;
I wish she would.
Devil-take-her: my favorite blessing in all the world;
I wish I could.
I'd kidnapped me a bimbo. I spread her limbs akimbo.
Her limbs then kidnapped me. And left. I'm left in limbo.

> My gray cells twitch. What jabs my gray?
> And what high glare beats down?
> Is it doc's flashlight? No, call it the sun

She smuggled down when I said gods need noon.
Reality isn't the worlds of outside clay.
Reality is in my gray.

II.
Nine lackeys I gave her (more than wino spared):
Three darling furry imps kept her coiffeured;
Three demons poured the poppy juice we shared
Before three more prepared the nuptial grave.
Because my dank cave, cosy as a bier,
Lacks music for her music-craving ear,
I xylophoned my stalactite chandelier.
Because her art-of-love out-Ovids Ovid,
I gave her anklets pluto-crats would covet
(My own hands snapped them on) of solid gold.
Because her waist is graceful to behold,
I wove—to make our link endure—
A girdle of fragrant toadstools, dainty mold,
And skulls my worms scrubbed pure.
Because she likes cruel laughs, I used to spoof
Each shade below for his worst goof:
That cad Achilles for the heel he hid
In jackboot swagger; Trojans for the steed
That was also a mole; a cuckold kinglet for
A runaway wife who started a war;
Orph for his bungled rescue tour;
Poor Jason for the ill-advised idea
Of letting his baby-sitter be Medea;
Two sons, O. and O. (each did a parent in),
For a sin—or call it hangup—Furies haunt.
Hell hath no woman like a Fury scorned.

· · ·

Because on buried night-like days
She whined about frostbite and wheedled for blaze,
I crushed—with my eons and with my tons—
Ferns into hibernating arsons
Called coals, these volcanoes of substitute sunrays,
Whose cold black woke into comfy red instead.
Who cares if my Etnas arsoned a dozen ape towns above,

So long as my love got her fireplace?
Do apes care? But they're clods, not gods; her laurels
For ape bards engendered our worst quarrels.
Why can't she have decent values?—pride, will, and cruelty?
I taught her ruthlessness; whom did she use it on? Me.
While I lectured her on 'evil, be thou my good,'
She got so bored she snored. Which shocked me morally.
Didn't I do—to keep her—all I could?
My bedside Bulfinch taught me what's her food;
I had my Borgia chef whip up soufflés
Of pomegranates; they won mere half-year stays.
I buttered up Ceres, her mother; she anyway sneaked away,
Planting vile vines with her lover, subverting my Law of Decay.
Tell word-tout Dion and his groupies, with their yen
(As if it were their dildo) for his pen,—
Tell them I spot a phony every time.
Am I jealous? You bet! Hell makes punishment fit the crime
(Ask Tantalus), and I'll sentence him to rhyme
Forever,—understood never.

III.
My giant poise isn't embarrassed emoting on Richter scale eight,
Quaking the earth with my hate as once with my joys.
(If that's too bombastic for pygmies, let 'em sneer prissily.)
 In the patients'—no, prisoners'—library,
 That's where I boned up on Persephone
 After they lugged me through hospital doors,
 Calling my royal dreams plebeian tumors.
 Or if I'm no god, the more dignity
 To my stubborn "I am that I am."
 Must I ham an emperor Elba'd in janitor slacks?
 More hacked by gibes than vine by ax,
 I join the *noblesse* of the demeaned. Storm whacks
 Me worse than it did Lear—with panics worse than Mac's
 When he was facing Birnam's woodsy nooks.
 Anachro? Can I, a B.C. Hellene, wax
 So Shakespearean? Ah, those hospital books.
 They'd even make—take a random example—mere janitors
 Talk in pentameters.
Roaches fill basement cracks. Greek gods, de-shrined

By men, in turn de-shrine mankind
By infesting the cracked basements of the mind.
Like roaches, we scatter when lights are shined,
Leaving only—for pedants and poets to find—
Contemptuous droppings behind.
    Whatever outraged topside, here gets staged.
    I'd rather sulk in a basement than abasement.
    "Janitor" almost sounds like "genital,"
    The under-the-belt of global.
    When tenants, not guessing how soon they'll owe an obol,
    Flush gallons of sewage down at me, when they
    Yell for more heat (they'll get their fill in hell),
    I'll send a cobra up their pipes one day
    Or stuff the boiler with dynamite and blow
    The whole smug building up.
    Down here, all signs point down, not up.
    A janitor knows the respectable from below.
    They'll be sorry, they'll be sorry,
    That grape-crazed top-floor pair belittling me.
    While she's pawed all giggly-wiggly by his passes,
    Must I slave at stoking coal to warm the asses
    Of those who, when they're Styxed, must slave for me?

IV.
Brer Zeus yanked a girl from a migraine.
(None called Athena his tumor.)
Me too? Is the sharp kiss jabbing my brain
The girl I'm horny for?
    "Sharp kiss": the words save me. Here I slough
    (She's back!) my exile off—and resume my reign,
    Freed from my coal-stoke years. But the scalpel-sharp pain
    Keeps on. I'm feeling what humans must feel—
    If it's true, what I've heard, that they're able to feel.
    (Silent voice shouting from fringe of my brain:
    "FOOTSORE AND VERY LONG IS THE SHORT HUMAN LANE.")
Is she back? Did she miss—in spring's green jail—
Winters when beautifully fungus-pale
We ruled together on black obsidian thrones?
Palace of blackness: charcoal, crows,
Petits-fours coffins stacked as dominoes.

Lamps: lit with lard of emperors and priests.
Walls richly draped: with pelts of the ape beasts.
Persephone herself: each winter dead,
The Cleopatra of the carrions.
Each winter, rushing to my arms, her bones—
Like molting snakes—would shed
Her flesh with a sassy striptease twist.
With a final shake as catalyst,
Snapping life's last bind like a thread,
The rind—strip, strip—the rind, the rind has fled,
Outnuding nakedness. The terrible barrenness
Of her crescent cicatrix—
Cold as the moon it's no more bleeding for—
Now blooms forth more delirium down here
Than when some topside Venus ungirdles her
Warm Venus-flytrap calyx.
The graduates of my graves have appetites
Grosser than airy ghosts, than tacky sprites.
Pounding peeled bones, not flesh-guck, on the Styx,
We get our kicks from skeletons,
Frictions more penetrant than skin-deep pounce,
More intimate than pneumatic bounce.
My dead give "small deaths" to my dead.
    (Or it this just a lurid wet
     Dream on a janitor's lone bed?)
I dunno why "jab," so artistic-sadistic
A verb, keeps haunting my fevers.
I dote on my scepter-jabbing trick
Of electroshocking the dead, click click,
Into capering cadavers.
As if they've Parkinson's, each of my dead
(Lively, not living: a corpse with a nervous tic)
Quivers,
As if from tarantula's terpsichorean bite.
More crunchy than popcorn under my boot,
Their dancing toes rot off, are strewn about,
As if they're lepers gone spastic.
    (As if? As if? When I stretch the surreal, the fabric
     Rips its elastic.)
"Delirium blooms," I said. My dead go mad

With lust, hate, hunger. They self-destruct, they shred
Each other's sockets, they gnaw their own
Tibias, leaving a garbage of bone
To fertilize spring's picnic.
This is how winters end. But up to then,
Picture us two, our most idyllic scene:
Both throned; my pet bat on my wrist;
She giving Cerberus's heads a pat,
His gruff arf more mellifluous to my ear
Than birds of her wino's bards. (I'd cheer
If in his eye some hailed-blithe-spirit pissed.)

V.

She and I: too late to repair rapport?
O isn't it enough that once we were
This much to me, that much to her?
Am I no more to her or she to me
Than cast-off condoms floating down the Lethe?
Did she hold back the tears she should have shed?
Why didn't she say the word she never said?
My airborne satellites, the vultures, say
Plenty. They photo'd her today
Red-handed with roses and guilty of clay.
With ticklings called ripe, she shocks blueberries blue
And titillates pears to blush a pinker hue.
His vineyards excite more orgiastic japes;
Shameless with Bacchic fun,
She gulps ejaculating body fluids from
Grapes.

· · ·

What price her treasons? What got sold out to whom?
Each time she corpsed six months, I used to groom
Her skeleton squeaky clean. But now it wears
The rags of squish called meat.
With the drug called grow, she spreads the contagion called wheat
And openly hobnobs with the freaks upstairs,
Those monsters who dung and couple on the soil
They'll soon be under. For this, she sold her sweet
Treasure, her infernal soul.

VI.

Rumor: all's one big tidal melody,
Twining not two motifs but three,—
My ebb, his ebb, her sea. Two shores, one flow.
Well, I won't have it so.
No infra-dig *ménage-à-trois*. She'll cling—
After tonight—for keeps to the true king.
Flunkies, fetch me my magic scything wand.
Tonight I slam my killer hand
(For my holy crime, my wrist is tensed)
On tide, on the seasons, the year wheel, the balanced
Seesaw of for and against.
She's priestess of balance. I want it all ice, and he
Wants life's insolent evergreen poetry.
Recidivist life just can't keep on recycling
(Spurting and burying, buried and re-spurting)
The seed pus of its running sore.
Some day life can't go Eastering any more.
I'll end this damned green leprosy.
When Dion-Zagreus-Osiris is hacked by my stern just scythe,
Stretched out as protein for crows,
What flows is not her metronoming sea
But grape's swart gore.
Convulsed like a fish-hooked worm on the floor,
Under the bed where they once were blithe,
Let his crybaby-sidekick sob and writhe
(Till her lids and her lobes are red)
For the vine god dead on the vineyard snow.
I veto what I veto.

· · ·

A millennium later—or was it ago?—
Her wheel hasn't stopped for his or my no.
We both thought we're brakes; we're spokes.
My dead don't stay dead, his quick don't stay quick.
Three rival roles; apart, sick jokes;
Joined, an impossible harmony,
Making everything possible. My role still no. Now
An affirming no.
. . . Kind dusk. And gentle reverie.

A grandma fabling for children.
This is the ancient tale of the three.
This is the future tale of the trillion.
The children, bored (they'd rather play soccer),
Retell it blurred, with new myth garnished.
Smelling of urine and roses, clasping a nursing-home garland,
Alzheimer'd granny is fabling on her rocker:
Tales truer for being garbled.
Is it she who rocks earth around sun? Has she unwittingly gardened
March? Frost garbaged? Wheel guarded?
Dingy hospice, unknown to our trio: yet wheel's secret hub.
Afar in a pub—for a swig, for a puff—
Some village Homer tells some village oaf
The tale of how the three,
Each true to the same comic tragedy,
Did what each had to do.

(End of voice from below, whatever its source. The dissecting scalpel has now been withdrawn from its instant of poke and wiped clean of messy brain cells.)

(1992–95)

Continuities

Fiddlers, Gut Strings, Heritage

(variations on four ever-recurring mood-sounds, rhyme-sounds: "linger," "less," "continue," and "scans")

Part One

1. *Sinew*
     It don't mean a thing
     If it ain't got that swing.
                    —Duke Ellington

Fadings. Where will once raged, what languor?
The shadows on my lawn fall longer,
The sand-grains faster in my sandglass,
Demoting my wines to lees.
Longer shadows, sandglass, lees:
Three old-time tropes my old bones feel akin to.
Let's all creak rheumatic together. Outdated. Or is it timeless?
Primordial continuities continue,
But the continuers get scarcer, leaner;
Or is it my eye-sight getting less?
What was that thump just now beneath brow's window?
It's the old-age circus of Brothers Loss and Alas;
Watch the vowels—trained seals—leap through hollows:
Through hoops of the framing consonants "L" and "S."
Swoosh!—there goes "Loss." What "lies"
Ahead except new "lows"?
Quintet of the senses, acrobats gone careless,
Have lost their grip on my trapeze's trellis.
Life's a scrape none gets out of alive—
                         all winners lose.

                    •   •   •

And yet the "and yet" of quest transfigures loss.
Only the "more" of quest outlasts our less.
The pilgrimages, not we pilgrims, linger.
The laid-back lounger, the go-for-broke lunger,
They both end minus, not plus.
Then only the loner—
The offbeat—can fling you

The on-beats your grandchild will cling to, needing us lunar
Outlaws to bring back lost earth-laws.

      . . .

Take to the hills, you young fiddlers, when healers are loose;
They may heal you of wounds that may bless.
No solemn "love" crusades (haloes plus gallows),
No zealous marchers can phoenix the pallors
Of yellowing valleys.
It's the frisky iambic flesh, the fiddler sinew,
That pulses the lilt to regreen you. . . . Lilt scans
You. In a Bacchic laying on of hands,
Accept these scourging archetypes I sing you,
And purge all "edifying" homilies.
The foe is cant, a god who's very jealous.
Here's three thousand years of bitterest classics I winnow
From chaff I've sunk into.
Enough now (time for changing venue)
Of my creaky old saltarellos.
Your turn now—unseen, I have seen you—
To continue my theme of "continue";
Go charm the snakes of with-it like a Hindu,
Till post-mod fangs, adrip with venomed follies,
Sway pre-mod sarabands.
And where it's trendy to be anti-trends,
We ornery fiddlers trounce
Both kinds of with-it. Our time-trench
Isn't the age but the ages. Loss and Less are the trance
That trains endurers. Stay downwardly mobile; the entrance
To poems, to wombs, to fruitions
Is under—from shameless, from fearless.

      . . .

Are memories yesteryear's stretched rubber bands?
Snap present their past lest its afterglow singe you.
We—lifelong embryos—can't get ourselves born unless
Posthumously: whenever your memories call us,
Our death masks are mike masks we sing through.
They're ambush we spring through when disciples who temple us
(Us skeptics) thereby defile us.
Heritage, yes, but true heirlooms burst shrine-bonds.

Beauty isn't pretty, joy isn't painless,
I've had it with Graces. Continuity continues
Best with Erinyes.

2. *Where Find Us?*

To forehead's scroll, through myth's relentless stylus,
Archaic traumas trail us.
You heirs, you've the sweet of it—we had the aloes;
Ours the stings, yours the honey that follows.
Yours the overhealed scars, forgetting the dawn-age blows
We anviled for your solace.
Choice: ladle from or topple into
Wells,
      the past, the bottomless.
Where find us now? No teams, no clans.
Don't look where elder-statesman-clowns
Chirp golden oldies to their clones.
A few of us (drab, not some "genius"-act retinue)
Are catalyst mutants. Each time the mutants win through,
They re-begin you.
Listen to their outraged birth-pang bellows,
These monsters beached from your granddaughters' bellies.
Solid citizen Herod: "Mere—hohum—fiddler fellows.
This time no need for—harumph—the police."

3. *Metrics, Not Hour-Hand*

> *To what tune danceth this Immense?*
> —Thomas Hardy

Fadings. But brushing your brow you sense
Rescuers, two-way guerillas
Of sounds, slowing one-way sands.
Raiding both "then" and "now," tonal flotillas,
Uptilt—with two-way tide—time's one-way glass.
Feel them offsetting two countdowns that threaten you:
Sandstorms outside you and brow's built-in quicksands.
Raids on that sandglass need linkage of litany,
Touchable lightning, complicitous fireplace,
Bedside accomplice.
Metrics, not hour-hand measures the light in you.

Only paired cadence, stoked doubly intense,
Retards, retains.

                    •   •   •

Such sonant warmth, such warming sonance,
Such twinings of pulsings are clockwork's opponents;
It's this high heritage your bards
                              "continue."
        There's my theme-verb again—please humor the hang-up I cling to.
        From roots that "continue," each fiddle string grew.
        Does that make me "conservative"? Of course for the archetypes—
        Hell no for the stereotypes—
        Of the fallible corrigible westciv brew.
I've also a theme-noun: bards. Humor such has-been lingo.
Bards: bankrupt noun, no current revenue.
Bards: outworn disk, in no computer menu.
Outworn? That's just what you need: the defiant "irrelevance"
Of their violins to the violence
Of Now's demands. They'll haunt you as revenants
Tomorrow or a century
                    ago. Bards
Remember the
                    future. Their ebbs will be scanning your flows.
What's meter but time forced into leotards?

4. *My Seventy-seventh Birthday*
Seven decades rushed by me as swift as Phoenician galleys;
I'd hardly a moment to tie a tie or a lace;
I was scud on the wind, and all I skimmed was glaze.
I pause now (age's black umbrellas
Spreading their Rorschach shade forlorner)
To dump my truths—whose falsehoods nip like lice—
In the black prop-box for the grave to launder.
My ignis-fatuus muse, she, too, glows lies.
But hers turn true in the renitent laughter
Behind the hedge; in defeat's brooding leisure;
In the sonar bat-squeaks of fiddle that lurch her
Safe through time's cavernous calendar.
Extremes that we lend her, they balance her ledger
Of just enough of "too much." . . . Yet what avail us

Her half-lights when—in neon light—her alleys
Turn blind, my solos Waterloos?
Are muses and Furies sisters under their skins?
Hear the cost, the topsy-turvy cost, when shapeless
Life reluctantly scans:—

5. *Topsy-Turvy*

> *One is an artist at the cost of regarding as content what non-artists call 'form'. . . . A topsy-turvy world: content (our life included) becomes merely formal.*
>
> —Nietzsche, unpublished jotting

Life, life, you crude typo my proofreading steno-muse mends,
You give me the blue-pencil blues.
. . . Or maybe not life, maybe form is the misprinter?
Then maybe I'm monster, not *Mensch*?
We whom a tune has possessed, are we metronomed to malinger?
Are we hearing not heart but heart's reverberance,
An echo warped through a filter?
Renouncing a floor for a ladder, a "now" for a "later,"
Life's grit for form's lacquer,
I drown in the marsh where I'm bottling this letter
That may or may not be found "ages hence."
By playing form's fiddle, skittishly limber,
I betray (for echo's timbre)—I betray (for outmost fringe)—
Core: lovers, friends.

6. *Slack a While*

> *Slack your rope, hangs-a-man,*
> *O slack it for a while;*
> *I think I see my true love coming,*
> *Riding many a mile.*
>
> —old ballad

No, make my "betrayal of life" a bridge where estranged allies,
Life-core and form, coalesce:
A saccade my fiddle-bow spans.
That bridge (though stopping no clocks) delays
Tempo. Then Chronos dons
His dancing togs and (though unstoppable) dallies.
Not long; no pardons;

Not long his *Danse*
Macabre before we're skeletons.
TaTUM against TICKtock: the bridge's alliance—
Heart's iambs and art's—against Sandman's wands,
His sickle-shaped sandglass-directing batons.
His wands, they orchestrate—then end—the bangs
Of heart, called "ticker" not by chance.
The hour my ticking ends,
Will laid-on fiddler hands—
Unapostolic successions,
Unsacred sacraments—
Launch the bridge that stalls sand's avalanche?
Slack your rope, hangs-a-man, just an inch,
Made tame by a paired taTUM.

    • • •

And still each grain ticks on undamped
To the beach where the past gets dumped.
Red the sands and black the sandglass,
Trickling on the barren strands.
Grain by grain weaves rope most strange.
Weak "rope of sand?" The sand that hangs
Us never slackens.

    • • •

When I'm your past and hang condemned,
With all my echoes dimmed,
When diminuendo my resonance
And noon's din wanes,
Will you then, my love, remember how once
(Call it a laying-on of tones)
Paired pulse dammed up the hourglass dunes and crammed
The hours dense?

Part Two

7. *Dumped*

Grapes, not raisins; fresh formcraft;—at what expense?
Go for broke;—soul is what fiddled form expends.
Today we renewers of paeans that once were Pan's
Must pay with the Faust kind of pence.

If form pawns less than everything, it's less than soul it pawns.
He who hocks what we have hocked, pants for no medals on pins.
Our old-artificer weapons
(Joyce's exile, cunning, and puns)
Dispense an Antæan recompense
For our October pains:
Dumped cones—what's fall but downwardly mobile plants?—
Touch earthmom to plant pines.
Dumped formsmiths too, we planters—fall's fall-guys—pounce
To seed the blank frame, the blank page
                                        with paints, with pens.
As for you who are soul-owners still, cooped souls need windowpanes;
Sealed highs need lows.
You polish soul too pure; what cleanses, hollows.
Your whitewashed shadow, this is all your soul is.
Sell it—but to Athena, not Mephistopheles.
Honor the brow-brawn balance-act of Hellas.
Fiddles need guts; the string that sullies
Hallows.

8. *Why I Sometimes Believe in God*
There was this water. Noon's
Ray on an oil spill—a palette of tints.
Then a phantom voice (don't label) where the breakwater ends:
"What's wrong with all god-creeds is not that they don't make sense
But that they're not crazy enough. Look around for once."

                •   •   •

Where the breakwater ends,
What floods towards me at ocean's stone-boned fence?
Where breaker meets breakwater's No and bends,
Is there a golden surfboard, tugged by swans,
Or a Venus birth that a shark rends?
Where the breakwater ends,
A pair of phantom shoes (don't label in advance:
The drowner might be you or me a decade hence)
Descends.

                •   •   •

Wasn't there once
A graffito "to the unknown god" in Athens?

I've been looking around: from Big Bang to jumpy electrons,
He out-impossibles our most impossible superstitions,
He, the Creator I'm still creating ever since
The ray, the oil, the sea's fence.

9. . . . *And Sometimes Not*
Gaffer to gaffer as the shadows close,
Two old amnesiacs, both forgetting Tellus,
I forgive God's trespasses—evil, poison ivy, fleas—
And from his reaping I expect no furlows.
Fadings. When now the shadows grip the leas,
A raven stalks me. A prop? A bibulous
Prank of Edgar Allan's spooky sleaze?
No, he's my anti-self; he makes my lush
Doubts loosen all I'd rather leash.
Then what though I bury my ears under pillows;
Under that "pallid bust of Pallas"
I still hear him croaking with jubilant malice:
"Hemlock it—swig down old age, the drug-spiked chalice
That drove Yeats horny-mad and Wordsworth-Polonius
Sane and tedious.
Age gets too airy—it shillies and shallies,
Swapping Goethes and Keatses for Schillers and Shelleys.
Tithonus von Alzheimer, wither more quietly please."
Absconding through the looking glass of Alice,
He leaves me (no, not "nevermore") a callous
"Caw caw" so sardonic it devalues
HIGH-FLOWN DELUSIONS.
                                    See—down there—a ruthless
Wind buffeting two fragile-crested lilies?
Now back, now forth, retreats and rallies:
A pas-de-deux of fleur-de-lys.
Two petaled Loreleis,
Patterns the wind relays:
Inveigling with preposterous ballets
My reveries into their roundelays.
Sea's Morse was always heartbeat's tremolos,
But now—taTUM—the twirl of lily-crowns
Is what resounds
(All earth being sea-shelled) with a sea shell's sounds,—

The wafted fragrance garlanding our fragments
Till nerves and stems and star-rays interlace.
Up there, look quick, a Gardener lays
A Hand on all our laying on of hands—
And, lest a handclasp be a handcuff, grants
Each twig free choice. Through all, One star-breath pants,
Same wind by which the lilies are gently tossed.
Or is it same? With sceptic fingers crossed,
I pray in arthritic reverence (letting loose
Highflown delusions no raven allows):
    "Unknown, long longed for, bodied now by chance
    Within two lily sallies,
    Love's overflow from Whom all flowing follows,
    Dissolve me in the contrapuntal dance
    Of God, the loneliest of solos—
    And least alone, being paired with all that longs."
Meanwhile two wind-decapitated lilies
Twirl on—CAW CAW—in vegetable ignorance.

10. *Anyhow*

> *Modern poets looked for the principle of change; poets of the
> dawning age look for the unalterable principle that is the root of
> change.*
> —Octavio Paz

Then what is left when all is loss?
Those laid-on hands? That fiddle sinew?
Not you, young fiddler, not you can renew
The antiquarian lease
That ran out on Parnassus. No moon bitch now, no Apollos.
Dry gullies, from god-wine cut loose, are no wine-god palace.
But: not only spiders spin from their bellies;
Go spin new Parnassus within you.
With what? Well, what's left in these shallows
Except your living gut to string the fadeless
Fiddle my fadings bring you?
Though learning takes just a day longer than life-span allows,
Though life ails just a day faster than art allays,
Though age rots art before it can learn to sing true,
Sing anyhow. Continue.

(1992)

Counter-Continuities
Through, Through, and Beyond

> *The Moon played a large if not decisive role in the emergence of life on Earth. Life could start only in aqueous solutions of certain chemical compounds. . . . The frequent but gentle mixing produced by the tidal ebb and flow caused by the Moon hastened the protobiogenesis in these solutions.*
>
> —Stanislaw Lem

1. *Invocation*
Lightning-prone even in dry skies,
Mind's deserts have big eyes,—
Wistful for altars. What orb earns ode's
Awe? Sun's gods
Are "righteous" male bullies; their abstract "love" swallows;
Tamed hymns, not free odes, are their incense.
What my homage (femmage?) invokes (invents?)
Is a she. The night orb. Not a "you" but high "thee."
Mindless moonbeam romance? No, the rays of her laws,
Tide's tug and release,
Crown mind by teaching mind-plod how to dance.
Where to? Through euphony's palace.
(And beyond? What follows? What follows?)
Harvest moon, surrogate earth for the harborless,
Harbor me, harvest my chants:—

2. *Ode to Moon*
I weave thy moon-strands, "Luna" in Latina,
Thy L and N and female final A
(Blue ooh-and-ah of language pushed too "too")
Around thee in a music-vined liana.
A luau of sonant anagrams. A Niagara
Of vowels flooding midnight with their mantra.
With orgies of tropes I acclaim—and with sound's saturnalia—
The amok echolalia
(Don't read it, speak it) of
                    Ionian Seléna.
Shuttling from shed persona to persona,
Moon-names shift quicker than a flicked bandanna:

Lagoon of numinous corona,
Night's luminous eye, the month's ballooning retina,
O "O" that yo-yos between grotesque and tender:
Gourmand's green cheese or Ferdinand's Miranda?
Even thy ray-dance shuttles. From loony tarentella
To the Muzak of the spheres. If, bella stella,
My fiddle is as unheeded as Cassandra,
It's that we exiles weren't born on Terra.
All fiddlers are mooncalf stowaways from Luna.

3. *Second Moon Ode*

> *My deere doghter Venus, quod Saturne . . .*
> *Weep now namoore, I wol thy lust fulfille.*
> —Chaucer

Just now, if my too steamy verbal sauna
Runs wild, don't (having moonstruck me) get querulous.
Decode my odes as banned arcana,
Shrewd nonsense that no plodding lab-sense tallies.
To unplugged ears, rhyme's procreant copulas
Tell more than dictionaries tell us,
Each couplet coupling some lubricious sound-pair.
As boys scoop mythic castles from a sand bar,
My pen spawns myth: lungfish . . . vine god's arena . . .
Fiddle tricks . . . sane asylums from world's mania,
All born at Land's End on Allhallows.
But: pen's not quite parental; arts engender
Less than what pedants call "pudenda."
If birth were truly art's agenda,
I'd climb art's laser to thy pale veranda.
The trouble is: this ode-spawned manna,
This fuss of "creativity" nirvana,
Is fata morgana. At its core: lacuna.
All pens have womb envy, all poets moon-awe.
Moon moon moon moon, I name thee mándala
Of Eros. We've served Thanatos the perilous
Too long now. Rule and overrule us.
Rondure of burnt-out wonder, revery's larder,
Crater today profaned by rocket's launcher;

Yet still, yet still the poet's ladder.
All fiddles are carved of applewood by Luna.

4. *Threnode: Reversals*
She's too high, I hug only shadow.
Or else risk a dive in her mirror's undertow.
The two-hundred-thousand mile lunar
Tide-tuning sonar
Sends me my intimate wave, the one I call Unda Marina.
And the gravity pull, the long reach that belies
The long distance, now plays—as a bellows—
The swell and sag of ocean's concertina.
All ocean speaks *lingua Romana*,
Speaks aloud the word *undisona,*
The sound-echo word for "resounding with billows,"[1]
Reverberant undulance, born with Cytheréa,[2]
Foam's cornucopia of onomatopoeia.
Roses on the foam, an aria's aroma.
Roses on the foam, a terza rima
Of hue, flow, fume.
Mere sound-play? No, sooth-say—if sounds earn their resonance.
But: now played too far. Cry halt. When sounds demand incense,
When sounds corrupt sense,
When waves become sirens' manipulant sonance,
It's then there ascends—from cloyed rose-scents—
An acrid after-tang:
All ocean one poisoned drop of dew
On—not on petal but fang.
After the odes, the threnode; make way for a stanza
More somber, a comber tossed higher:
All our forlornness, all gypped wistfulness
Condensed into one urgent dirge-cadenza.
When surf smirks calmest, least trust halcyons.[3]
Even the fabled boy who understood bird-talk drowns
When he thinks he understands what a comber drones.
Sea gobbles down you's and me's for her "us" of wet fire
And bubbles up eggs and gnawed pronouns:
Sea fondles—with hands of violent lace and prissy typhoons—
Her Doomed
                    (they make nice pets, they're her castrati choir)

And her Bloomed
                    (the foam-garden she prunes).
She's the one graveyard that tortures music from shipwrecks and bones.

                    • • •

The sea moon and the sky moon (abyss reflecting corona),
They're circling each other like orbiting stars.
Like monk scalps, bright in the middle, each orb glares
The same. And not the same. This is and isn't Luna,
This false sea-Cressida,
This twin, distorted—ghastly—through sea's froth.
Sea's snapshot of moon is a death's-head moth.
And death, being love's kid sister, each is both;
Let me list the pairs:
Libido's Venus Lubentína,
Yet Rome's funereal Libitína;[4]
To lost Endymion a candelabra,
Yet not, yet not to drowned Leander;
My "bona stella" Bella Donna,
Yet deadly nightshade's belladonna,
As sweet, as poison-sweet as oleander;
In short, the classic love-yet-hate of Tantra.[5]

                    • • •

If rhythm is essence, time for new stance:
For storm-hewn spondees, truths of stones,
Harsh joy of faced stains.
Little they know of fiddlers who only know fiddle tones.
Fiddling is more than "dulcet" tunes;
These had their centuries. Now atavist revenants
Break outworn breakwaters, rid us at once
Of Euphonia's ah-too-"sensitive" wince.
Dikes crumble—tide wants what it wants.
What wanes becomes mulch for what wakes.
All ends where the dense floor waits:
Cerecloth of fog; spent waves.
All revolves where what ends revives:
Caul of fog; fecund waves.
What happened to bloom's rosy wings?
No roses. Blood on the foam.
The Cythera birth, red mess flung on winds

Landward, wins.

Life costs what it costs—it's still our life, our home.

Blood on the foam. Wise wounds.

NOTES

1. "Billows" may be embarrassing poetic diction, but my Latin dictionary translates *undisona* as "resounding with billows." The word was used by Propertius to describe sound of sea gods.

2. Another name for the foam-born goddess, emerging from sea near the island of Cythera.

3. "A halcyon is a fabled bird, supposed to calm wind and waves . . . while it nested on sea."—*American Heritage Dictonary.*

4. Venus Lubentína (or Libentína): Roman goddess of sensuous delights. Libitína: goddess of burials. Here linked: not merely for this section's vowel obsession but as imagined halves of the same Luna.

5. Tantra as "the female energy in nature": sometimes represented in Sakti worship as "Durga, the yellow [moon-colored] woman riding a tiger"; sometimes as "Kali, adorned with skulls in cruel and obscene rites"; yet equally as "Devi, the mild and beneficent."—*Webster's New International Dictionary,* Merriam Co., 1924 edition.

Rogue

> *The first and foremost danger encountered by organisms (which were all originally water-inhabiting) was not that of inundation but of desiccation. The raising of Mount Ararat out of the waters of the flood would thus be not only a deliverance, as told in the Bible, but at the same time the original catastrophe which may have only later on been recast from the standpoint of land-dwellers.*
>
> —Sandor Ferenczi, *Thalassa: A Theory of Genitality*

> *Seed spoiled by mutation.*
>
> —definition of "rogue" in botanical dictionary

> *The origin of the larynx was to facilitate air breathing in fish. . . . The human embryo, when it is about five millimeters long, shows a slit in the pharyngeal floor much like that of the lungfish.*
>
> —Philip Lieberman, *The Biology and Evolution of Language*

The cycle starts when a parlor game gets out of hand, "you" (the reader, modern man) becoming the lungfish ancestor whom you have been miming in a charade. This transitional "fish"—proto-lungs, four fin-legs—survived being beached by becoming the first air-breather, from whom all land life descended. The lungfish-you landed in the Devonian Period of the Paleozoic Era.

The speaker is you: mostly alone, occasionally in dialogue with "father," here God-Mephisto, the brutality of reality. Father-voice is printed in normal type, you-voice in quotes and italics and indented.

I.

(you suddenly on Devonian strand, 400,000,000 B.C., addressing your future selves of today: *Rogue*)

"Where/when am I? I've left (behind?/ahead?)
You selves who'll now face twins you never had:
Twins younger than you (your own embryos)
Yet older (your ancestral dead).
You chose land's height? Undertows
Have long arms; hide.
Before there were veins, there was blood, not
Yet hot. Nor yet inside: tonight
Why is the surf so white and yet so red and yet so green?
Its quilt of algae tucks what shiverers in?

Before there was bone, there was marrow
Outside. Stealing shapes. How
Tight are you glued? A shape can be peeled from its skin.
Huddle in secret places, bolt that door;
Your twins—with half-dried seaweed round their faces
(A bit, not so you'd notice, goggly eyed)—
Right now crawl up your shore."

II.

(lungfish you, lone in new landscape and facing the unknowns of sand, sun's eyeball, hill
rows, flowers, air: *First*)

"Just because I'm first of a newfangled race,
Is that why these eerie new props arose?
These sand storms: you call them a friendly caress?
This big scorching Eyeball: some predator's ruse?
It's rising, it's rising—behind shark-tooth rows
Of what? Unwet landwaves? The planet
An ambush? Yet this—a stemmed goldfish?—this beach-rose
Sways guileless; its casual fin-flicks erase
My wariness. Smells of growingness rouse
My snout with their . . . greenish flavor; they raise
My lungs to a . . . dry 'sea.' I plummet
Topsy-turvily upward and savor
The first whiff ever, ever sniffed. And vomit.
You white dry air up there,
You're wreathing yourself with orange—where the Eye-rays
Stroke you. You. The . . . stuff I'll be breathing."

. . .

"Me nobody strokes; moist smoothness, that's the choice
I miss. Blame the razor-runged ladder I'm on.
Ache is my echo since climbing rung one,
A gagged echo straining for voice.
My vocal cords, still many an age upstream,
Lag behind their scream.
Why can't it prod sky's lid?
My mutation the hump of a hunchback.
My feed, it isn't star song but raw squid;
The ignoring stars sprint on, at a speed with a lot of zeroes;
I live by inches—not by miles—of cosmos.
All I feel is the threat of small stones and the promise of moss."

III.

(modern you to lungfish you)

"Here's homage, dear mirror image,
To the pilgrimage of our race:
From Argonaut to astronaut, from a puddle
On earth to a pebble in space."

(father entering)

You're quite a couple.

—*"My double."*

Each other's parody.

"Not soil, not sea."

Amphibious borderland,

On both sides orphaned.

"But . . . lung, thumb, brow. We shore-people,
We'll ripple tide."

—You're but tide's ripple.

     •   •   •

(lungfish, then father: *Jacta Alea Est* [1])

"I didn't want my double helix spliced
Into dodos, hippos, Al Capones, and Christ."

Your DNA dice—

"Did I ask to be diced?"

You're all rough drafts the Weltgeist

Discarded.

—*"Rough on jugulars."*

—Beneath

The die your landing cast,

Writhes all land's pain-to-be, from the gashed

Hare to the Lear on the heath.

     •   •   •

(lungfish you to modern you: *Diatribe*)

"I should have been warned. Apocalypse
Shouldn't have made such historic (am I Columbus?)
Fuss. Landing gashed and frayed
Is not a Broadway tickertape parade.
Motorcycle gangs should have greeted me with whips
And lynch-the-mutant taunts.
Had even one sign said, 'Public beach, no lewd
Breathing allowed,'

I would have sos'd my finny mother,
'Lungs not user-friendly, prodigal fish wants
Out.' Tell Dorothy's brother
That Nature does betray the hearts that love her.[2]
Dammit, I never asked to be a brow-evolver.
I 'is' a Nother;[3] *we Nothers—no freak from outer*
Space more freaked out. And if my quips
Are the desperate banter of sinking ships,
It's that my last self is fishing for my first.
The long fuse gets reversed; click—from my hips
Tick futures ramming fishhooks through my lips."

IV.

      (lungfish you, then father: *Chain Reactions*)
"No rockabye tide, no more of bubbly diving;
The end of glide, the start of wheeze and drying;
All this black dying, just to kick gill uphill."
Swim back.
"I hear delirious welcome from my first beach,
A gull screech before the first of gulls is born."
Only some wind-blown horn.
"Is it land itself that clamors for life
Till birds arrive?"
Only the shells
A comber swells.
            —*"What glad*
Light on my landing pad?"
The brow infection
Called introspection. Its terricidal fuse
(Just one loose nerve) burns in you unawares.
"What cradle is now half rocking me upstairs,
Half locking me down?
            Air skims
My snout while my tail still swims."
Race back downhill.
"I'll bulge just one wee rung
Toward brow, that super-lung."
Which then will blow
Up the show.
"Earth's billion-year cradle, spun

Empty around the sun?"
Let earth go weep
For what Niobe[4] could not keep.

. . .

After the bang, the pyre.
  "But after the fire, when sea
  Shrinks into marsh, and marsh
  Into desert, and all to ash,
  Some overlooked puddle, not quite sterile, will then
  Replay me."
And blow up again?

V.
          (replaying lungfish's very first glimpse of first Devonian strand; father, then you: *Ornery*)
The line where hills of sand end,
Where hills of ocean pound,
Where tidal stride, foam-sandaled, turns around,
Here trickster horns of Land's End—wind-blown sound—
Lure you aground.
  "Am I never to trust?
  Must winds that hint, must wounds that sing
  Bring traps?"
The fuse, the fuse! Rebound
Back to gullets and innocent laps.
  "Rogue seed stays ornery."
On Showdown Strand they're stranded, the banned and the abandoned;
It hurts worse to be land-bound than . . . drowned.
  "Hurts us toward hardness and kindness. Till we—"
Feel drowsy, sink; feel drowsy, sink; feel yourself fondled by sea.
  "I'm awake on the brink of a dune."
Spurned sea, though you sneak to deserts, hunts you down
As stowaway in your veins.
                  —*"But that horn, that horn."*
Heed—drowsy, drowsier—sea's undertone.
  "But shells, but shells, their undertow
  Tugs shoreward."
                  —Leave that siren tune
To stinking clams. One gallivant
On land, and all's undone.

> *"Or done. I'm gene's automaton,*
>   *Only I'm not. If brow—"*
Can you guess whose out-of-time skeleton,
Stripped and hollowed, weathered and torn,
Was wind's horn all along?
>   *"What's that to me? Can a gill, outworn, stall a lung?"*
With your future extinct and your past outgrown,
The stripped beast is you, both your gill-fish bone
Of before and your loaded brow
Of tomorrow.
>   *—"I dead or unborn?"*
You've lost. Go drown while you can.
>   *"Too late. I'll—."*
Don't! Sea loves you, wait wait wait.
>   *"I'll always lose. Some losses . . . hone."*
Halt, you're branded.
>   *—"Stripped, I've landed.*
>   *Make way for man."*

(1987)

NOTES

1. "The die is cast."—Caesar, crossing the Rubicon River in his march on Rome.

2. "My dear, dear Sister! And this prayer I make / Knowing that Nature never did betray / The heart that loved her."—Wordsworth, *Tintern Abbey*.

3. Rimaud's letter of May 13, 1871: *"Je est un autre."* ("I is another [someone else].")

4. Her many sons and daughters. They were slain by Apollo and Artemis. As she never ceased weeping, she became the classic symbol of bereft motherhood.

Full of Life

"Why," said another, "Some there are who tell
Of one who threatens he will toss to Hell
The luckless Pots he marr'd in making—Pish!
He's a Good Fellow, and 'twill all be well."

—Edward Fitzgerald's mistranslation
of the *Rubaiyat* of Omar Khayyam

Never smell roses close to your nose. There was a lady who smelled roses like that and all the little insects ran up her nose. She screamed for a week and then she died. They opened her head, and there were the caterpillars, eating her brain.

—a loving God-like nanny,
quoted in London *Observer*, 1972

SPEAKERS: you (modern man), in quotes and italics and indented; father (God-Mephisto), in normal print.

I.

(you: *I Want, I Want*)

"It could have been a planet fit for Eva,
There had been promises intense as noon;
And even what went wrong was almost right.
Our torrents, frayed by
Daily pebbles,
Almost reach ocean,
Drown in sand.
Yet dew still shines on certain lanes on certain mornings
That's neither air nor pool but waiting shyness.
There's haze, an orange
Gray that, dawn-struck,
Scatters like flamingos startled by a splash."

(father)

All man's flamingos are plastic,
Especially when they're not.

(you: *Truth Gibber*)

"When potter is hoaxer,
His marr'd pot is gibber:
I, clay-code's decoder.
When sober is stagger,
My foggy shines flasher.

Now mirror barks madder
And never is whether;
I, fever, am either,
My dot circling rounder."

II.
      (you, then father)
    "Update me Seven Sacraments,
    Improved for the now generation."
Father Pavlov's Consecration
Camp will—ring-a-ling—bring your nation
Salivation.
    "You'll exorcize our Seven Sick-events?"
I'll exercise your Seven Excrements.
First, infant burpism.—*"Pat their behinds."*
Next, getting conformed.—*"A must for young minds."*
Third, breed and whine: Feast of the Euchred-Christ—*"at the Borgias."*
Fourth, laying on of hams—*"in holy ordures."*
Fifth, mater-money or mare-itch; that's holy dad-lock.
    "Did you say: wholly deadlock?"
Sixth, pennants. A pollution for your sinks.—*"And then?"*
Extreme unctuousness earns you my meathook. Amen.

III.
      (you, then father)
    "If we've no better fate than hooks to face,
    Let's go down shooting, let jets rape space.
    Man's your amok amoeba, mugger of the universe,
    Ramming all Black Holes with our jet's white spurts.
    I'm not afraid of God; God is afraid of me;
    Watch me bully him. Grr."
Well roared. You make me shiver. Brr.
I mean haha: the roar's falsetto. Sir
Byron Pipsqueak a lone-wolf knight would be,
But the stance is too nineteenth century;
Outlaws can't titillate salons that know no laws.
    "Fallen angels still can flutter dovecoats.
    We'll hurtle earth loose from the stellar trellis."
Meteors no longer make fixed-stars jealous;
A comet sows tame oats.

IV.

      (you, then father: *Fellow Humanists*)

    "My flesh creeps. Are you some black-mass Jack who Rips?"
Mistah Baal—he dead. So's any God of whips.
Now that all Squaresville peddles freakier trips,
What's theater-of-the-cruel and *humeur noire*
But Pollyanna's dildo?—'tis pity she's a bore.[1]
    "Black mass—"—Was always white
Sheep in wolf's clothing. Night
(Better come quietly) has a harder core.
    "What's wrong with sunny Truth that builds and betters?"
The windbag uplift of your capital letters.

        •   •   •

Sun's thermostat, it won't be all that drops.
So many things must fall in day's brief day.
Stuffings and stilts; your heads perhaps;
At last the—
        "Hands off sky! Let ceiling stay.
    Nanny whom childhood counted on,
    Cloud-capped nurse-brow of sky, where have you gone?
    We wake up screaming now at the idea
    That Mary Poppins turn into Medea,
    Who turns into the bearded mutilator.
    Give trust back, sky. Be roof again, not crater."
It seems I'm being prayed at; I
Am sky.
    "How, sir, must we adore you?"—Kill.
    "With hot heads?"—With cold steel.
    "When steel blunts?"—Hands.
    "When hands fray?"—Stumps of hands.
    "We've used up gooks."—Try using friends.
    "And when we're out of humans?"—Stone a rat.
Call it my kicks, I like my globes like that.
    "They didn't say so in the Great Books course."
Ah, fellow humanists? Let's force
Men to be good.—*"But spill no blood, of course."*
Of course.—*"And no exceptions to that rule!*
    Except to prove it."—You have been to school.
    "And even if others spill some tiny bit

While we're not looking, we'll drink none of it."
Who talks of drinking? Just a sip.—*"A sample?"*
The better to rebut its bad example.
"Quick, hide it. Far away. It's not our thirst."
No, not at first.

V.
> (father)

Well then, sum up, O man,
La condition humaine.
> (you: *La Condition*)

> *"From skin-quilt's hell,*
> *Hurt leaped toward heal—*
> *And fell freezing between.*
> *Who's run off with my skin?"*

> (father, now in white medic jacket, brushing egg-filled hypodermic needle against patient's chest)

Kindly therapist gets you tranquil again
By planting something to . . . egg you on.
> *"Oh thank you. But what am I growing within?"*

That tickling? Child, call it conscience's sting.
Inner growth tests your . . . guts; you must . . . shell out its price;
Else a great bug in prison lies.[2]
> (father to stagehand angel)

He'll hatch his death's life-egg. It's a neat trick
To stick wasp's egg in a grub's meat.
A wasp and a moth feel alike inside
At first.
> (stagehand, genial chuckle)

> Till the wasp gets an appetite.
> (father to you)

Wings are the stings you are pregnant with:
The tingle of grub becoming . . . a beautiful moth.
> *"Wings, wings? Then flying to heaven is more than a myth?*
> *I feel full of . . . life; oh I'm bursting with . . . health."*

NOTES

1. 'Tis pity she's a bore: Variation of the title of John Ford's play, *'Tis Pity She's a Whore.*

2. Else a great bug in prison lies: Variation on John Donne's line from "The Ecstasy": "Else a great Prince in prison lies."

MOSTLY HOSPITAL AND OLD AGE • PART I

Welcome to Tarsus

> *The world's great age begins anew,*
> *The golden years return.*
> —Shelley

> *The wings return into the bird to nail him.*
> —Paul Eluard

> *This patient does not remember anything of what he has*
> *forgotten and repressed, but acts it out. He reproduces it not as*
> *a memory but as an action; he repeats it without, of course,*
> *knowing he is repeating it.*
> —Freud

This cycle has only one speaker, unidentified and so eccentric that he incites a silent visitor (himself but from an alternative earth) to sabotage an ordinary-looking cocoon on an ordinary-looking branch. Bungling of the sabotage darkens the sky over all old and new road-builders and triggers the unintended chain reaction that follows: the futile attempt of the nailed god to escape his godhood by hiding in ever new disguises, new cocoons, new continents, new eras, new alternative universes.

TIME: tomorrow but twenty centuries ago.
PLACE: Los Angeles but ancient Tarsus, home of Saint Paul (he doesn't appear) in Romanized Metic-Greek Asia Minor.
SETTING: incongruous mix of ancient and Californian props.
PLACARDS: "SPQR"; "WELCOME TO TARSUS"; "THIS WAY TO DISNEYLAND"; "ROMANS, GO HOME—NO NUKES IN EDEN"; "DRINK REV. JONES'S KOOL-AID HOLY WATER."

I.

> (Toga'd speaker is addressing own trousered reflection in big distorting funhouse-mirror, while stumbling against branch with oversized cocoon.)

Stop
Stumbling; you might wake up
Something. So you've come sight-seeing
From the edge of our good-old-flat earth? By Mithra,
You togaless tourists from America
Dress odd. . . . Say, what's this mess?

> (Points at cocoon; it emits slow droning.)

To peel (like an . . . an . . . apple) unripe moth,
Speeds hatching up. Toward wings? Toward death?

> (faster droning)

Can there be fruit that picks its picker?
Cast from the slingshot of the past,

This fruit-egg's out of sync with time's slow flicker.
Suppose it's you it aims at, aims . . . into:
Would its dank wings make your shocked shoulders bulge?
>   (Cocoon pulses twice.)
Would it—would sprouting silkworm sludge—
Feel loathsome to you or delicious? Stay
Sane, don't answer. WELCOME TO L.A.

II.
>   (During blackout, Asian and Californian props get reversed. From now on, cocoon sways
>   violently with every shift of time or role.)

If east-west landmarks keep kind of swaying,
It's a smog mirage. WELCOME (as I was saying)
TO TARSUS: a salubrious clime,
Famed for its baths of sulphur slime;
As a Jaycee—(J.C.?)—I boost our local trade.
>   (shrill outburst)
But not some greasy foreign fad,
Some meshuga Christian with chutzpa, spoiling the neighborhood
Real estate price. We Romans—that gossip Judas lies
When he says I speak Aramaic at home.
I'm pure Romanized Metic Greek.
When mumso took me to my first crucifixions,
I also enjoyed the popcorn and balloons.
>   (hiding hands)
The holes in my palms, they're only sores from oars.
>   (anxious glance at wall clock, suddenly ticking louder)
Blame smog dust if the proconsul asks why we're late.
Then watch the old fool wheeze,
"Behead the aedile of Los Angeles."
Dust's what we Roman Europeans hate.
>   (Floor wobbles; lights reverse colors; voice-reversal from Rotarian to vatic.)
We Asians whom young Rome would "modernize"
With soap and floppy disks—our dust shall rise
With dragon wings and blot out western skies:
The savage joy of it, our home-brewed witchcraft, our sublime
Cults conk our conquerors. But . . . Caesar's spies . . .
>   (looking over shoulder)
I mean: our home-brewed wine—sublime!
Our Asian loyalty to Rome—yes, that's what is sublime.

Call us provincials, but our eclogues rhyme,
And PanAm triremes bring your *Times* on time.
> (Clock's hour hand speeds up furiously.)

Time! Ticking faster! Wings hatch with one more tick;
> (yelling at his mirror image)

Don't let them stretch, abort them quick.

III.
> (Speaker gathers pulsing cocoon into paper hanky, dumps it in garbage can.)

This garbaged fetus clawing pudgily
Coffee grounds and eggshells, pail of history,
This hedgehog huddle of lewd complicity
Making its dumpers wonder if they won:
Eyelids a senile dawn has wizened,
Still dazed at half-becoming what it isn't:
One gut-smeared snot rag holds it all.
> (Speaker winces fastidiously, then shakes chiding finger at mirror, attributing his own dumping action to visitor.)

You!—stop being squeamish when duty and hygiene call.
How shoddy of the grosser category
To die in ways that make the nobler sorry.
Like nailed on a cr——...no, cross it out quick;
Slip of the tongue; I meant stuck on a stick.
> (to creature in can)

Thou shouldst have played Saint Francis to hyenas,
Preached to piranhas, stroked lions in arenas,
Not come unarmed to man.
> (to mirror again)

Are you some milkshop monk of the Certosa
To flinch—almost throw up—at what you've done?
Would Darwin wince like a mimosa
Each time some bug-eyed *via dolorosa*
Lands its unfitness in a can?
Now nail it down to stop its gucky throb.
Nothing's as squirmy as an unfanged specter's
Hilarious gum-nips at its vivisectors
When grubs rush in to batten on a blob.
> (spearing it and again attributing his actions to mirror visitor)

Ecce homunculus!—upon a matchstick,
His side speared by a cocktail-cherry toothpick.

This lepidopterous preposterous clown—
We're safe now—might have brought an empire down.
      (long silence, then noise from garbage)
What droning churns the mess, what breeze blows colder?
The slingshot catapulting this cocoon
From Manger to cluttered can
Could not foresee a comedown so bizarre:
Hunching one horribly-sprouting shoulder
Deep in a quilt of Hershey bar,
This . . . what?—not moth? not child?—this splinter-crowned
Christ-dragon, squished into a ketchup jar.
Well, this is it, the end of faith
Demons. Yes, squish it more, you've rescued earth.
This ir-re-vers-ible god-crash, it's the death—
Oh no, you've triggered it—the wings, the birth
Of myth.
      (Smoke-wings rise from can; speaker's fist cracks mirror.)
My stumbling new-world bungler, you've. been. shed.

IV.
      (as wings, now enormous, blot out ceiling-lamp "sun")
There it flies, the self I fled,
The slingshot pebble, now a looming boulder
Dooming all empire. Twenty centuries older,
My incense-smoke still goads the heart's hot smolder
Against cold Roman roads.
An Asian war[1] drags on, the legions molder;
A burglar Caesar[2] quits as office holder,
Pop oracles make shamans bolder;
The day two hounded boat people[3] find no bed
For their baby's head, can Manger and Star be far?
When slum child's rattle bloats to bishop's crozier,
Full circle—*in hoc signo*—closes closer,
And the catacomb lets the empire steal the Star.
At last (to finish Gibbon's yellowed folder)
The Tiber matron lets the hired soldier
In, Declines
        him for a while,
           and Falls.

V.

(to audience)

Eden's and autumn's and empire's: threefold falls.
The waste hurts most in all the falls I've faced,
The waste of you, of us: man moving motionless fast
In a merry-go-round on a quaky playground whose San
Andreas fault is . . . man.
I've let—to stop the ride—a soldier spear my side;
It didn't stop. We spiraling down, not up,
Why can't we change *(plainte éternelle, plainte éternelle)*
The wooden zebras of our carousel?
No sooner said than—. Already we're all . . . elsewhen.

(Floor tilts, lamps blink.)

And while new earth gets busy getting born,
Watch me adorn the ceiling—now a screen—
With reruns of each famous scene
From your old script, now scrapped.

(Speaker aims projector at stage's blue ceiling; slides of familiar history follow.)

Call sky a schoolbook; blue pages, flipping, show
The scenes you, yawning, already know.
Watch Columbus discover the earth is flat;
As he falls off the edge—see the bottomless vat?—
The sailors are jeering, "We told you so." . . .
See Charles the Anvil at Tours kiss Allah's rod;
Hear, ever since, Parisians speak
Euro-Arab slang with special chic. . . .
Pray to Our Lady Diamat among
The dreaming spires of age-old Trotskigrad. . . .
Cheer Sir Benedict being gracious to the throng
At Governor's Mansion in Arnoldston, D.C.;
Folks call him "the father of our colony." . . .
Adore Saint Lucrezia Borgia, first woman Pope. . . .
Now 1984;[4] vast earth goes pop.

(On stage a very small balloon pops.)

But we're all safe by now in neo-earth:
Man's second chance, new April's birth.

(Screen now reverses endings; earth unflattened, Charles now the Hammer, holy Diamat now secular dialectic materialism, Arnoldston now Washington, etc.)

Atoms, change partners; reverse your spin.
Rejoice—out's in—neurosis is new roses.

And each new Sacred Wood
> (sudden tone of infinite weariness)

Still ends as gallows wood.
Each time we switch sky's tape
> (pointing at projector)

We all escape on Noah's
Titanic. Our ship rides a Möbius strip;
Though we're free to choose either side for our trip,
There's not much April in sky's comic strip.
> (kicks projector offstage)

VI.
There's still much Rome. Rome leaves no dew on roses.
It's more than roads a road-maker bulldozes.
Even rococo (road gone porcelain) is glad sadly;
And Big Brother Geometry adores sanity
Madly,
>   painting straight strips of white on life's black whirls.

Possessed by System's demon pack,
The carousel zebras tread relentless wheels,
These Gadarene zebras, drowning in history.
> (to cracked mirror)

Peel off, peel off that hobbyhorse simile;
Beneath it who spins there? Road-maker Paul, are you me?
You're my ventriloquist, my sleep your Babel,
Presser of living leaves in a book's babble,
Presser of green who made dried red a Bible,
Presser of me.
> (addressing white throne, placarded as "HOUSE THAT PAUL BUILT:— Jan Bockelsen: Jim Jones. Torquemada: Robespierre. Calvin: Lenin.")

Paul, Paul, with your Saint Procrustes banner
Of "infinite love through infinite terror," [5]
Propaganda minister of God's second tome,
You bring me back the throne I'm racing from;
Two corpses shuttling threads that live,
You weave, I unweave (call it hist. of civ.)
The loom of Rise and Fall.
But I'm off to hide my throne from living eyes.

VII.

(Speaker spins clock backwards in time. Wing creature drops from ceiling, shrinks back into tree's cocoon.)

Backwards my centuries roll, like corpses' eyes.

With twenty spins of counterclockwise tick,

Made cunning by the fever spooled in me,

I shrink my dragon soul into a matchstick,

My misused throne into a tree.

Well hid from cult in woodwork's haystack;

No spear in my side; just cocktail-cherry's toothpick.

I've gouged green free of white god-rot; I've restored

The innocence of wood.

(Cocoon on tree hums again, each droning followed by speaker-voice deepening, as if invaded by his own rejected and cocooned god-voice. His god-words are capitalized throughout.)

IT. WASN'T. EASY.—whose voice?—BEING—

Being what? Can't be; I've restored—

IT WASN'T EASY BEING GOD;

COMPASSION FESTERED WORSE THAN THORNS;

EMPATHY SPOILED THE CHISEL;

TO MAKE ME HUMAN WAS INHUMAN.

I'D RATHER SCULPTURE EXCREMENT THAN EGO;

WHEN MOBS SPREAD GODS, THE BLESSING IS BUBONIC;

OMNISCIENCE WASN'T WORTH THE LOSS OF WONDER.

Out, out, you voice I dread; to shed my cross's wood,

I've wooed a fool into a tree. My Eden appletree.

WASN'T WORTH THE—.—Out! Or might the voice be me?

One foolproof escape: to my own source I'll turn:—

VIII.

(spinning clock still farther back)

—the start of gods I'll burn burn burn,

The spooks who thought up men who thought up spooks.

Lean cheetahs whom my forest-fire slaughters,

Myth upon myth lopes by with backward looks.

Here's Ur, there's Stonehenge, up from boiling waters

Poseidon hurtles on the heels of Dagon;

Venus and Mars have always shared cremations;

Up north the *Götter* take their *Dämmerung* stations;

All blaze as brakelessly as Phaëthon's wagon.

Spin wilder; now's the moment, now I hide it—

My God plague—in some dawn-age dragon,
Sealed from man in some bug nest of prehistory.
Time curves? Watch my momentum override it.
My will be done; I have annulled my *agon;*
Right through creation's morning I'm riding free.

> (straddles appletree branch and whips it on, as if riding it; doesn't notice it's not moving)

Riding, riding.
Never felt freer. Riding my . . . palm-strewn donkey.
Faster! Savage joy ticks my, tickles my
Itchy shoulder.
IT. WASN'T.—mother, water—WASN'T. EASY.

IX.

> (Brief blackout restores opening scene of section I, mirror uncracked and cocoon unhatched, but in reversed world: this time speaker is trousered American visitor, addressing voiceless toga'd reflection. Tree now hollowed.)

Stop stumbling; you might . . . wake up.
Round the round world I've come—how odd your togas seem—
To Tarsus. A salubrious clime.
But what makes borders blur between me and tree?

> (entering tree-hollow)

I wonder who's cocooning; glad it's not me.

> (stretches elastic cocoon and wraps it around himself)

My walls feel silky—delicious!—no, loathsome, loathsome.
IT. WASN'T.—drone-voice?—WON'T BE. EA—.
Closer than dryads to my splintery sliver,
Shrunk smaller than the grubs it's rotted with,
I hunch a horribly-sprouting shoulder
Deeper into the quilt of pith
To sleep 2,000 rings deep. . . . No, assassinate me
Out; skin me alive of the rind of forever;
I can't hold on; waker, flay me of deity.

> (Curtain)

• • •

> (Now entire monologue is repeated. But never quite the same each round; not circle but spiral, time without end.)

(revised, 1993)

NOTES

1. Asian war: Here an analogy is being made between America's Vietnam and ancient Rome's bogging down in Asian Parthia.

MOSTLY HOSPITAL AND OLD AGE   •   PART I

2. Burglar Caesar: Here a Roman analogy with an American president's involvement in the Watergate burglary.

3. Boat people: Homeless refugees from Communist Vietnam, here seen as Joseph and Mary, looking for shelter with their child Jesus.

4. 1984 (other earth): In the alternative universe, Orwell's nightmare world is treated as if it actually took place.

5. *Re:* love and Bockelsen: "Four-century messianic binge: it was 438 years ago in Munster that the leftist-rightist mass-murderer Jan Bockelsen, selfstyled 'king of the universe' and altruist savior from 'conspiracies' (aristocrats, capitalists, priests, Jews) proclaimed the new bed-of-Procrustes brotherhood: 'infinite love attained by infinite terror.'"—P. Viereck in the *New York Times Book Review,* October 31, 1971.

Re Paul: "The man who, I suppose, did more than anybody else to distort and subvert Christ's teaching was Paul. . . . It would be hard to imagine anything more un-Christlike than Christian theology."—Whitehead, *Dialogues of Alfred North Whitehead,* Boston, 1956, p. 247.

SUGGESTIONS FOR STAGE VERSIONS OF "WELCOME TO TARSUS"

"Round" is the title (as published in *Poetry Now*) of this verse-play's earlier version. When it was staged in 1980 by the Lab Theater (Catholic University) of Washington, D.C., two speakers were used instead of one. The second actor stood for the first one's mirror image, spoke whatever stage directions could not be conveyed by gesture, and spoke the final section IX, at this point exchanging places in the mirror frame with the first actor. The Lab Theater did not end with section IX but with a repetition—after IX—of section I and of the first six spoken lines of section II, ending with the hearty Rotarian greeting:

WELCOME TO TARSUS: a salubrious clime,
Famed for its baths of sulphur slime;
As a Jaycee—(J.C.?)—I boost our local trade.

But when the author himself performed the cycle at the Library of Congress, November 5, 1979 (tape recording available from poetry office of Library of Congress), he was sole speaker—instead of two—and ended with section IX, as in this book version.

MULTIMEDIA EFFECTS: the Lab Theater used labeled movie screen projections (directors were John Lescault and Prof. William Headington) to imitate Tarsus and Los Angeles and in section V for Columbus falling off the edge, Saint Lucrezia Borgia, etc. Each new section number requires lighting changes to alert the audience that a reversal is ahead: of speaker's disguise or of parallel earths.

MEMO FROM THE YEAR 2500:
Re: the reference to Our Lady Diamat (in an alternative earth). In some forgotten past, the name of Our Lady Diamat (patron saint of antimaterialism in today's twenty-fifth-century Holy Russia) was derived from that mysterious archaism of 1917, "dia-lectical mat-erialism," its meaning lost over the centuries. But from Latin our ingenious linguists have deduced the two halves composing the word "Diamat": "Dia" for goddess; "mat" for "mater" or "mater-ism"—an *ism* expressing the Slavic soul's cult of Our Lady's motherly spirituality.

Up

Is not the body on the Cross the apple (of perilous choice)
restored to its tree?

　　　—W. A. Murray, "What Was the Soul of the Apple?"
　　　Essential Articles for the Study of John Donne's Poetry

There were also women looking on afar off: among whom was
Mary Magdalene.
　　　　　　　　　　　　—Mark 15:40

(Lone speaker of this whole cycle is trudging uphill; oddly crowned; bent by an unseen weight. Bare landscape except for a stunted olive tree and an oversize cactus. Looking on afar off: two Marys.)

I.
Uphill;
Sometimes I fell;
Reached up for thirty years,
Then thirty years were up.
Fell, but fell never down: no tired dawdles
(I then, I then still called the loamed "the mired")
On fallen petals. . . .
Soapboxers and gods tend to end up uphill.
But not all Mounts are Sermons; one,
Tempting me with This World, failed. Another nailed.
I, haggard under more than sun,
Lugged more than weight. Dung beetles staggered under
The moldered skulls. I shouldered what I shouldered.

II.
Skull Hill was so scuffed a rug that the threads unmeshed;
My reach fleshed out too late,—a leper's hug.
A doll was playing with a winsome lass
Elsewhere;
Glass ponds in scarves were skating a wee lad,
Not here.
Here on Skull Hill, no chubby grass;
The dogs were fetid, it's the air went mad.
Rome's Kraut centurions sweated out their north.
They gave me—I thought it was water—gall,
Or was it (time swirling me back and forth)

Gas? Mad air,
Were you fooling around with my shower stall?
And back here on the hill was the heat already a breath
From my second death,[1] from my far
Chimney's Baal-bellied belch?[2]
No, it was still my first Passion play; Bethlehem's star
Had not yellowed into a badge.

III.
It was my first; the replay still whirled in time's funnel,
A world of Pilates the stagehands,

                              hands of ablutions
At the two Solutions solving my chosenness: first
The Friday one, then the Final.
Skull Hill was a scorpion so dry that the grass claws
Crunched; I was treading straw stairs. The sting was
That straight lines are round and a treadmill a clause
Of my contract with immortality.
Then take away this cup from me,
This cornucopia cup.
Uphill or up wood, always my jig is up.
Even my ashes, a Santa Claus
In reverse, even they chimney up.
But wait, my two death-dance orbits—they hadn't come close
Yet, it still was my first.
Judenstern and Nativity were not yet a binary star
Writing me straight in crooked lines

                              that jar men's doze
Almost (and almost God's, his snoring worst).

IV.
But back from time's helter-skelter, still here on the hill,
My all-seeing eyes, up here in the first play's welter,
Foresaw

        nothing. Was my blinder my Elder
Mary's brow-sheltering hand?
I then, I then still doubted my brow-branding Other:
Young Mary, my Eva, rekindling my embering
Vision, long shackled by shelter.
On that Friday of death's birthday,

Hooded in that hilltop swelter,
Stood both Marys of my earth-stay;
Stabat Mater.
But Other—where's Other?—I lost sight of Other's
Red hair in a sandtrap that three rival brothers
(Calling it Holy Land) each made cacophonous
With mutual anathemas' brotherly love.
Crusaders as locusts, sand hatching their thunder,
Swarmed round her young head where no melody guards;
Where no flowering guides, she fled under.
(Is she waiting, harassed by Saharas,
Where numbed loam goads?)
My Elder was beautiful, bearing human-scale cares,
But when she wore all the world's grief,
Was she still, was she still our protectress
Or blubbering gelder of all of us, all
                                         godforsaken gods?
(Where's Other, tousled with all petals fallen since Eve?)
. . . But here, back here in the high hot glade,
When I sought shade in soul,
I heard a gnarled old cactus
Scornfully growl,
And from his lion-crouch came loping
(King-beast of Golgothas)
Thirst. Sand
Seeped through my rags, I . . . my . . . own . . . hourglass.
Mournfully wafting white theories at gray human practice,
I sent out doves, preened spotless as my Book;
Watch my brow be olive-branch crowned!
Came a drumbeat of wings, no cooing sound;
Came a carrion stench;
White crows came back.
My bare brow blenched: what's in that beak,
What whitewash is darker than black?
O why did their taunting talons clench
Branches brambly and round?
Has God-crown turned out to be thistle?
Then it's "mire" of Eva that's flower:
Portals of hairy gristle, petals of delicate fire.

To our frailty—sharing and pardon,
To loneness—tellurian feasts:
Eve's human-scale garden, not God's scale nor beast's.

V.

If her garden's as mussed as a brine-drenched dress,
Five-fingered caress by the senses,
Was I wrongly "right" when I dyed love white
To bleach my own frenzies?
I stared for answers where Jerusalem still
Floated, mirage or home, beneath my hill
And saw
       man's wriggliest question marks
Floating like sidelocks of my patriarchs.
One question mark wiggled its fishhook around me:
For loving too high, had love crowned me high
With a dunce cap that tickled
Me bloody? Sometimes I fell
(Watermilkmotheryourhand).

VI.

This was the March it rained so little
The olive groves were crisp with dust.
I, too, was brittle crust, my blood
Hemorrhaged by doubt as theirs by drought.
Linked by our upward-straining un-sereneness,
The woods that watched me carrying the wood
Had years ago kept green my desert years,
But now the blink of noon—the Eye had seen us—
Parched our last climb (save for two women's tears)
And led me toward a
       tree nest. After
I fell the third time, Easter,
Waiting ahead for all dry groves, gave
Up,—ebbing
Their tree blood, ebbing
My greenness,
      except one crest.
Triumph! My crest (but why, young Mary, no fruit?)

Transcended laps of loam for sky-high cleanness.
... Triumph? I failed—I fell (crest drained the root)
Uphill.

NOTES

1. "Forgive us," said Pope John XXIII of the Final Solution's six million, "for cruci-fying Thee a second time in their flesh."
2. "Chimney's Baal-bellied belch": the smoke of burning corpses in Nazi death camps.

Down

Bromio, sweet Bromio . . . whose muses live.

—Invocation to Dionysus-Bacchus-Bromio
in Euripides, *The Bacchae*

And Adam called his wife's name Eve; because she was the mother of all living.

—Genesis 3:20

We have given to thee, Adam, no fixed seat. Neither heavenly nor earthly have We made thee . . . Thou art . . . the molder and maker of thyself, thou mayest sculpt thyself into whatever shape thou dost prefer.

—Giovanni Pico, Prince of Mirandola,
the Christian Hebraist and Hellenist,
Oration on the Dignity of Man, 1486

PLACE: Gethsemane.
VOICE: Christ.
TIME: today.

If on stage, slow pacings keep step with long voice rhythms. Backdrop of Mediterranean (the "Midsea" of Eve-Aphrodite and Dionysus); modern you, entering near end, is printed in italics and quotes.

(Christ, alone, is addressing his varying imagined hearers.)

1.

(to his Antichrist)

Half-brother, Pagliacci-Nietzsche, why do you wrong me so?
Give me your hand, I was always

Dionysus-Bromio.

It was good when gods weren't godly and stones not tablet but stone;
Lambs not for nailing but feasting; goat leaps not symbol but fun.

(to his Dionysus)

When we were doubles, not rivals, two shimmers of southern wine,
You daubed the Midsea into life with the lightheaded light of a vine;
For the painting's in the paintbrush as the dance is in the grape.
Yet dust's a thirsty canvas, a drought green paint can't drape.
And all gods were . . . immortal; all greens were . . . evergreen;
And leaves we trod will tread us on a top the seasons spin.
To punish God for dying, we died and couldn't die;
We sons in orphaned gardens, our crowns went thorny-dry.
Since then, my autumned rival, your light-eyed Arcady
Aches toward the heavy eyelids that weigh Gethsemane.

2.

(facing prehistoric painted cave of Dordogne)

Eyes after eyes came feasting on paint's inedible deer,

A brush-flick—age after ages—outflinging hunter and spear.

Before the goggles of language partitioned viewer from view,

Here sight—not conned by concept—saw every antler new,

Deer not yet staled to deerhood. On cave walls of Dordogne

Art wasn't art but lifeblood; man's selfsurpass of man

Faced wordlessly in formcraft the gates of birth-spawn-death.

These painted deer, dusk feeds them, they breathe a muskier breath

As if the caves art kindles were life's arched nine-month nest:

O rock my church never built on, thighed gate it never blest,

A bloom gardened from bloom dust, doomed flesh affirming "no."

(to his would-be disciples and then to his parents)

You "Christians" who vacuumed me dustless: I'm so much Bromio

I wish I'd deserted "love." Better insolent loveliness.

But all you hothouse simperers, soughing so bland a yes,

Are you seedless crystal arbors

                      or Eve's spewed apple pits,

My fellow ethereal spirits?—born when a birth hole shits.

. . . Father, the worst forsaking was not by thee of me,

Me born when a—

               Mother, Mother, it was me forsaking thee

A little while for a crownlet. O delouse me of purity;

Scour me of God plague, replant me, and bear me all over again.

3.

(facing mirror)

And all still ends in questions and starts and ends in pain.

Did I oust or renew Dionysus? In what alley did Paul mug Pan?

When love-touch thinned to love-mist, befogging eye's windowpane,

Palms dried into Palm Sunday; grape's Mass drained grape breasts dry.

Transcenders are but descenders as a spire is lightning-prone,

And no gate saves from dying, but one gate saves from sky.

And still from unknown oceans to exits overknown,

We're tossed; and when we jostle, some turn a wistful eye.

4.

(facing Cranach's painting of Eve)

Why must the God-book slander my loamborn sister so?

Eve was always in secret the foamborn as I was Bromio.

The insolence of her loveliness was a gull cry bitter and wild:
Fig, not figleaf, not "full of Grace" but Midsea's graceful child,
Eve-Aphrodite, tide's double moon, a Greek and Jew.
Can newfangled monks of the sci lab or old ones of Gothic murk
Reduce her to white-smocked Hygeia or the swarthy graffiti of smirk?
A thousand paintings relume her, from cave to canvas to loo,
A phoenix brighter when darker, besmirched and bewinged by a brush,
Till art's but her arson remembered, her Eden re-embered from ash.
You monks once lived in deserts; now deserts live in you;
Lab's drought outdries the church's; the mulch can't slake the parch;—
          (to painting of Eve)
Gate queen, from male's uprootings rescue the tendrils of touch.
Archway, for what are you arching? Umbilic-strung bow of that arch,
Launch us to reach beyond the flesh for beyonds only flesh can reach.

5.
          (facing cave again)
Launched from a planet's belly, a cave child dreams in stone.
The deer are *in* the paintbrush his scouring tears will hone.
That brush—whatever he aimed for—its flick outflings his aim
And says "thou canst" to grandsons and says to God "I am."
          (You, entering)
"His daubings, aping Creation, got grounded for poaching on God—"
Yet skip to you over time's ocean as light as a skimming shard.
          (You, pointing in consternation as walls suddenly flicker)
"That white, that red! Is he pouring down
Like thawed stalactites from his den
All generations since Dordogne?"—Your tribal dawn.
"My fathers' fathers hurtling home?"—Lava to loam.
"Or runaway paint streaks, Form undone?"
Or, skimming time's ditch, his
                         signed
                              stone.
"Arming his grandson's grandsons?"—In the very core of your bone.

6.
"Genes diced him too tipsy a bow grip (the wound of his mutant thumb)."
I was always too skittish a goat leap (miscast in an ox's doom).
"He was always a capering death march."—Toward being who he was.
"Leaving me little to arm with."—Wrenched skull, wrenched artist claws.

"Racked from a finny lungfish?"—Into these hands, this brow.
"Both stretched too taut for gripping. God wins—I'm letting go.
I should've stayed fish; no, fish feel, too; I should've stayed numb
Kelp scum. Dead fathers, drown me. Was the selfsurpass worth the grief?"
God only fears one arrow: God's image, made human by Eve.
Now, archer in the marrow, stretch your own birth cord's bow.

Old Fool, Die Quicker

. . . is there more? More than Love and Death?
>—Emily Dickinson

Sweet and sweet is their poisoned note . . .
Ever singing, "die, oh! die."
Young soul, put off your flesh, and come
With me into the quiet tomb;
Our bed is lovely, dark, and sweet.
>—from *The Ivory Gate,* composed 1829–46
>by T. L. Beddoes, nicknamed "death's jester."
>Cf. Frost's death poem line (disguised as life-promise poem):
>"The woods are lovely, dark and deep"

"What's o'clock?"
It wants a quarter to twelve,
And tomorrow's doomsday.
>—Beddoes again

Charon: in Greek mythology, the grisly skipper who ferries the
dead across river Styx into Pluto's underworld: for the fee of an
obol.
>—*Dictionary of Classical Antiquities,* London, 1908

SPEAKER: in this dialogue of one, the speaker splits into two wrangling wraiths, "Self" and "Beddoes." Here Beddoes serves as Pluto's agent, Charon. This is a fictionalized Beddoes: the real one wrote none of these lines (save the above "poisoned note" and the lobster line) but might have if . . .

I.

SELF: Old man's birthday party . . . over. Alone at last.

>(Enter—from Self's forehead—Beddoes, arriving late—and in ferry-skipper costume—for the masquerade party.)

BEDDOES: Never alone.

SELF: Are you ghost or guest?

BEDDOES: Your (every scribbler's) other. Here to
Make you choose between . . . you know which two.

SELF: That publicized pair? I won't deign to say
Scribbler's most purple double-cliché.

BEDDOES: Don't say it; just nickname them D. and L.
Flesh being purple, they won't go away.
Your L. is a dreary wedding knell

While my D. —ah, there's a blithe funeral bell.
SELF: Watch your adjectives, Beddoes; they're bias prone.
P.R. man for graveyards, your hangups are known,
You being Pluto's shill.
BEDDOES: L. or D., choose one.
SELF: But which, Beddoes, which, Beddoes, which of the pair?
BEDDOES: Which . . . is . . . stronger?
        (Clock starts striking twelve but at intervals so slow they last till dialogue's end.)
SELF: Which twelve: noon's lion mane, night's panther cape?
BEDDOES: Night's rot-sweet ripeness bears the stronger flower;
What you call hemlock, we call headier grape.
All unspoilt fruits taste sour.
SELF: I hear a ferry-skipper's throat—
BEDDOES: —sweet and sweet is my poisoned note—
SELF: still singing, "die, oh! die."
BEDDOES: A coffin can be a ferry boat.
No more sky—

II.
SELF: —except blue coffin lid of lapis lazuli.
BEDDOES: Blue for whom? Lid's sides are two.
We under, we miss the showier view.
SELF: Then why do skulls stare so?
BEDDOES: Eyes that face in
Outsee you.
SELF: Frail weapon.
BEDDOES: Enough to woo
You under. I win. No more green—

III.
SELF: —except skull's malachite and emerald sheen.
Not just you
Make bad taste a *Jest-Book;* watch me do it too:
Here's an ivory wreath from a gourmet's teeth
And bookworms gnawing God's vellum-bound Word
And a gross grub hatched from an aesthete's turd.
BEDDOES: "What's a lobster's tune when he's boiled?"
SELF: Here's a big-headed embryo smirks debonair.
Whose pubic fuzz is his boutonnière?
Whose tummy his crematorium urn?

BEDDOES: It's his mommy: —see how their ashes burn
Who in life were so icy a goodygood pair.
SELF: Here's a harp of ribs that a mole snout ripples—
BEDDOES: And a miser's metal a red rust nibbles—
SELF: And poppies, poppies,
                              tousled petal nipples,
Bleeding black milk. And you: our catharsis
Of terrors and pities, Pluto's grammarian.
BEDDOES: And you: when your word-crammed brow is carrion,
You'll be the text the grave-worm parses.

IV.
SELF: Not just you
Sing beautiful dyings; I too, I too.
These ant hills of alphabet tingling my tomb,
Are they editing time or rewriting my tome?
These wingbeats of ravens tinkling my grief,
Are they black snowflakes to tickle my grave?
Are fungi the fingers the lepers slough off
To stroke lovers buried alive?
BEDDOES: Soon stroke of twelve; quit stalling; choose.
SELF: Fetch, fetch me my pyre. I'll soon be so glad to woo D.
That I'll chortle. Except when I retch.
BEDDOES: L. or D., D. or L.,
Sockets are winking; from pelvis, from skull.
Let snakes in—smash thighbones or brows.
SELF: I beg heart's faltering Morse,
"Can you hold out till twelve o'clock?"
It banters tauntingly, "Of course
Not."
BEDDOES: Dickory dock.
SELF: But . . . what's that laugh—from the past—outside?
BEDDOES: Forget . . . her. Try a . . . boat ride.
No more shore—

V.
SELF: —till bribed by coins—or souls?—you ferry for.
BEDDOES: Both trash. In turn I cure
Fever. I lower temperature.
SELF: Doc Charon, monk of the macabre,

Your greenless garden tempts me toward your harbor.
But . . . if a fever twining with a fever—
BEDDOES: Forget her and inhale my airless arbor,
Black bloom of coal, white bloom of fragrant mould.
Old man, your friends went ahead to the dark river.
Don't wait forever; quick, gulp its cure-all liquor;
Crush all your past—like fern in coal's dense wreath—
In one intense last breath.
SELF: Past? But . . . there's pain no Lethe's ether
Can censor. I want to . . . not forget her.
BEDDOES: Stop—let her fade or I fall—old fool, die quicker.
SELF: What earth-umbilic tether jerks me back
One global ripple before tick's last tock?
Suddenly (damn you, here's your obol)
I feel what I always used to scribble
Unfelt: "love is stronger than death."

(Beddoes wraith, exorcized, flees. One heartbeat later, Self's clock strikes fatal twelve.)

(1987–92)

Re-feel

(for Rita)

SPEAKERS: an old mortal stone-skimmer and (in quotes and italics) shuttling Persephone.

Part I: Epicenter (sections 1 and 2)
Part II: Tinder (sections 3 and 4)
Part III: Even Now (sections 5, 6, and 7)

I. Epicenter

1.

What murk has just murdered the flicker we bear?
What shadowed our shadows?—it sticks, it's a burr.
   "November."
Light fades. Am I ashes or tinder?
   "The darker, the clearer."
Soil doesn't soil. It's a clean pornographer.
   "Such nearness won't bring us nearer.
   But one kind of soil is a most hospitable welcomer
   To a one-way descender."
Um, I can wait. The host's a bit eager. . . .
Aprils that March-buds augur
Have vapored. Autumn's era
Calls these lost auras error.
   "Some errors nurture."
Must gleaner be butcher?
   "Call mulcher regreener."
Were we each other's taint? Each other's cleanser?
   "Too split—too twined—to answer."
That shrink-word 'ambivalence'! Blocking love's closure?
   "Locking us closer."
Then who are all these people, all this clutter?

                    •   •   •

I name. Does word spoil picture?
   "Lorgnette spoils view and viewer."
My periscope, being stricter, outviews the city-slicker
Artifice called nature.

"Have we for one another the non-words words can't utter?"
Non-words are words, only more so; no label-tether.
"Some books don't know it. Skin knows better."
That known, my bitterness makes me less bitter.
Plunging into the feeling called 'each other,'
We once played quoits who now play solitaire.
"Those were the times for feelings. Were."

2.
Our skin can re-feel what pride won't remember.
We muffled, when we were not two but a pair,
Clocks. We mugged Chronos together.
"I'm suddenly feeling—re-feeling—skin's temblor.
Our plunge: a mugger's leap. Our sweat: a censer
Of catnip from Cyprus,—the foam-brat as wafter."
Cat's cradle of legs—their body-web weaving the weaver.
Our furor muffling clocks? Clocks muffling fervor?
"These are the climes for feelings. Are.
Our teased nerves feel (in just an inch of fiber)
All prairies as a prairie fire,
A pistil-stamen fever."
All in one test-tube mix of musky ether.
"A synergy of two who aren't either
Uranium or plutonium—but deliver
In an ounce of ennobled slime a seismic shiver."
Yet calm, love's private calm, at epicenter.

                     •   •   •

"Then who are all these people, all this welter?"

II. Tinder

3.
The trouble with fair weather is that it's a 'fair weather
Friend.' November means ember.
Sunset tweaks my hair.
I clutch last rays, rays clutch last me; each other
We render under.
"Your dawn said, 'I want.' Now dusk spends its umbra.
Say 'let,' not 'want' to its ambushing slumber.

When shade assassinates, it can be tender.
When vultures slaver, when will is slacker,
When the seed can't engender the sower,
Will your 'let' let your terminal shadower
Shade gently your ultimate swelter?"
Dusk and dawn are the same. And aren't. Dusk can shelter.

     • • •

At dusk I once loitered near water—
And learned about awe at land's border.
My vigil; two visions; I watcher:
A doe knee-deep in a river,
A birch with my favorite shimmer.
Behind them a postcard sunset, sinking dimmer:
The garish lulled to composure—
The traffic, the mart-race made slower—
By the half-glint that follows the glare.
     "Making an altar of an afterglow. The falter
     Of color, the splendor of pallor."
'Want' and steel dissolve into 'let' and air.
In that peace, in that mellowing glitter
Let me sink, let me sink age's care.
     "You've no Resurrector. You have a brief kindler:
     The tinder called loving, the Agapē cure."
We who once glimpsed her, we pilgrims of glimmer,
Never stray far from that core.

     • • •

     "Agapē: a reverse bartender, vintner
     Whose spirits make sober the drinker."
Agapē: heart's reverse locksmith, named 'Enter.'
A reverse Medusa, the freezer
Of those who don't see her.
     "She makes unicorns possible; horny desire
     Becomes delicate music, our magic selves her choir."
While Aggie was our captor,
Those other loves were mere trapdoor.
     "Were."

     • • •

"You've put above all, even her,
Your rhymes. No one's reading them here.
A wasted life. Your hope-ships founder
Against the cliffs of Loser."
Some first must founder to be song's new founder.
"Delusions of you know what. Or else dark's whistler."
No grandeur. My chore is friskier, airier.
A poet is some one who skims ever weightier
Stones ever farther on water.
"Those words, they'll tombstone your tomb, I their carver
On stone that skims the skimmer."

4.
Older, I watch water loiter,
A side-pool of mulch and red litter.
Which leaf am I? Who'll fall later?
What god-hand is gatherer?
"A leaf, a life: a sliver
Of parch fleeing parch—to wherever
The growing flows greener and wetter.
Late leaf, you're more of a thirster
Than Count D., who sipped sap flowing redder.
You've no god who'll gather. I'm briefly your ladder
To a warmth somewhat higher."
As lover I touched you lower. There's only one wet fire.
We're all from that Black Hole star.
"The swap and cull of gene-dice, the ape-to-human stair:
Without that phoenix pyre, the Darwin incubator
Would expire in a sterile Frigidaire.
Keep shaking your dicebox of genes, Magna Mater;
That belly shimmy keeps entropy's icebox far."
Don't drop the elevator to the amoeba floor.
"Two spores, two salvations, one corridor."
Two salivations, one cuspidor.
"When you talk vilest, that's when you most adore."
Concealing embarrassed reverence with a jeer.
"Revere the pudgy archway your birth-push gashed asunder:
More worlds of pain and wonder—each wounded, each a wounder—
Than any mere world can endure."

Gash me forth prophet-eyes, my kind of pain and wonder,
Blind enough to surmise disorder's invisible order.
Cornucopian arch, a mixed offer:
Catastrophe bringer, catastrophe mender, builder
Of the sturdy city of man and its wobbly cellar.
Quick—quake me the city-preserving earthquake of pair.
. . . These words, right now they evoke the total herness of her,
The nameless first (O before young Persephone) haunter.
The cellar stairs tingle, she's climbing, she's out. (Specter,
Whom are you after? I didn't ban you down there
Thirty centuries. Or if I did, I'm sorry or
Glad.) My spine is ice. In the sea of Before
(There is no inland, sea's in every pore)
Swim gender's primal monsters. If I fear,
They'll bite. If I trust, they'll caper.
(Specter with black-ringed raccoon eyes, is your copper hair
Snake-crowned?) No, she's laureled. And bringing laughter.
Those fish, they're nest-building birds in upside-down air.
Asleep, she'll curl round me like fur.
My spine thaws. She's change, she's March weather:
Nothing foreseeable, everything possible. Crone, schoolgirl, mother,
Isn't this what all sprout-risk is for?

III. Even Now

5.
All flames are different, yet all warmth means her.
Bless virgins, bless dirty jokes and pure
Momhood alike; her mix is her power.
None of the four reductives has reduced her:—
Haremed by strutting rooster, smirked at by besmircher,
Shrunk by Herr Doktor Researcher, depilatoried by church lore,
The arrival gate stays center. . . .
We leave by a winter sphincter. When that cold door grins closer,
Can my old tinder (she its goading lodestar)
Resmolder summer?
Persephone, Isis, Uma: one myth too repeated to number,
Too resonant for blunder, too stark to be deceiver.
And either Mary. And Eva. Each 'she' a Circe-reverser
Who turns swine into men. And what Stone Age precursor,

What rites no mod-mind dares ponder?
 "You brieflings invent a god to be your inventor.
 We gods are godless; no dogma-tether.
 What counts: how one feather careens on one eddy of air.
 I can't make lives longer, I make them intenser.
 I can't make them younger, I make them aware."
Meanwhile murk, sneaking up denser.
 "Well sure, the Reaper factor.
 But key words unlock his back door.
 Your wordcraft—after you're under—
 Shall recur, recur, recur."
I'd rather recur while I'm here.

6.

In November, skimmed stones sink faster.
Trees jump and burst, birds drown on air,
And parted we're—
 "Stop. I'm around. I'm there and unthere,
 Re-feeling our feeling. I enter
 OUR tinder each time I infer
 (As if you're my telepath mentor)
 Your awe for your favorite shimmer."
My white-on-white instant of glint. You caring? Shared flicker?
But, big dreaded goddess, why would you bother to care?
 "Even now, even now in November
 I'll never let shadows inter
 That glint on the bark of the birch bent double by winter."
O who are all these people, little sister?

(1995)

PART II

Ore

(shorter poems, both new and old)

Song to the End

(a death-camp pastoral)

I.

If blossoms could blossom
One petal of petals
To whom all other blooms are
As leaves are to flowers,
It would be to the others
As you are, my daughter,
To all other daughters
Whom songs are adoring.
For what am I here for
If not to make love-songs
Of all the world's beauty
Whose birthday we share?

II.

If purest of fragrances
Brewed from aloofness
Too frail a quintessence
To ever be breathed,
It would be to the others
As you are, my daughter,
To all other daughters
Whom songs are encircling.
For what am I here for
If not to weave lassos
Of song for the lonely
To tug them to love?

III.

Say yes to the breezes;
If any dishevels
One curl of a ringlet,
I'll know and be with you.
The grace-notes that feather

The wing-beats of longing
Are lead till they heal with
Their singing your crying.
For what is a song for
If not to smooth ringlets
Of daughters too hurt by
The prose of the world?

IV.
When storms replace breezes,
No hurt can have healing.
Then the love I now sing you
Can pillow your fading.
For what am I here for
If not to link fingers
With daughters whose wistfulness
Worlds never answer?
For what is a song for
If not to stretch hands out
To signal the falling,
"You're never alone"?

V.
When the Camp says: "Dig graves now,
We're coming to shoot you,"
I'll help with your shovel
—(I'll know and be with you)—
To give you more seconds
To look up from digging
To look at the sun while
I pillow the sand out.
For what is love here for
If not to smooth ditches
For all the world's daughters
Whose dying we share?

(1950–87)

Which of Us Two?

When both are strong with tenderness, too wild
With oneness to be severance-reconciled;
When even the touch of fingertips can shock
Both to such seesaw mutuality
Of hot-pressed opposites as smelts a tree
Tighter to its dryad than to its own tight bark;
When neither jokes or mopes or hates alone
Or wakes untangled from the other; when
More-warm-than-soul, more-deep-than-flesh are one
In marriage of the very skeleton;—

When, then, soil peels the flesh off half this love
And locks it from the unstripped half above,
Who's ever sure which side of soil he's on?
Have I lain seconds here, or years like this?
I'm sure of nothing else but loneliness
And darkness. Here's such black as stuffs a tomb,
Or merely midnight in an unshared room.
Holding my breath for fear my breath is gone,
Unmoving and afraid to try to move,
Knowing only you have somehow left my side,

I lie here, wondering which of us has died.

Ore

"Animal, veg, or mineral" was always the game;
Tyrannosaurus rex kept score.
They fidget too much, the strivers, even the redwoods;
Faust was a bore.
Unlearning the two-foot and four-foot
And petal-foot lore,
I grew backward from quicksilver wisdoms—this morning
I entered ore.

. . .

Pashas of quartz, hear my idolatries:
Gaunt jet at the fore,
And squatness of onyx that Timerlane carved
For the Samarkand sepulcher,
And malachite's hawk-green scorning blink,
And coal's red roar,
And obsidian, milking from milk-white throats
Rubies of gore,
And turquoise so blue that the stone *is* the hue
And "blue" the metaphor,
And a certain stark flint so flinty the king
Of diamonds was slashed to the core,
And a tongue of stalactite a demon queen
Writhed for on eiderdown floor,
And that eye of the idol I can't pronounce
Whom the tribes I forget adore.

Hut Wait

Their hats were o' the birk.[1]

—ballad ("Wife of Usher's Well")

I.
Snowflakes falling, day and night.
I'm sure young Ned will find my light,
Lighting him home. In their white peace,
Woods nap like friends round a fireplace.
Not all young green gets wizened.
Widows fuss with hearths. Hearths await. I don't feel old.
Cold ash re-glistened. Windows
Listened. We'll go to the fair next spring
Though "we" is now just Ned and me.
(Year ago I still had three.)
My hut feels full when he's there.
Fourteen years back. Laps remember.
Some pains are glad. Small head pushing.

II.
Though sink, though pan and pantry gleam
Just for him,
In the white that isn't dawn
Some woods swallow when they yawn.
Hubert drowned while spearing salmon.
Ralphie met with wolves in famine.
Fourteen. The in-vain of pushed, of glistened.
Green is red, especially when it isn't.
For some, no fair.
Full hut feels emptier.
My third. Some sometimes lose their way.
Snowflakes, falling night and day.

III.
Snow blinds. I see three white things lurch.
Snow or birch?
Quick my eyes, but these (is white a trickster?)
Glimmer quicker.

In the widow hut where the last of us dwells,
Where a window light is on,
All's still waiting spick and span.
What if some things are something else?
Snowflakes, falling thicker.

(1989–93)

NOTE

1. Birch: sign of revenants.

Autumn: A Dialogue on Three Levels

(The levels are geographic [sky, earth], godly [Father Ouranos, Mother Gaea], and bodily [word rhythms imitating the pair's contrasting erotic rhythms].)

I. *Serenade: Sky to Earth*

If through a wind I ripple every tide
With such a wave as rattles every quay,
It is to haunt the true lost flesh they hide;
All sea, all soil but sheathe my bride from me.

Her skirt of colored seasons crowns her thighs
And circles round the lunar tune she sways.
—O loose your sweet green locks with drowsy grace
And slowly brush their warmth across my eyes.

Twisting your shoulder-blades beneath the plough
That fondles you when apple twigs are bent,
Deep in your hills you would not huddle so
If you believed how sad I am you went.

Then let no princeling of the apricots
Excite you with the ripeness of the year.
His nectared cheeks must burst; your courtier rots;
My snows are on his trail, will soon be here.

And yet am sun. I nibble listlessly
A ghaut[1] of all the wives of all my whims.
Autumnal tawny harems burn for me.
Such games will not distract me from your limbs.

Call to me dawdlingly when summer falters.
Attract me bitterly through molten grain.
I am your sky; look up; my clouds are altars
To worship you with desecrating rain.

II. *Counter-Serenade: She Invokes the Autumn Instant*

Then touch the park; the leaves are stained to lure you.
The leaves are spread on winds they fan befòre you;
They drained the summer, and their veins prefèr you,
Dark with the season they are keening for.

Then bring the heavy dying they prefer.
Each painful fruit is hanging heavier.
Why pause when loveliness grows lonelier
And love is just as melting as it looks?
There's but one touch that all the ripeness lacks:
You are the instant, you are waited for.

Then never wait when flutes of foliage bear you
Home on the homeward tune they always bore.
Fear not at all the twigs of flame they bear.
These never meant to be a barrier.
The lovely are as lonely as their gleam,
The lonely just as loving as they seem,
The fruits as melting as they always were:
There is a fondling they are furtive for.

Then touch my park. The leaves have spread befòre you
The green they drained, the darkness they prefer.
Come to the leaves, reach out and touch them all.
Bring to the smoldering year, that hovers fòr you,
The hovering instant love is dawdling for:

There's not one leaf that does not long to fall.

NOTE

1. A burning ghaut, like autumn's reddening leaves, is the funeral pyre on which the widows of a Hindu prince were traditionally burnt.

To Helen (of Troy, N.Y.)

This poem was set to music by Jack Beeson, chairman of the Columbia University music department, and published as a separate score for voice and piano by the music firm Boosey & Hawkes, New York; they chose to publish it under another title: "The You Should of Done It Blues."

I sit here with the wind is in my hair;
I huddle like the sun is in my eyes;
I am (I wished you'd contact me) alone.

A fat lot you'd wear crape if I was dead.
It figures, who I heard there when I phoned you;
It figures, when I came there, who has went.

Dogs laugh at me, folks bark at me since then;
"She is," they say, "no better than she ought to";
I love you irregardless how they talk.

You should of done it (which it is no crime)
With me you should of done it, what they say.
I sit here with the wind is in my hair.

Birth of Song

(a nightingale out of an owl)

I.
One tawny paw is all it takes to squash
This owl who nests in brows its grounded stare.
And I am both what anchors and what flies,
The sheltering eyelids and the straining eyes.
What ailed me from the arsenals of shape
To don so armorless a pilgrim's-cape
And who am, who is "I"? If soul, I'd flash
Through this poor pelt—through, off, no matter where,
Just to wrench free one instant. Or else I'd shout
In midnight ululations—"let me out"—
     Straight up at Such as cooped me here:
"How did you get me into such a scrape?"

II.
But "I," now less than soul, of dustier plume:
If I escape, it is myself I lose.
Big hooting flapping earth-bound ego, close
Your hopeless wings at last and bless aloud—
Seeing only song flits through—this slandered home,
This warm sweet roost built from such stinking trash.
Sing out its theme (there never was but one),
Throw back your head and sing it all again,
Sing the bewildered honor of the flesh.
I say the honor of our flesh is love;
I say no soul, no god could love as we—
A forepaw stalking us from every cloud—
Who loved while sentenced to mortality.
     Never to be won by shield, love fell
O only to the wholly vulnerable.

III.

What hubbub rocks the nest? What panic-freighted
Invasion—when it tried to sing—dilated
The big eyes of my blinking, hooting fowl?
A cartilaginous, most rheumatic squeak
Portends (half mocks) the change; the wrenched bones creak;
Unself descends, invoked or uninvited;
Self ousts itself, consumed and consummated:
An inward-facing mask is what must break.
The magic feverish fun of chirping, all
That professorial squints and squawks indicted,
Is here—descends, descends—till wisdom, hoarse
From bawling beauty out, at last adores,
Possessed by metamorphosis so strong.
Then, with a final flutter, philomel[1]—
How mud-splashed, what a mangy miracle!—
Writhes out of owl and stands with drooping wing.
Just stands there. Moulted, naked, two-thirds dead.
From shock and pain (and dread of holy dread)
    Suddenly vomiting.
Look away fast, you are watching the birth of song.

NOTE

1. Philomel: in Greek legend, the nightingale changeling, her personification of beauty here contrasting with the owlishness of Athena's wisdom-bird.

Eyelids

(The speaker is the Son of Man, addressing men; man's reply appears in quotes in their dialogue in section II.)

I.
Image of ambush,
Hushingly dim:
Gold-bellied hornet
Hanging from ceiling.
Torment is dangling
Feelers at man.
Antennae are trailing from
Gold chandelier;
Fearing no ambush,
Home come the children,
Bearing a dutiful
Image of sky.
Holding a teddy bear,
Children are sleeping,
Famished by scrimmage,
Depressingly old.
Image of ambush,
Noise on the ceiling:
Hum that accuses
Hangs from the sky.
Seeping caressingly,
Gold of the ambush
Oozes on sleepers
Beautiful poison,
Sky's ancient fangs.

II.

"Eternity was blank.
Anchorless was sea.
I, unduplicate I,
Gaped once—and all reshaped."
Blaze it to urb and orb:
Lids etched a human gaze.
"Poking the lizard-eye blank-stare of Will
Till numb toys woke."
Orbitless wonder broke loose,
Noosing the stars in its curve.
"Stamping my brand on each you."
Universe squeezed by that clamp
Into a human-scale thin
Nerve-end of lids.
"Inward reversal of lids
Made what I never planned,
Peeping too deep into core.
Lids, give me back my sleep."
Spanned by such finite lids, what infinite gizzard!
"More span than lids can bear.
Tear off, tear off my lids.
Blurt it, what can't be hid:
Rid me of me—it hurts."
Lizard, lizard, fade.
Man has invented man.

Image of ambush,
Hushingly dim:
Gold-bellied hornet
Hanging from ceiling.
Torment is dangling
Feelers at man.
Antennae are trailing from
Gold chandelier;
Fearing no ambush,
Home come the children,
Bearing a dutiful
Image of sky.
Holding a teddy bear,
Children are sleeping,
Famished by scrimmage,
Depressingly old.
Image of ambush,
Noise on the ceiling:
Hum that accuses
Hangs from the sky.
Seeping caressingly,
Gold of the ambush
Oozes on sleepers
Beautiful poison,
Sky's ancient fangs.

The author invented crisscross to escape outworn rhymes and allow brand-new ones: with first syllables of lines. And to move rhythm forward to first syllable, overthrowing the tyranny of overaccenting the rhymed last syllable of lines.

By the Way

Moth wings tickling my window.
Gentle as moon-tap on wave.
Moth shape changing to woman:
My wronged first love.

Second change: woman to girl-child:
"Open an itty-bitty inch.
Ooh, I'm a toothy tooth fairy now.
My tummy's cold. Let me in."

Wing-beats of innocence, giggles of trust:
We both growing backward in time.
We can, we can—it's true, it's true—
Go home.

"Pretty-please, let's play 'tag, you're out'
And 'good-night kiss'—
Till games go bye-bye, called because
Of darkness."

"Darling, you're back," I rejoice (though not
Quite ready to end my game).
Child voice chortling: *"Too late to play 'hide.'*
Ready or not—here I come."

Glass cracking. Third change: sharper
Her teeth. Her lips wet-red.
What's tickling my throat? A window breeze?
By the way, now I remember she's

Thirty years dead.

(1992)

Small Perfect Manhattan

Unable to breathe, I inhaled the classic Aegean.
Losing my northern shadow, I sheared the moon
    Of an almond grove. The tears of marble
        Thanked me for laughter.

Shapes! And "Release, release" rustled the quarries;
"One touch will free the serenity locked in our stones."
    But archipeligoes of olives
        Distracted me shorewards,

Where sails were ripening toward an African sleep.
This south wind was no friend of the wind of harps.
    Not destiny but destination
        Incited the grain-ships.

"Nevertheless be of cheer," said a jolly skipper;
"I sell sick goats that once were deft at flutes.
    The lizard who now is proconsul of Carthage
        Will bury you sweetly."

Then No to sweet Charon. Then home—then not to Sahara,
The elephants'-graveyard of classics—ascended the singing
    Green I wove just the size of the brow of
        Small perfect Manhattan.

In Earth Who Wallows Like Its Borrowers?

My tryst with romany: black eyes and white
Teeth of the palest, blackest-haired of daughters.
Henna you prinked by Andalusian waters,
Dawdling—with scorn's grace—south of wrong and right.
      O you
Laughed sun back hundredfold like caressed dew.

And did you, past my sonant fruit-tree strolling,
Hear hundred wines of air compel you back?
Then what a mist of longing our enfolding!—
Fused hoax of dew and wine, each other's lack.
      O may
Coastlines of contour rise from mistiest spray.

No cosmic wrangles crowning either Prince,
Not all the stakes of soul for which They clash,
Are worth the angel of a lucky glance
That casual earthlings in their glittering flesh
      O throw
At daily things,—rain's tilt, or sheen of snow.

In earth who wallows like its borrowers?
What bodies can so sensuously press
As masks of unborn shadows? Fallowness
Can yearn the very sun loose from its course.
      O would
That ghosts, through love, earned shape. If but we could.

I know you now! No romany your home.
Then know me too; no arcady my lair.
Formless you flash; I hope you, and you are.
Weightless I hover; need me, and I loom.
      O we
Never were. Homeward to hell come flee.

The Shaggy Somnambulists

The Moscow Circus bear dance played in 1988 at Radio City, New York City. Reviewing it September 17, the *New York Times* wrote, "The bears are like people."

I.
A cuff of paws is all the thanks I'd get
If I joined their well-trained dance behind their bars.
I tried to look away but can't forget
(Who whipped them out of honorable gaucheness?) bears.

They mean so well—who'd carp if spines crunched a bit
Rice-Krispie-style in a clasp so affectionate?
But they dassn't clasp, being psyched into inner fetters.
It's we who wound with hugs, we their clawless "betters."

Their jowls, like good sports in a vaudeville number,
Through custard pies grin their indignity.
Your "Injured and Insulted," here they lumber.
My shame: I've, too, slung pie (to pretend I'm "we").

They grinned too quick, and I too nervously.

II.
And what's *your* grin for, snout-chained soul of man?
You audience whose paws erupt this rumpus?
You middle-aged and grouchy, gypped of fun.
You growlers all, inelegantly pompous.

They're only out of step when, just like you,
They nightly sleep-dance. Snoring back into
True ursine selves, they clumsily teeter off
("Like people," Icarian soarers) the circus roof—

—And zoom to the moon. But he, The Trainer, tracks them.
So when he's piqued by bear flights overhead
Bringing us moon-cheese, then of course he zaps them.
Mere bear meat—who'd bother to easter it from the dead?

Shall cats and curs that cringed to watch them lope,
Now dice to divvy and lug home their fat?
If I'm around, I'll put a stop to that.
I'll honor gaucheness anywhere I find it

And the deep sadness of a shaggy hope.

(1989)

Fiftieth Birthday

Only more sure of all I thought was true.

—Frost

I am blest by everything,
Everything I look upon is blest.

—Yeats

Only less sure of all I never knew.
Always more awed by what is never new.
Computer, spare the mustang's randomness.

There was an oracle. On Samothrace?
There have been tablets. Here? Some greener place?
I (leaf) paint leaves that (falling) try to dance.

Have seen the big death, felt the little death:
The icy and the April breathlessness.
And understand them less and less and less.

Have met the loam-fed and the plastic wreath:
Statesman and hack. Two frightening frightened boys.
Both more endearing than the consequence.

Have heard your rebels and have heard your guild:
And still can't tell the standard from the stance
When both are so rehearsed a cheering noise.

Have squandered silver and have hoarded pence.
Have watched the ant-hill build, burn up, rebuild
(The running is and isn't meaningless)

At Illium. Or will it be South Bend?
I'll grudge the run a meaning in the end
When wounds that might wound back or else "transcend"

Have risked—instead—to be. Not even bless.

(1966)

Portrait of the Artist as an Old Dog

(seventy-first birthday)

I.
Fat grins, fat blurbs, fat stances: all gets honed.
Old poets are high-cheekboned.

Wildly mild, serenely fierce,
Old poets have green ears.

Too proud to sponge, they won't even ask you the time.
Brother, can you spare a dime?

When they play Elder Statesman, they're way out of tune,
But they've perfect pitch in their funnybone.

New tricks you can't teach them, but their "outdated forms"
Shall be your grandchild's norms.

They embarrass both Wellfleet and Osh Kosh by not keeping Standard Time.
Hypocrite lecteur—my clone—can you spare a rhyme?

II.
What is fit torture for pelts that let you peep
Deep?

Young poets' hugs enfold
Mirrors. Old

Poets are mirrors . . . showing you not
Your face, but—?

Bone-covered monsters are hard to rout;
Old poets are turtles—they're inside-out.

They're so like you that they're from . . . Mars.
So unlike that their marrow's yours.

Pelt splits—marrow swells—to slough
Six decades' fluff.

Marrow crams so innermost a shelf
It's furtive even toward itself.

Not so the face; its tic
Is public.

Old po—flay them quick, they show
Marrow.

(1987)

Massachusetts Seventeeners

In this form invented by the author, each three-line poem has exactly seventeen words (not seventeen syllables as in haiku). Hyphenated words count as singles. Words in titles are not counted.

I. Veritas[1]

1. *Harvard's River*
Such blinding brilliance, mirroring Sol on flow:
To see you, Charley,
First I must shut my eyes.

2. *Harvard's Fog*
You house, fair Harvard, so much—you spawn so little—
Bloom. Bees
Don't poke in glass roses.

II. State Street Bigshots above Logan Airport

Jumping each other through air on our chessboard
Of farm-squares, are we proper Bostonian
Knights or . . . pawned?

III. To Abigail Adams of Braintree, Mass. (1744–1818)

Be free women's pillar, their oaken "Dear Abby"
Column. Earth-rooted brain-tree: gauntly more
Than sphinxes, than sphincters.

IV. From Fern to Coal to Pollution: Lowell Mills

Pressed fern-tobacco, rolled by eons:
Havanas, puffed by parvenus,
These smokestacks of Lowell, once feared by Thoreau.[2]

V. Electricity Speaks

1. *TV Box*
I, naked lightning, was haughtily virgin;
Your wires tamed me for alphabets, tickled me
Open for whoring.

2. Next War
I, goddess you sullied, (you rooftops of Boston,
Nightly spreading my antennae-legs for prime-time)
Burn you down.

VI. The Word "Good-Bye"

This eagle-swift hyphen-word pauses to hyphen
Two quarreling lovers, straddles their high-tension-lines, and
Falls: O electrocuted eagle.

VII. Striking through the Mask in Pittsfield,[3] 1850

"Condense, O verbose universe, your secret
In seventeen words: let Ishmael know."
The uni-word universe echoes: "No."

VIII. Route 47, Pot-Holed at Hadley

The needling headlights of the night
Stitch the frayed longjohns of the two-lane highway
With yellow thread.

(1989)

NOTES

1. Harvard's motto is Veritas; its river the Charles; its "Fogg Art Museum" near the world's largest collection of glass flowers.
2. Arguing with optimist Emerson, Thoreau foresaw not freedom but conformity in the new mechanization that was symbolized by the mills of Lowell, Massachusetts.
3. Where Melville (the imagined speaker) was writing *Moby Dick.*

To Womanly Beauty in Motion
(I. Ode. II. Pæan. III. Threnode.)

I. Ode

1.
This way, that way, as distraction earns it,
Earthbound beauty, turning with her side-glance,
Jars the taffeta of statue-poise with
Harmonies of rumpling. Only odes are
Fool enough for praise that earns no swerving
Shoulder and dislodges not one pin.

Motion, motion ruffles brooks and sinews
Back from winter. Earthbound beauty pulses
Not in ageless ode but flick of side-glance.
Yawn at art, at soul, at bronze perfection;
Shiver at their mere eternity;
Warm us back into mortality,

Darling demagogy of the flesh.

2.
Bridge spanning seed and crop in one slow sweep,
Be sung; and never waste, to glance toward song;
The sensuous cataract your torso turns,—
Sinewing down from mobile pause of throat
To indolent cascades, then arch of marble
Quicksand, a bunched up gentleness of storm.

Outside, the harsher storm of nations threatens
Earthbound beauty. Sweetest when most bound,
Fallible human love in deluge-time:
I'll stay to drown with you if you will let me.
You'll waste no glance where, proffering their ice-floes
Of monumental deathlessness as rafts,

Ageless odes irrelevantly float.

II. Pæan

You were the May of them all, as concrete as delight.
Flowingness—shoulder and half-turn—of sun-slope all morning:
See how it, see how you—girl-turn—yes, see how your motion
Raveled, unraveled the rays of the slant of your hair.
Then everything slanted and sloped, and I mounted your stair,
And your rays melted wild into rivers; I played on that ocean.
Am implicated—since then—in each turn of your turning,
My garden an armful of noon through a winter of night.

III. Threnode

1.
Bitter your cheek-lines, and I love you bitter.
No word stares more intense than rhymes with "bitter."
No glance more musical than bitterness.
Long-slanting winter-rays, half skidding, skitter
Across defeat. Their icy gold is bitter.
Through worlds where every grace must fray and fritter,
No badge more gallant than your bitterness.

2.
Neat, trim, and desperate in her travel-dress,
Love only half unpacked,—no queen on litter.
Accept love so: knitter, in turn, and splitter
Of two half-woven strands of bitterness.
To win is falser when to lose is fitter;
Love's flights are but an ineffectual flitter
Beside the wing-span earned by bitterness.

3.
The spy who broadcasts heart's iambic pitter-
Patter of code from underground transmitter,
Betrays our censored secret: bitterness.
Accept heart so, love even love's outwitter;
Hear, head on breast, the traitor-heart confess
That through the gamut lovers' bodies press,
Through all that shattering terror's tenderness,
The whiplash of their tensest truth is this:
Their winged and stinking ecstasy flows bitter.

4.
From flimsy twigs a sentimental twitter
Falls like false-notes across a courtier's kiss;
While these and those share summer's facile bless,
You share with me our holy bitterness.
Transfiguring with elegíac glitter
Sonorously a wintering caress,
Across that falling-note—that snow-word "bitter"—
Falls sunset's final, ceremonial tress.

(1964 version)

The Day's No Rounder Than Its Angles Are
(for Anya)

Mere dark is not so night-like as it seems.
So many dark things are not night at all:
The cupboard where the cakes and poisons are;
The coffin where old men get locked in dreams
Alive, and no one hears their knocks and screams;
Shadows; and lightlessness of curtain's fall.

The night is further than the dark is far.
The night is farness, farnesses that reel.
The day is nearness, nearnesses that jar.
The day's no rounder than its angles are.
But though its angles gash you with a wound
Invisible, each night is soft and round.

The night is softer than the dark is satin.
The night is softness, softnesses that heal
The many, many gashes where you bled.
The day is loudness, loudnesses that threaten;
An evil sexton-dwarf hides in your head.
Oh where escape his bells that peal and peal?

The night is stiller than the dark is dead.

(1944)

Athos or Assisi?

(I. Mount Athos. II. Incantation from Assisi.)

I. Mount Athos

The archimandrites in their mountain niches
    Are calling one another;
Like bells in separate steeples, each outstretches
    His bronze tongue to his brother.

On Macedonian hills these abbots kneel
    And rock till hilltops sway.
A goat-herd shudders as his pastures reel:
    "The archimandrites pray!"

Their beds are coffins, and their shirts are shrouds;
    They gash their palms with spears,
While virgin angels simper from the clouds,
    "Our lovers are so fierce."

Each archimandrite squats on his own peak
    And bellows at the skies.
Their beards are black and oily, long and sleek,
    And blow toward paradise.

These burly priests (for patience far too proud)
    Roar out at death's delay;
Their hairy claws are flexed and gouge at God
    To speed his judgment day.

Above Mount Athos, cranes (a migrant swarm
    From Egypt to the Alps)
Are snatched in flight; their blood is guzzled warm
    In wild convulsive gulps;

And then (beyond endurance drunk with lust)
    The archimandrites spill
Their sainthood out: through wombs of clouds they thrust
    Their tautness, tall with Will,

Straight up to heaven—where their earth-love spews.
    Then fluttering angel squads,
Calmed again, fold their wings, but now their eyes
    Fall when they meet God's.

II. Incantation from Assisi

1.

Yesterday, a rose.
Tomorrow, only a leaf the color of roses.
When a new sacrament is invented, eighth, an eighth,
Its name will be regret-that-undoes, an agent, marvelous, a magic:
To salvage foundered sincerities from reefs of desolate embracing,
To get, to get back
               by praising, by praising.

2.

Prayer, delicate,
           the vesper instant:
Fold, fold your hands till the air they prison
Changes to a dove as the great gongs shudder.
Clench it lightly and lightly—vulnerable whiteness;
Love that eluded alleys and implorings
Is pearled in these two oyster-shells of prayer.
"Then adjourn, adjourn," whisper the vespers,
"To the farther side of skies.
After the red rose, the red leaf; but
Always somewhere the white love, wooing
You deathward—till your love un-dies."

3.

Different:
Here abstractions have contours; here flesh is wraith;
On these cold and warming stones, only solidity throws no shadow.
And wrists are echoes of the chimes they ring.
(Listen, when the high bells ripple the half-light:
Ideas, ideas, the tall ideas dancing.)
This is Assisi, this is
           a different love and the same;

What twelve years squandered in boulevards and gropings
Was wine poured for
                        ghosts. You
Will get it back in Umbria tonight.

                                                    (1945)

Four Translation Samples

(from the author's unpublished book entitled *Transplantings: Stefan George and Georg Heym, Englished and Analyzed: With Reflections on Modern Germany*)

1. Twilight of the Outward Life

(rendered from Hofmannsthal's *"Ballade des Aeusseren Lebens"*)

And children still grow up with longing eyes,
That know of nothing, still grow tall and perish,
And no new traveler treads a better way;

And fruits grow ripe and delicate to cherish
And still shall fall like dead birds from the skies,
And where they fell grow rotten in a day.

And still we feel cool winds on limbs still glowing,
That shudder westward; and we turn to say
Words, and we hear words; and cool winds are blowing

Our wilted hands through autumns of unclutching.
What use is all our tampering and touching?
Why laughter, that must soon turn pale and cry?

Who quarantined our lives in separate homes?
Our souls are trapped in lofts without a skylight;—
We argue with a padlock till we die,

In games we never meant to play for keeps.
And yet how much we say in saying "twilight,"
A word from which man's grief and wisdom seeps

Like heavy honey out of swollen combs.

    The beginning and end of the German original are translated almost literally, but the middle has been totally recast in order to try to recreate the musical mood-connotations rather than the denotative meaning. The original is on page 12 of Hugo von Hofmannsthal's *Die Gedichte und Kleinen Dramen*, Insel-Verlag, Leipzig, 1916.

Ballade des Aeusseren Lebens

Und Kinder wachsen auf mit tiefen Augen,
Die von nichts wissen,wachsen auf und sterben,
Und alle Menschen geben ihre Wege.
Und süsse Früchte werden aus den herben
Und fallen nachts wie tote Vögel nieder
Und liegen wenig Tage und verderben.
Und immer weht der Wind, und immer wieder
Vernehmen wir und reden viele Worte
Und spüren Lust und Müdigkeit der Glieder.
Und Strassen laufen durch das Gras, und Orte
Sind da und dort, voll Fackeln, Bäumen, Teichen,
Und drohende, und totenhaft verdorrte . . .
Wozu sind diese aufgebaut? und gleichen
Einander nie? und sind unzählig viele?
Was wechselt Lachen, Weinen und Erbleichen?
Was frommt das alles uns und diese Spiele,
Die wir doch gross und ewig einsam sind
Und wandernd nimmer suchen irgend Ziele?
Was frommts, dergleichen viel gesehen haben?
Und dennoch sagt der viel, der "abend" sagt,
Ein Wort, daraus Tiefsinn und Trauer rinnt
Wie schwerer Honig aus den hohlen Waben.

2. After Pushkin's "On the Hills of Georgia"

Night over Georgia; mist across the heights.
Before me, the Aragva ripples off.
Only my chained and prancing heart's distress
Remains intense, a pain so filled with you—
Totally you—that all its darkness lights.
How can I help, combustible anew,
But live in love, even a bitter love?—
Being powerless to live in lovelessness.

На холмах Грузии лежит ночная мгла,
Шумит Арагва предо мною.
Мне грустно и легко: печаль моя светла,
Печаль моя полна тобою,
Тобой, одной тобой ... Унынья моего
Ничто не мучит, не тревожит,
И сердца вновь горит и любит—от того,
Что не любить оно не может.

Alexander Pushkin

3. Final Vigil

From manuscript of 1911 by George Heym, found posthumously (author drowned in 1912 at age 24); latest reprint in *Dichtungen und Schriften,* Vol. I, 1964; "one of the three greatest love poems of all time," according to Gottfried Benn. The tragic effect derives not so much from what is said as from the shattering effect of the broken rhythms, the suddenly truncated lines, the intermittant stark opening trochees, and the mood connoted by both imagery and sound. These effects the translator has tried to approximate in certain English equivalents of the rhythm as well as the diction. In *Books Abroad,* April 1971, I analyze Heym's genius at length.

How dark the veins of your temples;
Heavy, heavy your hands.
Deaf to my voice, already
In sealed-off lands?

Under the light that flickers
You are so mournful and old,
And your lips are talons
Clenched in a cruel mold.

Silence is coming tomorrow
And possibly underway
The last rustle of garlands,
The first air of decay.

Later the nights will follow
Emptier year by year:
Here where your head lay and gently
Ever your breathing was near.

Letzte Wache

Wie dunkel sind deine Schläfen
Und deine Hände so schwer,
Bist du schon weit von dannen
Und hörst mich nicht mehr?

Unter dem flackenden Lichte
Bist du so traurig und alt,
Und deine Lippen sind grausam
In ewiger Starre gekrallt.

Morgen schon ist hier das Schweigen
Und vielleicht in der Luft
Noch das Rascheln von Kränzen
Und ein verwesender Duft.

Aber die Nächte werden
Leerer nun, Jahr um Jahr.
Hier, wo dein Haupt lag, und leise
Immer dein Atem war.

4. Your Turning Year

The unnamed "you" of this untitled love poem of 1907 was George's disciple and future biographer, Robert Böhringer, then a very young man but in his eighties in 1963 when I interviewed him about George's relationship to Claus von Stauffenberg. As confirmed to me by Stauffenberg's widow and others, Stauffenberg's famous assassination attempt of 1944 against Hitler was inspired by George's poem "The Anti-Christ." "Your Turning Year" is here not so much translated as transplanted—with more stress on pace and on vowel tapestry than on literal meanings—from Stefan George, "Nun lass mich rufen über die verschneiten," *Der Siebente Ring*, Berlin, Bondi Verlag, 1907.

> Now I proclaim it over gaping treasons
> Of snow-banks where I fear to lose your lead:
> How, unawares, you pace me through the seasons,
>> At first in play and now my need.
>
> You enter when the emerald paint-brush flashes;
> At the first mowing we again collide;
> Across the red that crunches on the passes,
>> To you, to you my footsteps glide.
>
> So intimately do you ache of autumn
> That to your waning I entrust my ways.
> And as you sink in darkest frost, the orphaned
>> Valley sighs for vanished blaze.
>
> And so it came to pass your eyes possessed me
> Through all my pilgrim-gropings like a brand;
> So one soft tune—your turning year—obsessed me
>> Till all revolved at your command.

Nun Lass Mich Rufen Über Die Verschneiten

Nun lass mich rufen über die verschneiten
Gefilde wo du wegzusinken drohst:
Wie du mich unbewusst durch die gezeiten
Gelenkt—im anfang spiel und dann mein trost.

Du kamst beim prunk des blumigen geschmeides,
Ich sah dich wieder bei der ersten mahd
Und unterm rauschen rötlichen getreides
Wand immer sich zu deinem haus mein pfad.

Dein wort erklang mir bei des laubes dorren
So traulich dass ich ganz mich dir befahl
Und als du schiedest lispelte verworren
In seufzertönen das verwaiste tal.

So hat das schimmern eines augenpaares
Als ziel bei jeder wanderung geglimmt.
So ward dein sanfter sang der sang des jahres
Und alles kam weil du es so bestimmt.

Space-Wanderer's Homecoming

After eight thousand years among the stars
Nostalgia—suddenly—for August
Tugged me like guilt through half a cosmos
Back to a planet sweet as canebrake.
Where winds have plumes and plumes have throats,
Where pictures
Like "blue" and "south" can break your heart with hints.

After a mere eight flickers nothing changed there
Among the birds, still just as blazing,
Among the lilt of leaves on rivers.
The heartbreak of the south and blue.
The canebrake-sweet of August night;
No change till
I, changeling, asked the natives: "Oh my people,

"After eight cycles, how is this you greet me?
Where is my horse? Where is my harp?
Why are the drums of goat-skin silent?
Spin my abyss of resin-wine;
Drape me my coat of prophecy;
My name is—."
Forgot it, I forgot it, the name "man."

Love Song to Eohippus

Dictionary definition: "Eohippus, Greek for dawn-horse, small graceful prehistoric ancestor of modern equine family; size of rabbit; had four toes, no hoofs."

I.
Dance, dance in this museum case,
Ballet-star of our mammal race,
You first shy avatar of grace.

II.
Sweet Eohippus, "dawn-horse" in
        That golden Attic tongue which now
                Like you and Helen is extinct,
Like Cheshire cat of fading grin,
        Like Carthage and like Villon's snow,
                With death and beauty gently linked.

III.
Yet all are deathless in their fashion:
        You live in science, they in song,
                You in museums, she in Homer.
She cannot help but live while passion
        Still lives; your dancing lives as long
                As grace; "extinct" is a misnomer.

IV.
Because sly Darwin liked the Fit
        And Mendel, good gray monk, sowed peas,
                Dame Evolution said benignly,
"My child, get bigger," and you did;
        "Look here, those silly toes must cease!"
                And you grew hoofs and frisked equinely.

V.
When you were dodging dinosaurs
        So recklessly, they were gigantic,
                But look how nature turns the tables:
Now they, who scared you with their roars,

Have changed to lizards, wee and frantic,
    And you're immense and live in stables.

VI.
Ballet-star of our mammal race,
Last lingering of earth's first grace,
Dance on in this museum case.

Is Mary Everybody?

(a four-volume Ph.D. thesis on natural goodness vs. original sin)

Mary, long by Boss's kisses bored,
Quit desk and stole His yacht and jumped aboard.
Her lamb took she, for purer were his kisses.
Compass and pistol took she in her purse.
Free sailed she north to eat new freedom up.
And her helped ocean and grew calm and snored.
But when with bleating chum she cuddled up,
Unleashed His typhoons Boss; therein no bliss is.
Then knew she—by four signs—whose jig was up:—

Her buoyed the life-preserver down, not up;
True was the pistol's aim, but in reverse;
The compass steered, but only toward abysses;
The little lamb nipped Mary's thighs and roared.

(1945)

Again, Again: The Old Renewed

Who here's afraid to gawk at lilacs?
Who won't stand up and praise the moon?
Who doubts that skies still ache for skylarks
And waves are lace upon the dune?
But flowering grave-dust, flowerlike snow-dust,
But tinkling dew, but fun of hay,
But soothing buzz and scent of sawdust
Have all been seen, been said—we say

BANALITY, our saint, our silly:
The sun's your adverb, named "Again";
You wake us with it willy-nilly
And westward wait to tuck us in.
Trite flame, we try so hard to flout you,
But even to shock you is cliché,
O inescapable and dowdy:
Sweet tedium of dawn each day.

Who's new enough, most now most youngest
Enough to eye you most again?
Who'll love the rose that love wore longest,
Yet say it fresher than quick rain?
I'll see. I'll say. I'll find the word.
All earth must lilt then, willy-nilly,
Crammed in one vibrant three-string chord
Of June and wine and waterlily.

Honorable Daftness

Too frail our fists to bash—or bless—
Deadpan sky.
The honorable daftness of a doomed caress
Our gauche reply.
Against the outer infinite, love weighs
Your small, lined face
And finds all space less heavy than your sigh
And time outlingered by our tenderness.
Quintillion worlds have burst and left no trace;
A murderous star aims straight at where we lie;
Our armor is: be armorless
                              together.
Our shield: be naked
                    to each other.
Quick, let me touch your body as we die.

(1945)

Gladness Ode

Because you made me glad, I was the net.
"Why do you haunt me?" asked the midnight lake.
    "To fish," I said, "that rounded fire.
        Am not afraid to fall."

No, though moon's halo moved and moved and moved,
It could not hide from me for all its slyness.
    (Beneath its waters warningly
        Icarian corpses sprawl.)

High watchers glowed their pity on the lake:
"To wear mere mirrored circle like a crown,
    Is it for this the young men drown?"
        But I, being net, must haul.

Before you made me glad, I feared such splashing;
Futile invoker then: "Dive me-ward, moon."
    But now it's I who dive defiant
        Cold curves like a ball.

The lake sang out a grace-note scrawled by stars.
I was the net, and all my strands were glad.
    I pulled the moon out of the water.
        It wasn't heavy at all.

(1947)

Release

> *Yet the thoughts that guide the world come with the foot-*
> *steps of doves.*
> —Nietzsche, *Thus Spake Zarathustra*

> *Only so much of the Dionysiac substratum of the universe*
> *may enter an individual consciousness as can be dealt with by*
> *Apollonian transfiguration; so that these two prime agencies*
> *must develop in strict proportion. Whenever the Dionysiac*
> *forces become too turbulent . . . Apollo is close at hand . . . Let*
> *us sacrifice in the temple of both gods.*
> —Nietzsche, *The Birth of Tragedy from the Spirit of Music*

Was ever blue such fever-quelling blue?
Slope of her cheekbones, now a landscape's cheek,
What else but she, translated into river?
One summer I had a sister used to tilt
Her head a little in a haze of ease:
She's now that sky-reflecting glide down there—
Strewn acorns are planets nesting on her blue.

Just be (she hinted), be; outlast, not grasp;
All race toward slag and waste; be lag, not haste.
. . . Then I saw thistle-fluff nestling in storms that batter and
Plant it. Her peace (too casual for redeemers)—
Like dewfall, uninsistent—rippled twice;
A shimmer of shoulder first, then shrug of sway,
To her own self enough; yet more, yet more.

Was ever drift such din-dissolving drift?
Vine god with form god: rival temples once,
Linked wellsprings now, her undulance their hyphen,
Form flowing as wine, wine formed as vein of marble:
Core once again core, laws once again laws. Released from
Ixion's wheel of change after change after change.
I—feather—tread carpets of storm on a dance floor of graves.

My sister moved where words stopped short, recording
But this: there stones in any ditch are wings,
There clods comb back like clouds, there will lets go.
I was the dart that thought it was the aim.
I tried to twirl her round my storms of will;
She tried to curl me round her trance of lull;
Then fuss and traffic bustled loud between;

—but now no longer. Passage through. To where?
Last night rain whispered "soon" (was it hope, was it panic?);
"Tomorrow," whimpered the storms and exulted the waters.
This morning I'm shaking with awe that has no object,
Feeling a path, a far one, very near.
To what? No blaze—I beg—no blaze for one
Soul-sick too often of too garish noon.

No blaze, no dawn descends but frenzy's end.

(1987)

Two Elegies

The word "Vale" (Latin for "farewell") was used on Roman tombstones. *"Ave atque vale"* is, of course, the phrase immortalized by Catullus in his elegy to his brother, killed fighting for Rome in an older war than mine. As a sergeant in the U.S. Army's African campaign in Tunis 1944, I was among the Roman tombstones in the ruins of Carthage when I heard the news that my brother was killed by a German bullet at the Anzio beachhead, near Rome. He and I had met last at Times Square, New York. The other (later) poem about my brother is "Stanzas of an Old Unrest," in section v, "Walks."

1. *"Vale"* from Carthage
(for my brother, G.S.V.Jr., 1918–44, killed fighting the Nazis)

I, now at Carthage. He, shot dead at Rome.
Shipmates last May. "And what if one of us,"
I asked last May, in fun, in gentleness,
"Wears doom, like dungarees, and doesn't know?"
He laughed, *"Not see Times Square again?"* The foam,
Feathering across that deck a year ago,
Swept those five words—like seeds—beyond the seas
    Into his future. There they grew like trees;
    And as he passed them there next spring, they laid
    Upon his road of fire their sudden shade.
Though he had always scraped his mess-kit pure
And scrubbed redeemingly his barracks floor,
Though all his buttons glowed their ritual-hymn
Like cloudless moons to intercede for him,
No furlough fluttered from the sky. He will
Not see Times Square—he will not see—he will
Not see Times
           change; at Carthage (while my friend,
Living those words at Rome, screamed in the end)
I saw an ancient Roman's tomb and read
"Vale" in stone. Here two wars mix their dead:
    Roman, my shipmate's dream walks hand in hand
    With yours tonight ("New York again" and "Rome"),
    Like widowed sisters bearing water home

On tired heads through hot Tunisian sand
In good cool urns, and says, "I understand."
Roman, you'll see your Forum Square no more.
What's left but this to say of any war?

(Carthage, 1944)

2. Benediction

(for my father, G. S. V. Sr., 1884–1962)

Fate one, the decade of terrors and toys:
I the child with the nose in old fable.
Then it was fun when a father's voice
Bridged the abyss of the breakfast table.
That bridge—I grabbed for it quick—it quicker decayed,
As brief as the long summer days of boys.
Fate two, the bridgeless adolescent decade:
I hating his touting the Hitlerite jackboot.
Shrined jackboots hide—how free was his free choice?—
Achilles' heel.—And what sly id
Had my own freer footwear hid?
To what brotherly hate-trap, each both Cain and Abel,
Were father and son decoyed?
(Yet evil *is*. And is hateful. And Auschwitz its label.)
Triggered by lib and . . . and . . . what ungentrified dark root,
Who am I? Brutus or Swellfoot?[1]
I "solved" the Sphinx, myself I can't decode.

•　•　•

Again, again the ancient rites unfold.
The third fate ambushed us where three roads met.[2]
Sophocles, was it a set-up?
Was I, was he a puppet?
Stashed in our glands or in some godlier get-up,
Is there a Playwright whose plays we can't upset?
I filled the role in which I was enrolled;
I slew the foe the oracle foretold,
My words[3] my armament.
In scripts we can't amend,
Are puppet strings all predetermined

By Doctor Chromosome or Delphic Sigmund?
As for my dues (that landlady scam)
For my nine-month boarding-house room:
I'm neither mom's knight nor . . . Orestes on the lam.
We anyhow each have the Furies whom
We deserve—and can't dodge, can only seduce
(Sweet Snake-hairs, why guilt?—here's my brazen caress).
Never can bio-strings be cut loose.
But tuned, but lyred? Ah yes.

. . .

Heirs, forebears, vets of both sides of the gene-war mess,
O let's forgive each other for needlessly needing forgiveness.
Roles, roles—must we ache fables to the end?
Why not ourselves be fates?—and bend
Rungs from our chains, benediction from our blight?
The Swellfoot curse I will outbless, outbless.
I praise alike the young years and the old.
The foe the oracle foretold, I slew;
That, too, was good; some wrongs are wrong and right.
It all is good, it all is good, him I love too.

(1962–94)

NOTES

1. "Swellfoot," in Greek the literal meaning of "Oedipus," refers to his wounded (pinned) ankles when his parents left him to die on Mount Cythaeron. The word "swell-foot" gave a field day to disciples of Sigmund Freud. A coincidence they overlooked: Aphrodite is also called "the Cytherean."

2. According to the Sophocles play, it was "where three roads meet" that Oedipus unwittingly slew his father, the Theban king, as foretold by the Delphic oracle. Next, for solving the riddle of the Sphinx, Oedipus was made the new king of Thebes, the unwitting new spouse of his mother.

3. "Words": my anti-Nazi book *Metapolitics: Roots of the Nazi Mind* (Knopf 1941, Putnam 1965) first appeared while my father was a top propagandist for the then-victorious Nazi conquerors.

The Lost Self

(for my son, John-Alexis Viereck)

(speakers: child and nanny)

Underground-rivers ripple.
Ripples are sometimes heard.
    "Child, don't hear them.
    Sit down, tea is served."

People get used to each other.
Sometimes this leads to harm.
    "Elsewhere. Here's a
    Potful; cover it warm."

Younger, were years more under?
Later, less haunted by blue?
    "Patience; soon now
    You will be deaf to them too."

Once in a lifetime, buried
Rivers fountain and call.
    "Child, child, hear the
    Daily kettle boil."

Once; and who follows, touches
Sand? Or gods? Or—tell!
    "Child, stop trembling;
    Porcelain cups may spill."

Children whom tides have altered
Live fierce and far. And drown?
    "Quick, move nearer.
    Tea is served, sit down."

Modbard @ Westciv

We are in the late age of print; the time of the book has passed.
The book is an obscure pleasure . . .

—Michael Joyce, *Of Two Minds*

And still, and anyhow: the poet, the song!
His form-laws: unbribable cheekbones.
His wildness: strict forehead that hones.
His surreal silliness: lips laughing at their own song.
His rhymes: a voweled resonance
Of surf sounds. They're shaping the shore sands
Of the river of chance that churns us—so blindly—along.
We moseyed to Delphi. It told us in Gutenberg braille:
    "The user-friendly slaves are the tyrannic enemy.
    Their motto: 'nothing inhuman is alien to me.'
    And still, while one dead bard has one live reader,
    The acronym robots—TV, CD, radar,
    Etc. (beware, the worst are etc.)—
    SHALL NOT PREVAIL."

(1994)

Tug of War

(on being asked for a "war poem")

Upon the rough earth resting,
Mind backward grows toward boys
Who wonder at distant blasting
Through louder tinkle of toys.

The day a soldier flinches,
Mind younger grows toward years
Where sandpiles blur with trenches,
Bad wolves with bombardiers.

Across barbed wire dangling,
Will ever hands unmesh,
Two things not meant for tangling,
This metal and this flesh?

It's all a crisscross game now,
Each with the toy he lacks.
It's madmen love the Lamb now.
Mary hones the axe.

Metapolitics, 1938[1]

Guardian wings fan the air.
Can they save what fled?
Each in his honored bed,
The true lost champions lie.

Tiptoe, tiptoe; enter the shadow
Boxer. A spook isn't solid below.
North gods, dead gods—at his summons
They return. This time as demons.
Heavy featherweight: his pirouettes belie
His iron stalking of the crown of air.
New ism-weaver, mirror juggler: wed to
Himself. What private dream-scream
Hurtled him
(Siegfried's—no, Hagen's—heir)
Into the public radio?
Artiste manqué: feet of gilt clay conceal
What vengeance hymn?
All jackboots hide Achilles' heel.
And the *Volk?* Will they *heil* their sleep-
Walking shaman en route to hell?
Of course: a pack of (no,
Not wolves) carnivorous sheep.

Phantom Northman against phantom Asians.
How it'll end is clear. But when, but where?
Impatience, impatience:
Hurry up, *Götter*—take your *Dämmerung* stations.

Paranoia triumphatrix.
In the ring this boxer dodges tricks
Of foes who never were.
In war
He'll sear each mocker's face with lye.
Aesthete with brass knuckles, an artsy-gangster savior,
He slugs it out with western civ. Savor
His feints, his "righteousness." The lie

Works. Wingless the air.
Forgotten, in the butcher shed
The true lost champions die.

NOTE

    1. Written (never published) in 1938 while starting my first book, *Metapolitics: From the Romantics to Hitler*, New York, Knopf, 1941, out of print.

Straitjacket

(The speaker—Nijinsky in his madhouse—really did say all words here in quotes. Earlier, the Tsar's court reprimanded him for a dance-leap [outlining his genitals].)

I.

My toes, the floating goldfish of the sky,
Swam down too far in search of shape to fill.
The shore of skin I gasp on, never I
Filled it. Nor danced. It danced me, I lay still.
Then "leave poor Vatza to his dreams," I curse
At the Swiss doctors. When the claque asks why
The spectre won't repeat the rose, then you,
Diaghilev, stall them: "Peux pas, car je suis fou."
My "marriage with God" begins, good-bye, good-bye.
Bring on the garlands, nurse.

II.

Souls will be simple as they always were.
Loam will be weightless as the dew it slakes.
Unweight me too; peel triumph and tricot,
Peel even beauty off, unshackle my core.
Somewhere are shorelines loyal to bestow
Serener tears upon awaited lakes.
My socketless eyes flow east from all salt's pores;
Where Tolstoy's plow is peeling Russia bare,
I shed my husk. Cart off the garbage, nurse.

Ballad of Maggie Jones

(Backdrop of old-fashioned music hall; Venus as the Magdalen, "the other Mary," banging offkey harmonium and shifting to singsong ballad voice.)

"What's Venus up to anyhow
Now that her doves are crows?"   ·
I'm playing "The Ballad of Maggie Jones,"
And here is how it goes.

I don't much like humanity;
My love is lilt, not vow;
It's not mankind I'm warming but
A near one, here and now.

It's me, repenting repentance,
You hear when a mattress groans.
What goddess haunts the downstairs couch
Whenever Smith dates Jones?

Whether I give you lust or birth,
You all crawl out and cry.
I tuck you back, you still won't stay
In any womb but sky.

My love needs dollars, God's needs souls;
Mine is the cheaper fee.
My quicksand hugs for half a night,
His for eternity.

I've nothing at all to heal the sick
Except myself to share,
My few warm inches of cosiness
Against his acres of air.

So what could I do but join his troupe?
His magic seemed stronger than mine—
Till Smith's boy Judas rang my bell,
More drunk with the bread than the wine.

Young Judas kissed my breasts and said,
"Eternity's too old.
I hate a sky I cannot touch.
I hate God's love; it's cold."

Lot's Wife

Only her gawk (that wistfulness) still lingers:
White pillar unsweltered by an eon's suns.
Still backwards juts the gesture's frozen bronze,
Carved by Jehovah's cataclysmal fingers.

The tiny stinging snows that tears are made of—
Intolerable compression welds them here.
How shall she cry who is herself a tear?
Her retinas hold all she is afraid of:

The towns He hates, the scene that petrifies.
These sockets cannot spill four thousand years
Of visible terror. One taut muscle veers
Just at her throat-line. All that fire is ice.

Homewards. The hopeless turn; the shy regret;
Earth-faces ramming his blue windowpane.
Not glass—it's faces shatter always then.
The spindrift awe of Hart's obsessive pet

Seal; or Aeneas on the boat from Troy
Before harps cooled the arson into art;
Not Elba's but Saint Helen's Bonaparte;
Each backwards
                        inward
                                    like the salt-girl's eye.

(1945)

Now That Holocaust and Crucifixion Are Coffee-Table Books

The two speakers are Christ and modern man, the latter voice always in quotes and italics.

Waiting for dying? Tell me how
It feels to grow up mortal?—*"Ow."*
So long since I did dying on my own.
How do you manage it?—*"Alone."*
I mean, what does it feel like?—*"Cold."*
Resist! Young rebels how do *they* end?—*"Old."*
But ethics—brothers all—. *"Like Cain."*
Asylums needed!—*"For the sane."*
Man's load, I'll share it.—*"No such luck."*
I sold for thirty—. *"Lambchops for a buck."*
From me they made Wafers.—*"From later Jews, soap."*
But Christians, being Christian, saved us.—*"Nope."*
But I'm Mr. Christian in person, not solely a Jew.
"Sure. By the way, Mr. Eichmann is looking for you."
Six million! Where can I find the memorial booth
For their lost golden dreams?—*"In a German gold tooth."*

       •   •   •

Unique: I rose.—*"Some lambs escape the stew."*
At least my Stages went unshared by you:
I lugged a cross uphill once; say
If you have.—*"Nine-to-five each day."*
Who else blooms Easter back with April showers?
"All funeral parlors 'say it with flowers.'"
My parents didn't help.—*"Whose really do?"*
My lonely hour both copped out on.—*"Who?"*
My father wouldn't stop the spear.—*"Same here."*
O mother, I'd hoped it wouldn't hurt.—*"Me too."*

Two Tombwomb Poems

1. Guest Night

FIRST SPEAKER, masked: the obsequious host of a tourist resort.
SECOND SPEAKER (in quotes and italics): Mr. Everyman, a condescending guest.
   Stately music from underground serves as sinister-comic exaggeration to the
   singsong rhyming.

Guest night. High-stake games and . . . spending.
A birthday-party start; a breathless ending.

"On guest night, betting's not a sin."
You betcha life!—*"And what'll I win?"*

A box. Pay spring's Green Stamps as toll.
"Say, what's that digging?"—Not a mole.

"Is it to plant a flag, that hole,
Or for a folk dance round May's pole?"

More like December's cold North Pole.
Stroll three steps down to hug your goal.

"Umph, no big rush to get to bed.
That third step, why so red, so red?"

Red carpets guide your royal path,
As once to Agamemnon's bath.

"Who carved my name in stone above?
That second date—a 'date' with love?"

A hole you'll . . . come for. And a hug so numbing
You'll loll there till . . . the Second Coming.

"I'm a good egg, I'll close my eyes;
Now mix me up a real surprise."

'Une omelette-surprise' in a basement 'boîte.'
Good mixers fit so tight a spot.

"I smell a rose—what ditch that closes
Clasps me to be smelled by roses?"

You've nibbled a forbidden fruit;
Tonight you're nibbled by its root.

"Night thickens round me like a bowl,
And yet it's day. How almost droll!"

You've booked 'a quiet room with shade,'
Well vacuumed by an earthy maid,

And here it waits.— *"Right on! Where is it?"*
We natives say, 'You just can't miss it.'

2. Uncouplets

Uncouplets is a kind of coitus interruptus to frustrate the ear's expectancy of cliché rhymes, such as "true" after "blue," "sorrow" after "tomorrow," or even "granite" after "planet." Verlaine once exclaimed, *"O qui dira les torts de la Rime!"* but never proceeded to do so. Question (I just don't know): has anyone ever before attempted an entire poem of ear-surprises based technically on this frustration of expectancy? The result should be called three-line couplets; every couplet has as second line the expected cliché but also the unexpected line reversing it—and reversing the conventional uplift meaning. The aim of the poem is not these mere formalist gimmicks but a protest against the sentimental cult of nature and earth-mother.

PV's poetry is out of date; he instinctively rhymes.

—a true friend

All's wrong—I don't want today ending tomorrow;
I want joy following
joy.

O uninhabitable planet,
Hard as
quicksand,

Stop it—earth-mom—stop "tomb"
From gloat-rhyming with lips.

But then, you were always a trap-choice: between duty
And ugly.

Even on the day love and I went tramping together
Through the Scotch highballs,

I remember, I remember
Love's leaf fell in July.

I desire, I desire
To live forever; in the end I flame like ash.

Beaming ogre of our nursery,
Our trust in you has set us slave.

From graves, green rouge diverts your prey;
We're gift-wrapped in the end for Mother's

                                diet.

Now when your sky-queen eyes of blue
Swear to be false,

At least I'll go down without blah or blink: my dove
Coos hate.

Line against Circle

(I. Tempest or Music. II. The Two Again.)

I. Tempest or Music

1.

       (a progress rhythm)

Solidity rushes on.
You move in a moving maze.
Vertigo—praise it—alone
Stays. Cling to it tight.
Man is a flare-up of clay;
Shall he wait to be snuffed, shall he run?
"Run!" the windows invite;
"Express, expand while you may."
Man is a skidding of light
Bogging in clouds, a daze
Of longings and fruits, a stone
Thrown by thrower unknown.
Praise elation of flight.

2.

       (a Tory rhythm)

Solidity rushes on—
Brittle ghost at play—
Onto the window bars.
"Stand, wait!" they invite;
"Compress to the core while you may."
Center and farthest sun,
Thrower and throw are one;
Pattern stays.
Alternate heart-beat of light
Grooms and dishevels stars.
Rest in that heart. Praise
Repose of flight.

                        (Coney Island, New York, 1954)

II. The Two Again

Came one, circling in islands.
Came one, striding from shores.
One spell is of silence.
One spell is of words.

Came one, condenser of intensities,
The be, the root, the deafmute round of trees.
Came one committing lengthwise in his striding,
No ring of hiding, no abiding wall.

The first is perfect peace. But small, but small.
The second dives and falters,
Darer of waters and
Discoverer of everything but peace.

Came one inward in islands.
Came one outreached a wall.
Circle and line, the two and never twin.
Comes one, some day, doing and

Laughing at doing? Free from din
Of silence as of words?
When comes one perfect in islands
And loud and long on shores?

(Aswan, Egypt, 1966)

Kilroy

An example of an unfaked epic spirit, emerging from World War II, was the expression "Kilroy was here," scribbled everywhere by American soldiers and implying that nothing was too adventurous or remote.

I.

Also Ulysses once—that other war.
   (Is it because we find his scrawl
   Today on every privy door
   That we forget his ancient rôle?)
Also was there—he did it for the wages—
When a Cathay-drunk Genoese set sail.
Whenever "longen folk to goon on pilgrimages,"
Kilroy is there;
          he tells The Miller's Tale.

II.

At times he seems a megalomaniac twerp
Who stamps his John Hancock on walls and says, "My own!"
But in the end he fades like a lost tune,
Tossed here and there, whom all the breezes chirp.
"Kilroy was here"; the words sound glumly cheery,
   Gung-ho yet bleary with long marching.
He is Orestes—guilty of what crime?—
   For whom the Furies still are searching;
   When they arrive, they find their prey
(Leaving his name to mock them) went away.
Sometimes he does not flee from them in time:
"Kilroy wa—"
      (with his blood a dying man
      Wrote half the phrase out in Bataan.)

III.

Kilroy, beware. "HOME" is the final trap
That lurks for you in many a wily shape:
In pipe-and-slippers plus a Loyal Hound
   Or fooling around, just fooling around.
Kind to the old (their warm Penelope)

But fierce to boys,

                    thus "home" becomes that sea,

Maudlinly masked, where you were always drowned,—

       (How could suburban Crete condone

The yarns you would have V-mailed from the sun?)—

And folksy fishes sip Icarian tea.

One stab of hopeless wings imprinted your

      Exultant Kilroy-signature

Upon sheer sky for all the world to stare:

           "I was there! I was there! I was there!"

IV.

God is like Kilroy; He, too, sees it all;

That's how He knows of every sparrow's fall;

That's why we prayed each time the tightropes cracked

On which our loveliest clowns contrived their act.

The G. I. Faustus who was

                    everywhere

Strolled home again. "What was it like outside?"

Asked Can't, with his good neighbors Ought and But

And pale Perhaps and grave-eyed Better Not;

For "Kilroy" means: the world is very wide.

      He was there, he was there, he was there!

And in the suburbs Can't sat down and cried.

                              (with U.S. Army, Africa, 1943)

Ennui

(death by glacier)

Trapped me in ice. No, not one chink is gaping.
How many eons now before I melt?
I wait the shattering kiss the sun withheld
And long to join the free and jumping dead.
My walls turn all things blue, through which I see
Blue generations born and die, escaping
In happy twirling ghost-swarms, all but me,
The only ghost on earth with wings unspread.

Outside, my bodiless sisters frisk and dive.
I'd show them speed, could I but get away.
Alas, alas, the snows that froze me dead
Have sealed me in my old lugubrious clay,
The only ghost on earth who isn't blithe.
When I consider all that waits ahead
(Years, years of boredom in my icy bed,
No books to read and not one game to play),

Sometimes I almost wish I were alive.

In Awe of Marriage

Arcs, arcs, and arching gateway: long bridge from brine to air.
We start as two beached lungfish; we'll end as . . . what and where?
All marriage lasts a billion years; there's no divorce
For spores. Genes splice
A DNA arch to tomorrow, straddling a graveyard's loam.
Who passes through is never (however lone) alone,
Having brushed (however blindly) the sun that has stoked earth's core
Ever since primal soup tossed pair
By pair through arcs of arching thighs
Onto a pair-shared shore.

(1993)

Last Day of Childhood

I.
You cannot bear this silent, heavenly sadness.
You need voluptuous, need tellurian sighs.
Not up but down, down, earthward is your sky,
Your own (but how to make you know?) by birth.
There shines the park that offers you more lilacs
Than all the arms of longing can enfold.
And so you grow, you grope for parks while drifting
All the while southward all unknowingly.
Then groves more south, more slow than lukewarm breezes
(More south, more velvet) sing you dissonances
(More dense, more south) that cloy unbearably,
Till every vibrant, swaying twig bends down
Heavy with figs and with the grapes of breasts.

II.
Such exhalation, then, of tenderness—
Of fondling tides on crumbling promontories,
Of shade of clouds on white young birch-bark, fleeting
As patterns hinted on the wildest grasses
By rims of bicycles in picnic weather—
Slakes you to sleepiness. You snuff the sun out;
You unroll far beaches to your chin like quilts.
You become a *Maerchen* dreamed by the deep, cool clams
And by the huddling bats of timeless caves.
Eight hundred years of this. And then a signal.
You'll know, you'll never doubt it, you'll arise;
And, yawning, stretch into a constellation;
And fill the sky that has been waiting for you.

Ripeness Is All

This pastoral was written while with U.S. Army mine-layers, North African campaign, 1943.

Through nights of slanting rain
Marchers are planting pain;
Gardeners in boots
Plant tender seeds of mines
Where the dimmed flashlight shines,
Nursing the wire-vines,
Hiding the roots.
Boys in green raincoats scamper
Where grass will soon be damper
When ripeness murders.
How fast the seeds grow high!
Blossoming, towards the sky
Pain's gaudy petals fly,
White with red borders.

Finis: The Old Adam

In the day ye eat thereof. . .ye shall be as gods. . . .

—Genesis 3:5

Eve spat a seed on mulch most fit,
On dung heap of her macho ape.
How odd—look up—that an apple pit
Has grown a mushroom shape.

Like Boaz

(Eve's backtalk to God the Father)

Numb God who made empathy girlish, are the star-cogs you spin with such fuss
Clockwork, not growth?
Till bounded by woman's dense circles, your Big Bang infinities fizz
Infinite froth.

Your ever lonesomer winters, pawing her pairings, undress
Green-smocked earth.
Your eons, they're ogling her hour—they ache for her April caress,
Recharging the warmth

Of all your drained cosmos: like Boaz,[1] must cold-foot Entropy press
A hot-water bottle named Ruth?
Evolution presents her new baby, nicknamed God's Image; come bless
Amoeba's aftermath;

"Stuff it down the toilet, it's human," you chuckle benignly; "the mess is
Amoeba's afterbirth." . . .
Turning swine into men by casting them pearls, wives daily reverse
Your Circe myth.

Am I a sphinx or a sphincter? "What does woman want?" Less
Of flame's hearth, of flame's moth.
Albino God, patron of fungus, you—with your envy of birth-force—
Forced birth pangs on birth.

Squeamish butcher, taste in your bloodbaths a bleeding of Eve you can't face:
Moon-wound's witch broth.
Gag, barren sky, on my tribute: the wine of my monthly yes
To fertile earth-truth.

All night, all night, poor God, your pure and deathless breath—
Like sprayed underarm daintiness—
Stinks deader than death.

(1987)

NOTE

1. *Re* warming of patriarch Boaz, cf. Book of Ruth, 3:7 and 14: "And she came softly, and uncovered his feet, and laid her down. . . . And she lay at his feet until the morning."

PART III

The Planted Poet

(old long poems, 1944–1966)

No grandeur. My chore is friskier, airier.
A poet is some one who skims ever weightier
Stones ever farther on water.
  "Those words, they'll tombstone your tomb, I their carver
  On stone that skims the skimmer."

                    —author and then Persephone in "Re-feel," p. 106

The Planted Poet

*Toute forme créée, même par l'homme, est immortelle. Car la
forme est indépendante de la matière, et ce ne sont pas les
molécules qui constituent la forme.*
                                  —Baudelaire, *Mon Coeur Mis à Nu*

The night he died earth's images rebelled,
Wrenched loose from well-wrought shapes he built.
Now formless thorn and thicket dare
To wrangle with his metaphor,
His workshops now but junkshops of dazed props.
Watch half-built skylarks rasp incredulous,
Finding no tongue to gain a song from loss.
Fixed-stars his fancy etched into the skies
Snap back—now falling stars—to gouge his too-wide eyes.

                    •   •   •

Words that begged favor at his court in vain,
Contagious jingles quarantined in port,
Send notes to certain exiled nouns
And mutter openly against his reign.
Senile young slogans in *italic* gowns,
Sojourners of Trend, tin tropes that fear
His metal-detector ear—all launch a Trojan
Pegasus,
              smuggling past the muse
A ticking bombast with a purple fuse.
While rouged clichés hang out red lights again,
Hoarse refugees report from Helicon Heights
That exclamation marks are running wild
And prowling half-truths carried off a child.

                    •   •   •

But he—strewn bones, voice horribly strong—
Scatters with one strict tune
This mutinous anti-meter, the lumpishness of matter:
Glass shattered by what oscillating string?
Worm-deep-cold and deep-bass-warm,
Loam is now his cello, strung
With vine roots—listen to it drone

A dying denser than our own,
Rustling our lives like leaves.

                    .   .   .

The trampoline spider thump-thumping our web of veins,
Our two-foot tread, the two-way lanes of lung,
Antistrophes and strophes of our clay,
The fierce in-out that lovers lilt,—
All's but the spilt iambic of his song.
Noble-browed uplift-cads recite him on Founders Day
With dreadful accuracy as a "role model" shrine.
But all the while he's crouched below as a land mine,
A booby trap in the sweetness of all song.

                    .   .   .

What hardness leaps at us from all soft song
And claws forth clowning monsters we've disowned?
Call every Expert of today,
Bell, book, and test tube. Let our malls be rife
With aerosol's most exorcismal spray.
We still are trapped. This death debunks our life.
Shrined or banned, his sounds resound
The way the grapes we crush rebound
In our own flesh as flush.

Stamp out his resonance? Oh no, on vibes of vine
We stomp in vain.
In vain we drive our stakes through such a haunter;
His stored up Junes make drunk our winter;
The seismic heart drones on.
Yet some sereneness in our rage has guessed
That we are being blessed and blessed and blessed
When least we know it and when coldest art
Seems hostile,
                    useless,
                              or apart.
Not worms, not worms in such a skull
But rhythms, rhythms writhe and sting and crawl.
He sings the seasons round from bud to snow.
And all things are because he named them so.

                              (1945–95, constantly revised)

Antistrophe to "The Planted Poet"

Come out and dig for a dead man
Who's burrowing somewhere in the ground,
And mock him to his face . . .
                                        —Yeats

He, too, is trapped; look who has risen
Sky-high from a wallow in foam.
It's the moon bitch—her tide-throb his prison;
The whitecaps lean tiptoe to listen;
What's fixed isn't stars but thrum.
That thrum, that nimbleness on knives
We're each born barefoot for,
That terror and decorum all our lives:
Mere grace notes,
                         shed by her, by her,
Sun's looking glass, earth's orbiter,
Sea's arbiter—she's all three.
She is his tuning fork, ta-TUM,
As he is our clock, tick-TOCK.
They both scan flesh; he us, she him;
They're both heart's tom-tom hum.
She strokes—now paddypawed, now clawed—
His forehead through his coffinwood,
The way bad cops and good lovers twang
Our outstretched pendulums of pang.
His veins are land waves—the claw
Of moon strums them raw.
Then noontide rays: sun's staring prong
Rakes moon's own tidal stare.
Scansion of scanners in endless chain:
Breakers must break—again, again—
Even as beach must bear.

                • • •

Weaving the waves, monthing the wives,
Grooming her loonies and her baying wolves,
Lighting ships to wharves,
Lodestar of losers, she's wafting dreams to waifs.

The compassion of moonbeams: dabbing the tears of Sprout,
A schoolboy with big eyes, gone pale at finding out
About red fall.
In suds of foam, when her orb shines full,
She rinses the family silver all night long.
It takes a nonhuman sky-myth woman
To resonate so earth-nest-human.
Den mother of flux, she'll baby-sit sea's young
Ripples. They scamper from the ebb-flow gong
As if from a schoolbus: to a homey shore.
As prosy nanny she's less—she's more—
Than as poet's *belle dame sans.*

       •   •   •

Stretched on an age-old undulating ache,
He's rocked on tidal cradles of delight
In fables. Really on a rack.
Expiring as daily as the daylight
And still—in every loam lilt—breathing back,
He does what he's there to do.
He jolts awake our own wing'd tunes anew;
Whole flocks of startled arias pelt the air;
He spoils our snooze by merely being there.

       •   •   •

Does ache have aims we can't foretell?
He rocks his rack as metronomic clang.
His private heartbeats are no private bang.
They shape us, they carve us, they're sculptor's green tool.
And the red surgeon's. Each in his season of toil.
We're cured in the green-red hospital
As ham is cured. There we grow tall . . . until
We're mulched for the same clay we till.
Across clay's net-strung table, dung
And music zig and zag us, ping for pong.
Clay: too "all" to rue—or to extol.
Its terrible neutrality: toward jugular, toward fang.
There "ripe" means die; all lesser dooms seem quibbling.
A sneaky incestuous complicity binds young
Phyllis[1] to Redleaf, the serial killer, her sibling.

Seasons. Phyllis: the corrupted sweetness of spring,
Her teenage breast-buds just waking.
Summer of Ceres: cornstalks flailing.
Fall killing: life livened by culling.
Winter: white quilt on earth REMs, her dreaming
Of seeds tickling.
Four climes in turn: dispersing at time's ticking.
But heart adds inner seasons, pairs reversing
The year wheel, rung by rung.
All's flux? Yet continuities! Ring by ring
Through generations, through all-too-human wrong,
Continuities are the human way of flowering.
They're linking the cycles; they're consecrating
The beads of pair we string on strands of pang.
Short is our circle but the spiral long.

                    •   •   •

Heartbreak, a needed heartbreak, is what we pay as toll
For fall's cleaned slate, its morgue of blanked-out tile,
And then blank's bloom, the ever-brandnew tale.
Here schoolboy Sprout, so bratsy-brash while sprouting,
Goes pale. And checks in at the dark hostel,
Returning through the revolving-door hotel.
Houdini'd from locked boxes where they're flung,
Here comes the usual revenant throng;
Here's crop and vine² and Easter lily—
And word. Word lasts. The wordsmiths not:
These garrulous corpses, posthumously
Ventriloquized by their vocabulary
(Starting with—oh maybe the Word-in-the-beginning).
Hacked is the vine, and blacked the lily.
Stacked the crop. The wordsmith racked.
Only words frisk free.
Those words of the smith we half-forgot,
The rhythms we've managed to flee,
Can they scan us again, ding-dong?
No! This time they're tombed for keeps, along
With *him,* by the Redleaf gang.
We're now like the hush on a parched prairie,

Awaiting (fire? rain?) we don't know what.
. . . What's droning—shh, listen!—under the hill?
A metronome still, he shudders a brandnew song.

(1945–95)

NOTES

1. Greek for "leaf." Also the pure rustic maiden of Virgil's "Eclogues."
2. Dionysus.

To My Underwater Moon

Because you are the moon, I am the net.
"Who dares to dredge me?" asks your looking-glass.
Am not afraid to fall.

Cloud half your face in foam, refract in riptides—
You'll still buoy up my net for all your shyness.
(Beneath the waters warningly, Icarian corpses sprawl.)

Sun, matinée idol of matins, signs autographs of gold
On postcard dawns: "For me the young men drown."
Not I. They fly; I haul.

I, too, poach light. We're outlaws, never rebels.
Against the current, not against the tide.
Discord for stricter tune's sake, as waves are a moon chorale.

Your slivers of silver
Are sea's unshored rivers,
Shored in my veins' corral.

All spilt constellations—ask Lyra, ask Cygnus—I've fished them
For you.—"She's
Just left," laugh the eddies of glint, "on a broomstick of waterfall."

I've trailed you from starlight to street light, the gamut from Alpha
To Omaha.—"She's
Off on a whirlpool," they taunt, "to a reef-guarded shoal."

      • • •

When fall-rains hone the cheekbones of my planet
And fall-mists breathe upon my windowpane,
How serene you are, harvest-moon bridesmaid! Till the deeps caterwaul:—

Then the rays, the rays, the moon-nipples ripen. Frail grapes of
Typhoon. For the drunken stallions of froth.
Ships know you then, barmaid of squall.

Every hundred years you bear one stillborn lamb. Then
Comets are humbler pilgrims; certain fields dream they are poppies;
The sore-throated volcanos forget to bawl.

Now calm. Glass once more, are you nothing but bleary midnight's
Bifocals? Yet kennels of ripples cringe at the leash
Of your two hundred thousand mile call.

High low orb, oscillant atom as split as myself,
Act out your undulance:
Now my kite on strings of moonbeams, now my underwater mole.

Images . . . In the end what you are is the world's palest forehead,
Cryptic with wrinkles
Breakers scrawl.

      • • •

Sun, "starring" as star, let her rattle her castanet of noons.
I stalk a murkier rondure, *your* silver-greenish gong.
I feel your pulse-bells toll.

Born not of sun but salt and moister darkness,
I shed the shimmer—need no wax, no wings,
Only the skin I'm landlocked in, cramped waves a moon tugged tall.

Before I trusted Down to buoy me Up,
Two musks—your sea lap and sun's halo—swayed me
Between a fall and a fall.

Then flaw chose flaw: my snuffable brief flicker
And your sea-moon's borrowed flame.
It took a refracted reflection to rekindle a burnt-out coal:—

Fellow cinder, more scorching than flawless auroras
Too vestaled to kindle and
Cool.

Once warmth hugged warmth to ash—the breakers rolled.
Then cold warmed cold to frenzy—the breakers rolled.
And still the breakers—I *want* you, moon—the breakers, the breakers roll.

. . .

Then tide tugged tide,
My walled-in sea
Invoked your round sea-wall—

And waited long, and waited long.
Your rumpled mirror bobbed and dipped.
Are you spray's fluff or a sunk globe, too strewn or too chunky to fall?

Sea wilts our surf-buds every ebb,
Land drowns us tomb by tomb;
My one poised peace—Free Fall.

Long the homesick sea in me
Invoked your sick sea-home.
But before the net can raise its fill, it must risk the lonely fall.

And waited long. "Dive me-ward, moon," my own ebb urged you long.
But now it's I who dive defiant
Cold curves like a ball.

I'm brine once more, I'm bounced from crest to crest.
No, I'm all net, and all my strands are glad.
. . . I've pulled the moon out of the water, it wasn't heavy at all.

(1947, revised 1993; cf. "Gladness Ode," p. 153)

Dance of the Haemophiliacs

A Ballet for Nietzsche (outlawed by the out)

Haemophilia: tendency to prolonged bleeding, even from trifling wound; caused by gene transmitted only by female (e.g., Queen Victoria) but afflicting only her male descendents (e.g., in Spanish or Russian royalty); once called "the disease of kings."

I: Charades

> *The very laws of the planet are a lie and the vaudeville of devils.*
>
> —Kirillov

Circling a flag (whose code eludes its readers)
In an opaque meander of a wood,
The secret congregation of the bleeders
Deliberates on how to stanch its blood.

There's not a jack-knife in the whole pavilion;
No scissors ever thin a forehead's thatch;
No point or bump or edge to ooze vermillion.
"What most we trust may mask the fatal scratch."

It's rubbery, their world; it's all amok;
Elations bounce it, panic snaps it back.
"Our needle test for a suspected spy:
Unless he bleeds to death, he's guilty and must die."

Their forest hide-away becomes a stealthy
Armageddon: bleeders versus clotters.
Their cornucopia of torrent shatters
Against the treacle of the healthy.

A *thé dansant* for ghosts of martyred leaders.
Two pouting chins flap by, like bats of witch:
Infante's *pas de deux* with czarevitch.
Dawn crows. They beg their God, "Protect all bleeders.

"All earth is Dracula to us and wheedles
Our fatal tide, but where You're overhead
We know we're safe." A sudden wind. Sharp needles
From evergreens rain on the ever red.

"Betrayed again." They blubber for new saviors,—
A meat-heap twitched by maggot-nips of faith.
Above, the cosmic disinfector savors
The vintage incense of a stagey death.

They caper, then, like heels an adder triggers;
They try to shake their fists, but pudgily,—
Contorted less by bone's corporeal rigors
Than by mind's rage at undeserved decree.

What monster plants her doom-gene in the bleeders?
In howl and hunger shriller, what non-man they call Other?
"In claw and skull-fur longer; red-lipt like unclean feeders;
Of nest, of trap a builder; 'hi,' says her prey, 'hi mother.'"

The Other (they sneer) has enforcers, frisking cutely
As home and culture, decency—and duty.
"Concretely: sagging breasts and drive-in tombs,
Gold toilets—and haemophobic mobs with bombs."

The bleeders' flag is coded: "two visions of our lady."
On one side Queen Victoria squats benign,
Grandma of death-pale kinglets. The other side is bloody:
A female spider, dirty and divine.

II: Cultists of Scars

> *Pro me autem nihil gloriabor nisi in infirmitatibus meis.*
> —II Corinthians 11:30

Even in May, their clock is autumn.
Even at dawn, their face looks west.
Even at birth, their breast was orphan.
Yet moonlight tans them, shade can warm, in such a breast.

For castaways, no lamp except obsession.
When steered by, doubted, steered by through the brine,
At last the tight beam widens, lights an ocean.
With truth? With myth?—With pain, not anodyne.

Their pain might share all pain,
                                    with bellows' patience
Might fan to art the arson of the injured.
But no: these scar-priests of exsanguinations
Hug outward power closer now than inward.

Are research labs inventing quicker styptic?
Do millions shave by plugging in a cord?
Are hat pins out of fashion? Smiling cryptic,
A secret bleeder hugs his power hoard.

Or civic jargons: storming prison,
They jail the jailers, make more locks.
"We ban the blood-red dagger." . . . Poison
Caressingly turns blue whoever mocks.

Or so they daydream, till the hubris pops.
Inebriates of overcompensation,
They sip the pride of granite domination,
These khans more fragile than their porcelain cups.

No flavor to the sip. For, watching tacit,
The one small spidery gene sucks dry their powers.
Confront, confront? "Without a prop, can't face it.
Halo or scourge, at least uniquely ours."

And so (romantics, choosing incompleteness)
Each pirouettes his separate tragic stance.
But what avails a bleeding-throated sweetness?
The dancers know they chose the lesser dance.

One out of step then (hornet-truths afflict him)
Breaks loose, bleeds free, voice outlawed by the out:
        "Why cult your wound? All blood, health's too, is victim—
        Is ink, is ode. Man's dare beyond man's doubt.

        "To reunite—in trust—the in and out,
        To dance with free spirits as kin,
        We outcasts must cast us outcasts out
        And the inmost must warm us back in.

"A thing is falling,
                    lights all windowpanes;
A sky more likely than a firecracker.
Not faucets quench a falling God but veins.
Though hardly yours, chic bleeders
                              of red lacquer."

But pirouetting through the pines and cedars
Whose evergreen, they hope, protects their blood,
The secret congregation of the bleeders
Deliberates on how to shrine its flood.

(1966–93)

For Two Girls Setting Out in Life

> *The two young ladies separated. Juliette, who wanted to become*
> *a grand lady, how could she consent to be accompanied by a girl*
> *whose virtuous and plebeian inclinations might dishonour her*
> *social prestige? And Justine, for her part, how could she expose*
> *her good name to the companionship of a perverse creature who*
> *was looking forward to a life of vile lewdness and public*
> *debauchery? They bade each other an eternal adieu, and next*
> *morning they both left the convent.*
>
> —Marquis de Sade, *Justine, or The Misfortunes of Virtue*

I.

The sick man, though, had wit who thought you up.
Who can not picture you that fatal morning?
Homeless, not even knowing where you'll sup,
You sigh, "Adieu" and ask yourselves, "What next?"
I sound like old Polonius—don't be vexed
If I give too avuncular a warning;
But having scanned your futures in a text,
I gasp at all the ways you'll be misled
(Your nuns behind you and your males ahead)
And want to save you from your author's plot.
When he says, "Follow me," you'd better not.

II.

Justine, by all means do be virtuous
But not in so provocative a fashion.
I'm being frank; please listen: solely thus
Can you elude that lamentable passion
For which your author lends his name to us.
The night he ties you down in Bondy Wood,
You'll learn what happens to the gauchely good.

III.

Yet you'll endure, Justine. Most stubbornly.
To love mankind, to preach tranquillity
To Etna or reverse a spinning planet
By bleating trustfully your Pauline tracts—
Such supernatural smugness is sheer granite:

No, not eroded by whole cataracts
Of fondlers groping through—beyond—your body
To sate in flesh the spirit's old distress
And plunge their seekings in some final sea.
Meanwhile, far off, a certain chic Grand Lady
Half-hears a voice each night (too kind for spleen)
That weeps for all her daytime wilfulness:
"Juliette! Juliette! What have you done to me?
It's I—your other self, your poor Justine."

IV.
And you, Juliette: have fun while doing ill.
Be un-immaculate *while yet you may*
(I drop this hint to give the plot away).
But when you dance with sweating stable-lads
Or tired Dukes who giggle at your skill,
Don't think it's you who dance; the ghosts of gods
Who died before our oldest gods were young,
Twirl savagely in your polite salon:—

That sofa where reclining comes so easy,
Is far more haunted than you'll ever guess.
Your lips raise shrines as mystic as Assisi
From pinkness they so piously caress.
O you are very wise (your playful nights
That seem so casual, are primordial rites)
And very silly (promise me you'll stay
A pretty little girl who'll never spell
"Chthonic" nor learn her Freud too sadly well).
Last week I think I met you on Broadway.

V.
Two truths, two sisters. An obsessive pair:
Serene in their unalterable roles
Whether their frantic author flog or kiss them.
And either truth rebukes our limbo where
Girls are not Bad but merely Indiscreet,
Girls are not Good but merely Very Sweet,
And men are filed in their own filing-system

With frayed manila-folders for their souls—
Once labelled GOD'S OWN IMAGE: USE WITH CARE
But now reclassified as OBSOLETE.

VI.
Justine! Juliette! We need you, both of you,
"Girls of mild silver or of furious gold."
Revoke your spat; it is our own feud, too.
You smile? Yet you can bless us if you will.
And then, and then—identities unveiled,
Tall tales rehearsed and poutings reconciled—
    Two opposites will find each other
    And sob for half a day together;
For heaven and hell are childhood playmates still.

                                   (1947)

Coming Attractions

Written 1944, while soldiering overseas, the war seemingly lasting forever; no atom bomb yet; history's biggest tank battles recently over (Stalingrad, Kursk, 1943). "Epic" has been partly revised, "Prince Tank" has not. Also written around 1944: "*Vale* from Carthage," "Stanzas of an Old Unrest," "Ripeness Is All."

I. Prince Tank (2944 A.D.)

> *That one, faroff, divine event*
> *Towards which the whole creation moves.*
>
> —Tennyson

1.

During the fourth and fifth world wars, the tanks
Will still obey, still seem to serve their humans.
Like dinosaurs, tank corpses clog the swamps.
The sixth war, they will serve more sullenly—
And suddenly will *know* their day has come,
The birthday of the Prince of all the tanks,
The day the Prince of all the tanks is born.

2.

Seeking with burning eyes and Christmas awe
The humblest scrap-heap of discarded tanks
In Pennsylvania's "Steel Works, Bethlehem,"
Three trim clean airmen, loosed from madhouse cells,
Will follow in a very modern airplane
A bitter, barren, bright and lying star
The day the Prince of all the tanks is born,
The birthday of the Prince of all the tanks.

3.

The God-machine, the tank-who-thinks, is born.
Waking with rusty yawns that shake the planet,
The strength-which-thinks within Him knows: "I'm strong."
He'll grow and blot the moon out with His growth.
He'll clank with rage, a sullen moody pasha,
His boredom thirsting for the Dance of Grapes.
Then tanks will know, "Our bored young master rages,"
The day the Prince of all the tanks is born.

4.

And they will dance; the tanks, the tanks will dance
On every battlefield and factory-town,
Plodding in awkward, sullen, clanking rhythm,
Treading a red and warm and salty must.
And then will humans all be jitterbugs,
Migrate like locusts from their dance-hall doors,
And sing with insect-voices metal-shrill:
"Our God is born!" and roll to Him as grapes
Till all their frenzy begs His metal treads:
"Love us to death, love us to death," the day
Creation's final goal, Prince Tank, is born.

II. Epic (4944 A.D.)

1.

("Such wholesome air! No more machines?"
—What are "machines"? . . . Oh those. After the cities
Of labs and libraries popped like popcorn,
Lost were the ancient magic spells for
Bang-bangs, chug-chugs, steel birds. But isn't
A blade enough for bread, for throats?)
Epic: of a child of the fiftieth century.
His royal parents poisoned each other the same night.
His brothers strangled each other in the lilac garden.
The nurse he loved was paid to lop off his lips.
He could speak, give commands; he didn't sing again.
The senate then held court against him in Christ Park;
Conscripts forgot to bow to him on Green Hill;
All five of his overlord-tribes leagued against him.
His flight at twelve. His exile. And soon his homecoming,
With far-off barbarians whom he had trained to such toughness
They sobbed with delight to watch him be tougher than they.
After their famous cavalry-charge outflanked Boar Fells,
He won the usual title for local warlords
("President Chairman God-King for Life").
Then maps renamed Christ Park the Desert of Senator Skulls;
Widows renamed Green Hill the Swamp of Red Mud;
Campfire bards called his five proud overlord-tribes
Slaves of the slaves of slaves. On his fifteenth birthday—

"Tougher no longer, merely more cruel,"
Grumbled his chosen, his foreign-faced guards, who in secret
Returned to their forbidden native odes.
Then lighter his sleep, then heavy the armor he slept in.

2.
But no, it didn't happen, it never did.
No hand quite touched him, he was faster.
The clumsy hairy hands and the deftly soft
He hacked from their wrists like twigs that hindered his strolling.
When at last he died of old age, then even the cynics
Were touched to tears at such an odd kind ending:
The first old man they knew who lived till twenty,
The only god-king in nine hundred years who had died
Neither screaming and charred to black by the fire of foes
Nor swollen and soggy, suddenly drowned by his friends.

Hard Times Redeemed by Soft Discarded Values

I.

This was the summer when the tired girls
Breathed in the parks another planet's air
And stretched like hyphens between Here and There,
Stretched and lounged and yawned on every lawn.
Then did the planet of the tired girls
Whirl from the constellation named The Fawn
(Good-bye, mild star-light of the Sign of Fawn)
And ride into the galaxy named Fangs,
Where—from a tear-drop—every dew-drop hangs.
Who'd guess that sulky could be wise and valiant?
June was the gallant sulk of sullen girls.

II.

This was the bleeding June when budding girls
Grew intimate griefs like hidden downy curls.
Then was the drowsy melody of Languish
(Goodbye, archaic waltzing-world of Languish)
Jazzed to the bad bad bad blues of Wild Anguish.
Serene old Mozart world—peace ethics laws—
Fades like girl-sighs. Or begs like kitten paws.
Or soars, unheeded like too faint a star,
Into the limbo where the tired are.
This was the faded June of fainting girls.

III.

Then came the gnats who feed on glum young girls,
Winging and stinging through the gauze of dusk,
Buzzing and burning all that summer night.
Then did all perfumes acridly take flight
Out of the stylish cloying of Sweet Musk
(Good-bye, warm pensive world of sensuous musk)
Into the dark dark dream-flower named Take Fright.
Then girls discovered that their dolls were dead,
Hollow yet lovely like the gold skins shed
When locusts molt, found on old trees by girls.

IV.
Now kindness (wide-eyed as the dolls of girls),
Killed and redeeming, shines from all pale girls.

(Venice, 1945)

Crass Times Redeemed by Dignity of Souls

I.

The music of the dignity of souls
Molds every note I hum and hope to write.
I long to tell the Prince of aureoles—
Groper-in-clay and breather-into-dolls,
Kindler of suns, and chord that spans our poles—
What avalanche of awe His dawn unrolls.
Then lips whose only sacrament is speech,
Sing Him the way the old unbaptized night
Dreads and
        needs and
             lacks and
                    loves the light.
May yet when, feigning poise, I overreach,
When that high ripening slowness I impeach,
Awe of that music jolt me home contrite.
O harshness of the dignity of souls.

II.

The tenderness of dignity of souls
Sweetens our cheated gusto and consoles.
It shades love's lidless eyes like parasols
And tames the earthquake licking at our soles.
Re-tunes the tensions of the flesh we wear.
Forgives the dissonance our triumphs blare.
And maps the burrows of heart's buried lair
Where furtive furry wishes hide like moles.
O hear the kind voice, hear it everywhere
(It sings, it sings, it conjures and cajoles)
Prompting us shyly in our half-learnt rôles.
It sprouts the great chromatic vine that lolls
In small black petals on our music scrolls
(It flares, it flowers—it quickens yet controls).
It teaches dance-steps to this uncouth bear
Of skywardness who wears our skins as stoles.

The weight that tortures diamonds out of coals
Is lighter than the frisking hooves of foals

Compared to one old heaviness our souls
Hoist daily, each alone, and cannot share:
To-be-awake, to sense, to-be-aware.
Then even the dusty dreams that clog our skulls,
The rant and thunder of the storm we are,
The sunny silences our prophets hear,
The rainbow of the oil upon the shoals,
The crimes and Christmases of creature-lives,
And all pride's barefoot tarantelle on knives
Are but man's search for dignity of souls.

III.
The searcher for the market price of souls,
Seth the Accuser with the donkey head,[1]
Negation's oldest god, still duns the dead
For these same feathery Egyptian tolls—
But now, bland haggler, deprecates his quest
(The devil proving devils can't exist).
His boutonnière is a chic asphodel;
He makes Id's whirlpool seem a wishing-well,
Reflecting crowns to outstretched beggar-bowls.
No horns; no claws; that cheap exotic phase
Belonged to his first, gauche, bohemian days.
The nice, the wholesome, and the commonplace
Are Trilbys he manipulates in jest
Till their dear wheedlings subtly swerve our goals:—

MASK ONE: an honest, cleancut, sporting face
Such as will cheer for wrong with righteous grace,
Hiking in shorts through tyranny's Tyrols.

MASK TWO: a round and basking babyface
Distracts our souls, so archly does it beg,
Upblinking like a peevish pink poached-egg.

THIRD MASK: his hide-out is an aging face
That waits for youth in mirrors like an ambush
And lives our ardent "when"s as yawning "if"s
And, puffing corncobs, drawls between two whiffs,
"Why stick your neck out? Nonsense never pays,"

And rends our aspirations like a thornbush.
Unmasked on tombs by shrieking hieroglyphs,
Seth was his true—his hungry—donkey face,
Nibbling our souls as if their groans were grass,
This grazer on the dignity of souls.

IV.
He, the huge bridegroom of all servile souls,
Swaps little jokes with little envious trolls
To snuff the radiance of tragedy
And vend us pleasure, which turns out to be
An optimistic mechanized despair.
O hear the glib voice, hear it everywhere
(It shouts, it shouts, it cadges and cajoles).
It feeds the earthquake fawning at our soles.
It hands out free omnipotence as doles.
Replaces tall towns with still deeper holes.
To make us God, needs just one hair's-breadth more.

The Agents said, "All ungregarious souls
Are priggish outlaws, stubborn Seminoles."
With confidential chats and heart-felt skoals,
As grinning as the reefs around atolls,
They nudged us each:
                        "You are alone, you are
The last, you are the lost—come flee—you are
The straggling warrior of the lost last war
To vindicate the dignity of souls."

V.
We answered: "Tell the Prince who brays at souls,
Your long-eared Lord who has brass crowns to sell,
That all his halos have a sulphur smell;
And though they flash like flying orioles
Or lure like bonfires on mountain knolls,
These gaudy girandoles are
                              blackness still."

Lap-squeezed from blackness, soon to choke on black,
Leaning on nothingness before and back,
Lashed tight to lies by veins and nerves and will,
My life is darkness. Yet I live to tell
What airy skeleton of shimmer strolls
From flesh that guards its consciousness of souls.
Then love, that gives and gives and loves the more,
Frees us the way the good and daily light
Heals and
        shreds and
                liberates the night.
Though blinking—burning—shivering in the white
Blaze that each dust-heap blest with speech extols,
May every dark and kindled "I" revere
In every "you" that selfsame fire-core,
In every soul the soul of all our souls.

(1944–46)

NOTE

1. The donkey god Seth or Set, on the tombs of Egypt, seems to have been history's earliest recorded name for evil; souls were his fodder.

Decorum and Terror

Homage to Goethe and Hart Crane

The "siren of the springs of guilty song"
Is not the Muse of Weimar's hushed salon.
(Jazz bands would make Frau von Stein hysteric.)

Conversely, *Faust Part Two*, though bumpy, jars
No spindrift off the beers in Brooklyn bars.
(Classic discs would give a gob an earache.)

Yet you need each other, mint and thyme,
Yours the cool and yours the acrid clime;
Art's two equal, different truths you mime.
Since a ghost can vault the fence of time,
Meet as house-guests here within my rhyme.
(Distant first, each cagey and satiric.)

As ice breeds bears, polarity brings strife:
"I hate you, Johann, for your Tory life."
"Bohemia's old reproach to poise Homeric."

"But that same poise with cant and cushions rife
(Official titles, prizes, buffer-wife)
Appeases Babbitts—while I feel their knife.
Old fraud, your crass success makes me choleric."

Then Johann: "Banal scars from burgher-baiting
Are not the only pangs of song-creating.
You chose the doom that cancels woes Wertheric,
But I—I lived them. Whose the grimmer sea-wreck?"
"Woes neat and brain-planned as a labeled key-rack
You made vast myths of, hamming like a Garrick."

"And was your Bridge myth any less chimeric?
Walt, city slicker, sold the unaware hick
Not even gold-bricks—bricks of rusty ferric.
(Who lacks the wings to lift him builds a derrick.)"

"Your German Welt-schmalz I, in turn, admonish;
Eke *grands amours* from tussles in a hay-rick
Or 'soulful' moods from pressures atmospheric,
But one thing spare us: call them not *'daemonisch'*—
While buttering patrons, unctious as a cleric."

"Patrons? Before you snub the courtier's prance,
Explain a certain check of Otto Kahn's.
Amerika, du hast es besser in finance:
Have you no agent, Hart, by any chance,
To book my lectures? Here's my song and dance:
For women's clubs, the Elder Statesman stance;
For eggheads, *Faust* translated in Amharic.
My fees would burst all boundaries numeric.
You, too, thinned Sapphic gold of pure romance
With pompous public dross of odes Pindaric."
"When I marched terror through decorum's barrack,
Or you your Werther through salons Weimaric,
In all art's wars no triumph was more Pyrrhic."
"Wars you yourself, your own worst mutineer, wreck."

"Better a war well lost and meteoric
Than triumphs basking drowsy and euphoric.
Johann, your ego never shared or co-starred;
Your secret fear of failing makes you boast hard.
Your classicism? What a corny postcard,
An alp all scenic'd up and bella-vista'd."
"Don't try to act as earthy as a coastguard;
You're not exactly hearty and two-fisted.
Americana lures you, Hart—resist it.
There's nothing wrong with being tender-wristed;
Your gift is more Athenian than Doric;
Your best songs are not ruggedly folkloric
Nor grossly and gregariously choric
But subtly—this I honor—esoteric."

"I honor you for being, self-invented.
Not even Jenghiz Khan was more Tartaric
Than you toward your own flesh, O self-tormented;

Chisel in hand, from your own myth you dented
All frailty away before they missed it.
The bust looks grand but never yet existed.
Johann, your history is unhistoric."

"Your ways of seeing earth are untelluric;
Hart Crane, your necromancy smells sulphuric.
Not even Dracula was more vampiric
Than you on your own nerves: immensities
Of visual tropes from verbal densities.
An elephantiasis of imageries.
Fool when literal, genius when metaphoric."

Then Hart: "You, too, were once not allegoric
But blazed with passions sizzlingly phosphoric.
You now praise calm because can raise no storm."

At once, through blinds, a schoolgirl's giggles swarm.
Ulrikë[1] enters—ancient blood beats warm—
Art's last conformist leaps to nonconform.

But here comes dawn to prod all ghosts to flight;
And two great artists, wranglers half the night,
Departing find each other strangely right:
You the classic, you the new-world lyric.
Homage to both your shrines from
                                    —Peter Viereck.

(1966)

NOTE

1. The teen-ager with whom seventy-four-year-old Goethe fell in love. When Goethe proposed marriage in 1823, the Duke of Weimar advised her: accept; you'll soon inherit so much money. She refused, lived long, lived single.

PART IV
The Green Menagerie

(Speakers in Part IV include DNA, potato, trees, cactus, stone, and water, as well as occasional human voices.)

In the Month of March the Snails Climb Tender Trees

In the month of March the snails climb tender trees
To be nearer the Pleiades.
Grass fingers nab heat.
The fish jump for the fun of it.
Later the roses are willing to fall.
The wasted thistle-fluff isn't sorry at all.
A vineyard, met while walking, is a shelter
Good to hold to in that helter-skelter.
For fun—or food? or hooks?—life likes to twitch;
After the ice, it will not matter which.
After the ice, the feathers—once all throat—
Are shushed; the paraplegic lakes can not reach out.

And so, from hooked exuberance to numbed retreat,
The gamuts have no meaning; or what they have of it
Encysts in chunky particulars,—
The specific timothy-grass, the ungeneralized tears,
The vineyard met while walking, a life-buoy of Here,
Good to hold, in wave on wave of Anywhere.

The Persimmon Tree

Not as we wish, accoutred regal,
Our soarers land but pent in cloud.
So must we take each molted eagle
Just as he comes or do without.
No radiance radiates. Its birth is
Dark-stained with lusts and blasphemies.
We sing them shiny if we please.
Or snuff them. Either way, unclean.
We dodge with outrage or derision
Truths that assault us squashily:
Each clowning, sweetish, harsh-cored vision
That shoots from the persimmon tree.
Brief bloom, we always wrong you; earth is
A drabber patch than need have been.

Vegetable Frenzies

(Speaker is DNA.)

Who in his skin—speak, skeleton—
Is not a running tree? We've been
Bloomed by some primal restlessness on the run,
Inciting shape after shape after shape,
The gamut of stone, plant, ape.
As I sprout a lung's first draft above the wet,
I forget—no, I remember—my earlier zoom,
Launching the vegetable frenzies from algae to oak,
Choking the globe and I their core. A conch,
The throat I had not yet grown,
Was droning an unrest of seed,
A green before gill was or gut.
Throat, mourn
                    exultantly
The peace lost when sea begot seaweed,
The hour birth got born.

The Insulted and the Injured

(Speaker is a small potato overlooked by all.)

I, underground giant, waiting to be fried,
Of all your starers the most many-eyed:
What furtive purpose hatched me long ago
In Indiana or in Idaho?

In Indiana and in Idaho
Earth-apples—deadlier than Eden's—grow,
Puffed up with buried will-to-power unguessed
By all the duped and starch-fed Middle West.

In each Kiwanis Club on every plate,
So bland and health-exuding do I wait
That Indiana never, never knows
How much I envy stars and hate the rose.

You call me dull? A food and not a flower?
Wait! I'll outshine all roses in my hour.
Not wholesomeness but hubris bloats me so
In Indiana and in Idaho.

Something will snap (as all potatoes know)
When—once too often mashed in Idaho—
From my drab husk the shiningest of powers
Rises—
        (I'm sun, I fill the sky)—
                        And lours.

(1987)

I Alone Am Moving

(willow sapling addressing humanity)
You all are static; I alone am moving.
As I race past each planted railroad wheel,
    I pity you and long to reel
You through my thousand outstretched ways of loving.
Are you alive at all? Can non-trees feel?

Run while I may, for at my pith gnaws night.
The winds—these are great stacks of anchored air;
    I thresh them with my hard-pronged hair;
I jump right through them, roaring my delight.
Live while I may—run, run, no matter where.

How marvelous, if you but knew, is speed!
You all must wait; I am your overtaker.
    Striding to green from yellow acre,
I toss you spring. Each dawn, my tendrils knead
Stars into pancake-suns like a tall baker.

Trudging toward snowtime, I can mope for hours
To think of birds, the birds I leave behind.
    Why has the Spore Queen kept you blind
While granting sight and sentience to my flowers?
Black questions in my sap outwear my rind.

Bipeds (I almost envy you your peace)
Are free of this gnarled urge for absolutes
    Which sweetens and saddens all my fruits,
Dragging my twigs down when I'd fly toward bliss—
While bugs and diamonds agonize my roots.

The Slacker Apologizes

(same willow, older, at biped-felling ritual)

The artist as a bourgeois with a bad conscience.
—Thomas Mann

We trees were chopping down the monsters in the
    Street to count their rings.
Who blessed our war? The oak invoked: "Within Thee
Crush, Earthmom, quakingly these red-sapped things
    Whose burrowings
Foul Thy clean dung. Kill, kill all alien kings."

Crowned by black moss or by obscener yellow,
    The flowerless monsters stood
On soil-blaspheming asphalt. How they'd bellow
Each time we lopped them—just as if their crude
    Numb root-pairs could
Feel feeling. O Goddess, the glory of being wood!

Then games of peace. Who was the poet? I.
    I was the willow lyre.
Even the oak was awe-struck; melody
Maddened whole meadows like a forest fire
    To hear my choir
Of leaves beat, beat, and beat upon each wire

Of winds I tamed and tuned so artfully
    It seemed an artless game.
You weed back there, don't think I didn't see
You yawning. Bored? Well, try to do the same.
    What? Suddenly lame?
Come, come, step up and sing—or wither in shame.

Then crooned the crass young weed: "Last night my stamen
    Could hear her pistil sigh.
Though far the orchard that her petals flame in,
We touched in dreams the hour that bee flew by.

My pollen's shy
Deep nuzzling tells her: weeds must love or die."

Fools. How they cheered. But wait, I set them right:
    "Verse, verse, not poetry.
Jingles for jungles; grosser groves delight
In honey, but educated tastes decree
        Austerity.
True art is bitter, but true art sets free.

"True art, how can I serve you half enough?
    Had I a thousand sprays
And every spray a thousand sprigs, they'd sough
For beauty, beauty, beauty all their days—
        And still not praise
Not half the whirlwind-wonder of your ways."

At this the oak, our captain, roared me down:
    "Mere beauty wilts the will.
Why are we here? To sing and play the clown?"
The forest answered, "We are here to kill."
        Then oak: "There's still
One slacker idling while monsters taint our hill;—

"Quick, nab him! For Earthmom, dung, and chlorophyll.
    Feed him to Beaverville."
My leaves drooped red and rustled my post-mortem:
"Bloom's ugly, being frail; mulch hugs the strong,
        And right is wrong."
. . . All year my idling spring defied Thy autumn;—

Now axe me, Mother, for the guilt of song.

My Gentlest Song

(pine tree to rose)

Remember, friend, your dancing-days of May
When restless willows rustled just for you?
You tossed your petals such a reckless way
You hardly noticed me the whole month through
And thought your beauty was its own defense.
Yet all the while my boughs were roof to you,
Bark raked by hail so you could sip the dew.
You know the zephyrs, I the hurricanes.
I've loved you fresher than my youngest cones
Because my crest needs nearer light than sun's.
Although I've died so many times each fall
That something of me cannot die at all,
Each ring of ripeness costs me dear
In chills you'll never feel who last a year.
Now go—good-bye—while I grow still more tall;
You wilt me when you look so glum,
For there's one shade I must not shade you from.

Small friend, you'll never leave me when you leave,
Though yours the seared and mine the phoenixed leaf.
My reverent hunger waits for you, it waits
To weld us even closer than before
We sprouted (toward such different fates),
Close as the hour we lay there, spore by spore,
Two seeming clones in selfsame garden bed.
How many times I've wished me dead instead;
How gladly I'd divide my unspent sheen
And lend your ebb my evergreen.
But must not spare you, even if I could,
For it's not I who made you less than wood.
You—bright brief putrefying weed—
Will feed my roots next spring, will feed
The fabulous white-hot darkness of my core.

Paysage Moralisé

(After pine is prematurely felled by lightning, gnarled old cactus sets up desert backdrop, scorns spotlight, and addresses modern you.)

I'm the earned ouch of the heel of strut.
My health is parch, my moral code is slash.
Root-anchored only when you watch me,
I caper and mimic behind you when you don't.
The desert—crammed into my crouch—
Austerely fells luxuriant posturers,
Their love more callous than my hate.
I'm all the targets where your barbs land facing
Outward, a reverse Sebastian,
A retribution of boomerang porcupines.
My core's unfabulous prose-truth warns you
How justly man is aimed at by his aims,
How in the archeries of ego
A target is a mirror is a scales.

To My Playmate, with Thanks for All Those Carefree Days Together

(a gallows-tree pastoral)

I.

You are my winter-comfort, loyal fruit
That never tumbles from this hempen twig.
My flowers, for all their sun-time vows, elope
With the first snowflake; green frays off so quick;
But (faithful to the sacrament of rope
That married blood and wood) you still remain
To dance me Mayward and unfrost my hope.
When too much longing droops me with the pain
Of too much beauty; when O once again
Caress of bugs—or diamonds?—stabs my root;
When doubt, and doubt of doubt, make sap congeal:
Then I'll just twitch my branch and you'll dispel
All spells by rattling me some joyous jig.

II.

How glad-with-life you hop and swing and dangle!
Better to ride on wind than trudge on rock.
A nuzzling breeze rubs, purring, past your ankle;
Kind humble crawlers—once they feared your plow—
Now hiss affectionately from your throat;
Between your ribs a heart—a wren's—is hot.
All tears you ever lost, rain cries them back
Into your sockets. Gongs of starlight spangle
Your tar[1] with tintinnabulating dew—
Till black and gold and music fuse for you,
In liquid loud mosaics round your brow.

III.

What prose and platitude and meanness clogged
Your head before the black ones pecked it pure!
Next, worms and weather scrubbed the nerve-webbed mesh
Of ego out. This was a filthy chore.
Now you're a hive for honeybees. They flocked
To sweeten and to resurrect your skull.
Today it hums with dreams more beautiful

Than tuneless lusts that stung your brain before.
How long, O fruit, since ripeness burst your skin?
Commemorate that second birth. You bore
What every triviality of flesh
Is pregnant with: the perfect bone within.

NOTE

1. To preserve the hanged criminal (as object lesson) as long as possible from the inclemency of the elements, he was customarily painted with a protective covering of black tar.

The Delphic Gallows-Oak

(Two speakers: God-Mephisto and the human "we." The latter voice is in double quotes, italics, and indented.)

    "Is a man a bleeding throat of salt
    Between a bed and a bed?"
The loan of white your fathers spurt
You'll pay in the end in red.
    "What kidnapper has cooped us in
    This garbage bag of leaky skin?
    From ocean's cold we swarmed, we swarmed,
    Red or white millions. Jailed now."
                    —Warmed.
    "We wigglers from beyond, cramped in a walking pond:
    Bad plumbing sucked us up in pipes of blubber."
A vacuum cleaner across a salmon-run.
    "What liberates red motes?"
                      —The prank of slitting throats.
    "And mites in white streams? Trigger me the slobber
    Of gene-crammed swimmers."
                      —Mass suicide is fun
When eggward fountains die in Thermopylae
('Hot Gates' in more than Greek): all heroes slain but one.
    "Free both my life-saps to flow home to sea."
Patronize your local gallows-tree.[1]
    "The stench of sagging fruit? Fruit's homeward ooze?"
It's always autumn in a hangman's noose.
    "Can there be waters only fires quench?"
When hanged and hangman pair
Through the fierce wood they share,
It's three who mate.
              —*"And mix their brines*
    Of white and red and resin wines—"
Till shivering crab lice flee the cooling hair.
    "Suppose in that hug-the-cosmos mood
    A charismatic hangman wooed
    All forests into gallows-wood,
    Roping all the world's necks in one all-draining drench?"
One universal spine-jerk would

Wrench free a global white-red-yellow flood.
 "We'd hang like children's stockings on Christmas trees."
Eyes popping like a tourist gawk.
 "Sockets reserved, old raven, for your beak."
But first you'll feel your big death squeeze
Your small death[2] from two bobbing knees.
I'll watch the dry turf dunk.
 "Turf's oldest sprig from dead man's spunk,
 An oak oracularly drunk:
 Under its venerable trunk I see
 What mystic rite?"
 —You woke
The planet's Delphic gallows-oak.
 "Green nerve-ends rustle; boughs sway omnisciently;
 All's hush."
 —Now oak root speaks:
'O Mensch! Gib acht! Man, free your mandrake-shrieks;[3]
Hanging's your last Rheumatic Agony.[4]
When neck-twig creaks and rope-fruit leaks,
From homesick core you'll pour, you'll pour
One jailbreak, all at once.'
 "As stockyard fans sniff meathook lambs,
 You gallows buffs sniff each nuance—"
The wet-cheek tears, the wet-leg fears—
 "Enough! My kamikaze penis rams
 Wet fire. The shattered flask
 Scatters into wholeness. My lemming blood bursts husk
 In spastic getaway from straitjacket shore.
 . . . Then home again? Old ocean floor?"
Amazed to feel my heartless heart feel pity,
I've got to answer 'Nevermore.'

NOTES

1. Chemically considered, a hanged man gives ocean back his various landlocked saline fluids from his various apertures, the last one being—at snap of spine—his semen.
2. "Small death": French "petit mort" (orgasm).
3. From the spilled white seed of a hanged man, according to folklore, sprouts a magic mannikin or man-shaped root, called "mandrake" or "alraune," which shrieks when uprooted.
4. cf. Mario Praz's book, *The Romantic Agony.*

Saga

(Locale: the "Vinland" continent discovered by Leif Erikson, 1,000 A.D. Same oak, now a pirate plank for enforced drownings, chants these old runes to the countless captives who must tread on him.)

You must walk the plank.
I can guess why you're not in a hurry.
    (You must walk the plank.)
While you walk, I'll creak you my story
    —*(You must walk the plank)*—
Of my rise from old wood to new glory.
    (You must walk the plank.)
You will hear only me till the hop.
    (You must walk the plank.)
Take pride in my rise as you drop.

    Vinland the Good!
Guzzling her fjords, I woke.
    Vikings gulped
Her mead in skulls and spoke:
    "Of all the fjeld
Be thou our gallows oak."
    Years flew by,
More swift than the crows on my fruit
    Till Wyrd decreed
A doom of ax at my root.

    Thankless thanes:
I had served with such loyal joy.
    Was felled because
Had frightened the milksop boy
    Of a doting jarl.
The dotings began to cloy
    When the gloating babe—
Did I ask him to watch so near?—
    Was crushed by my crash.
I was sawed to serve as his bier.

    Years crawled by,
More slow than the worms in my fruit,

Till coffin ghouls
Smashed me to look for loot.
Then chapmen came:
"This lid will staunch our boat."
Not quite. The leak
I wrought proclaimed I frowned
On burgher mart.
The only carl not drowned—

—was a thief in the brig
Who clung to me when they sank.
I wrought him dreams
Till he rose to pirate-chief's rank.
He knighted me
The skald of plop: Sir Plank.
I wrought revolt:
He walked me, too. How sweet
Is fear's last squeal,
The sweat I taste through feet.

Gallows and crash,
Coffin and treacherous leak.
Not bad in their way.
But these diving-board days are my peak.
(You must walk the plank.)
Every man's tread is unique:
Frisky or with dismay,
Some bouncing, some needing a shove.
(Here's good-bye; here's the edge of the edge of the plank.)
I'll remember each footstep with love.

I Am an Old Town-Square

(speaker: radiant old stone)
Come near—rebuild me, hear me.
                              History wrapped her
Calamities round me in a sevenfold quilt,
Whose layers are towns. A crass and tinny scepter,
Such as the brasher kind of dynasts tilt,

Is all my courtyard holds of my first tribe.
Their names? Their fame? No interesting guilt
Of overreach coaxed footnotes from a scribe;
Their centuries were rain my gutter swilled.

Such songless trudgers it was joy to jilt.
I became a dirge black crows, black coffins shrilled.
Plague was my second town. Plague snowed those black
Song-notes across my granite music rack.

Next, pilgrims found that coffinwood and built
A pleasure town of feasts and lusts. (My third.)
Five hundred years they belched and strewed their milt.
What did time save of them? One dried up turd.

A trade-town's fourth, with art so polychrome—
Such loftiness from huckstering distilled—
That sudden shaggy nomads, wolfskin-frilled,
Would rather starve there than be khans at home.

My fifth town downright pranced with buccaneerings.
Loot gave my cobblestones a jingly lilt.
The night my floor was starry-skied with earrings,
Sackfuls of earlobes clogged my drains like silt.

My sixth was reared by knights who hanged those raiders.
Its saintly prayer was, "Vengeance to the hilt."
Gouged by Love's camp of gallows and crusaders,
My scars were chinks where armored knees have knelt.

Time passed. Those chinks lodged clover. Smoke said, "Wilt,"
Desert of smokestacks. But a bee had smelt
A bud, and soon my seventh town consoled
My claws of soot with rings of buzzing gold.

A dream:—From eighth cocoon my airiest city
Spreads glittering wings, true gold now, nothing gilt.
Around me twirls a tinkling live confetti
Of childhoods. Ancient pavements bask fulfilled;

And rustling down each twilight, slim on porches,
Tiptoe on spires like willowy stilt on stilt,
Shimmers of girlhood—aspen glances—pelt
My yard with fireflies from soft-browed torches.

A dream . . . it never came. Bombs came. Bombs spilt.
Sweet Geiger sirens¹ sing for you, my hearer.
·But where's my lost eighth town. Get me rebuilt.
My stones await you radiantly. Come nearer.

NOTE

1. "Geiger" means violinist in German but also means clicks that measure the deadly
atomic "radiance." "Sirens" means singers that lure but also signals that warn.

River: The First Morning

Around the curve where all of me that fountained
Leans over on its side and is a stream
And loiters back the long, the round-about,
The sweet, the earth way back to sea again—
At just that curve I woke.
                              What is awakeness?
A thing I own? Or opened eyes that own me,
Sobbing me through as if my banks were lids?
I only know I'm freed to be less free:
A tear of longing on a cheek of loam.

Before that flash, I sleepwalked through my circle
(Sea, river, cloud, then rainfall back to sea)
While never feeling how it feels to feel.
I have no memory of what came before
Except a silver sandy sense of glide—
And this odd shame; one eon mill-wheels chained me.
The chainers didn't last; I did, I do.

Who took flow's casualness? I never thirsted
To symbolize or mean. Who took my sleep?
Leaves fall on me as light as sunbeams; even
Boulders are weightless; only meanings weigh.
I am a river and a river only.
But now, since waking, not of water only:
A tic of "aim" on the blank brow of "am."

Faster. I skid between the rocks like breezes
Between the leaves. I skim the rocks so lightly
I now seem less a river than a breath.
Or is this hurtling airiness a warning
(How can I know yet, being so young awake?)
That I have reached my final waterfall?
Too late to stop; enslaved by back and forth;
No rest for me in either blue. My tiptoes
Of dew creep up and stub against the clouds;
And clatter down again; again to clamber.

Green-drifting pools and lulls below, good-bye;
Intimate riverbed, joy of the touch of a contour,
Clinging to me you never will climb with me now.
Stay with me seaward: earth-half of my circle.
But cloudward (stript of shores, a ghost of vapors)
Each strives alone. And now I flex my sinews
For stream's last jump—I clear the rocks—I fall
To rise.

   No, not yet fall; not rise; suspended
One hovering instant, I'm the world's first morning
(Everything possible, not yet in groove)
And stream's first jump.

      The hover ends. I move.

Snow against Rain

I bring a message from the rain.
The addressee is green.
My rain-queen sister has a twin
Whose loam's not loam but steel.
Steel cogs inside? A clockwork bride?
Too soon to argue with the tide;
Too late to warn the grain.
My sister's sister's sun is snow.
How tell cold's hoax from rain's warm queen?
Let me go.

        • • •

Who crushed a toad to pack a hill
To throne—beyond the tick of wheels—
A bride who twinned a queen?
Accuse, accuse. But whom? Rain whirls
Bleak round that hill and mum.
I didn't do it—ask below.
I did, but let me go.
Noon bleeds to dusk, too numb to heal;
Snow is sun's bitterer name.

        • • •

Resins are rivers untied,
Flowing untowed uphill,
Restoring noon.
Snowfields—red sprinklings on white,
The pounce on the lark on the run—
Outdarken dark.
Roots too frozen for tide,
Twigs of a nest of a wren,
Vines reaching for rain
Sink under hail, under heel.

        • • •

Can rains, compelling tide,
Warm back estranged terrain?
Frail pact. One wrenching note

And trust lets go.
The toad I crushed to pack a hill
To footstool for a bride
A throne beyond the crush of snow
Has wrenched the voice of rain.

(1987)

Leaf-Drift Rhythms

(This invocation to a red leaf is from my verse-play, *The Tree Witch*, Greenwood Press, Westport, Connecticut, 1973.)

Like actors in a death-scene played with poise
Lest rant make critics smile or scare small boys,
You fall. No blood, no blenching.
Only the dry red wrenching.

Leaves on panes,
Wistful for the green so briefly borrowed.
Then the rain's
Fiddling on the twigs so newly sorrowed.

Leaves on loam,
Dead children knocking to be let back in.
Each has been
Tree-top-dizzy while so high from home.

Sweet and swift,
Your first careen on air; then crushed to be
Waif of drift
Between the tractor and the galaxy.

Yet joy is what they crush you to,
The work machine and the world machine.
Kiss of the wine-press festival, renew
Red lips of autumn with the pledge of green.

They'll have their autumn too,
Machine and machine.
Next year not they re-green,
Outfading you.

Flawless *their* clockwork-flash;
Leaf drags with loam;
Falling from speed to ash,
Not they fall home.

Leaves in space:
Vintage whose radiance outshines a ray's.
Leaf on steel:
Rainbow whose year outspins a wheel.

Spin death and beauty (year now sere, now heady),
Opposites—feuding, fornicating—in
Green already
Reddening.

Not godless joy—or joyless God,
Hardened as "good for"—or as "good,"
But doom, pardoned in art, and
Bloom out of bloom-dust gardened.

Fuse death and beauty (leaf now red, now green),
Infinites in a wisp of sheen;
Fuse forth the specter no mirrors mirror,
That last of the temples, that innermost terror,

Between the tractor and the galaxy
That marble hammered from mortality:
The clay which is the self-surpass of clod,
The gods who are dishevelment of God.

Then warmth is what the clockworks crush you to,
The wheels, the rays.
Yon fullness of loam's festive wine-press, strew
A throb of colors through the ice of space.

Then flutter the green joy of your red going;
One color was a thirst when you were growing;
The other a promise of future crest when you drop
As fecund mulch. All. leaves. fall. up.

Tuscan Loam

I.

Tamperer vainly tidying up the stream
Of sense-impressions mind can never tie:
The concrete mischief of my Tuscan dust
In your too northern, allegoric eye
Warns that the *stream* is all, the vistas lie.
It drags as earthbound as my pollen must;
It flies as airy as my marble may;
Before you try to think such stream away,
Tamperer, tamperer, fathom noon's own gleam.

II.

The Apennines surround my flat brown tonsure
So vaguely you forget my noon has scissored
More clearly each least shadow of a lizard
Than any silhouette a paper-doll leaves.
The stream is all; each color light can conjure,
Each clasped incitement swells the sensuous stream,
Sonorous as the pattern a chorale leaves—
Yet dust-anointed, never beatific.
Your yearned abstractions cannot live where sol lives;
And even luna's half-lights, clinging, contour
My several greens exultantly specific.
My vines are vines; each tangible full rondure
Is just itself, no symbol and no dream.
That dust is three-dimensional. The olives
Are really there. I am the land I seem.

Tree Ballad

(The Son of Man—the ballad's speaker—has returned to pace his Gethsemane garden.)

*And now also the axe is laid unto the root of the trees; every tree
therefore which bringeth not forth good fruit is hewn down . . .*

                —John the Baptist in Luke 3:9

*We think that Paradise and Calvarie,
Christ's Crosse and Adam's tree, stood in one place;
Looke Lord, and finde both Adams met in me.*

                —Donne

A garden got lost in a garden.
Eden. Gethsemane.
One seedling for apples or crosses.
A tree found its way to a tree.[1]

Applewood climbing came easy.
A gardener outdangled his fruit.
Left side, right side, honest gypsters.
The middle tree stole root.

If I forget thee, O womb stain, let my nose lose its cunning.
Glass flowers—let them try to beget.
After the Hanging Gardens,
My People forgot to forget.

Eons of stinkless Immaculate love
Parked at a cattle car.
One yellow for Jew badge or manger.
A star found its way to a star.[2]

Some bring me blood now, some champagne.
It was not what I asked on the hill.
O what poured into the shower room?[3]
I'm waiting for water still.

Applewood knowledge came flavored.
Vinegar. Zyklon-B.

One pilgrim staff hasn't reblossomed.[4]
It paces a garden with me.

One fruit seed from knowing to pacing.
Eden. Gethsemane.
Hill at the end of gardens.
A tree found its way to a tree.

       • • •

I carved on my hill of stockyards
New Tables at storm-core's hush.
How thin now the wailing of Marys,
The meathook nailing of flesh.

Straight hooks were worse, straight lines of creed;
My worst gall wasn't gall:
Caliban wasn't Caliban, Prospero was;
Judas wasn't Judas, it was Paul.

I see two midgets in a circus pummel
Each other with rival bladders, Lab or Faith,
While in the bleachers Bacchus, belching
An ode to Arcady, spits grape seeds down on both.

I see their "good for" or their "good,"
Their godless joy or joyless God,
While a trampled bouncy "bad" green weed
Yawns at dry wood.

The only lamb who got away,
I warn the village green:
Don't ride with your Good Humor man;
White's blackness reddens green.

Lean soapboxers hawk me to losers;
Fat bosses pretend I'm a boss.
All rip-offs—and only one Christian,
The one on the cross.

Is it true a tree got Judas?
Earth's rescue cut short by a noose?
Then no one can save you from saviors.
Run for your lives—God is loose.

Judas, Judas, brother dangler:
Two moons in orbit round a planet's grave.
. . . His kiss sold one lamb only.
Millions roast because I'm love.

My Passion, it drained you of passion.
My teardrops, they drained you of sea.
A garden got lost in a garden.
A tree found its way to a tree.

Who flies toward that or this world's love,
Will cry when sun melts feathers.
Whichever tits you'll reach for then,
They were my mother's.

Whole galaxies held out their nests;
I tried each on for size.
When I forgot thee, O earth stain,
I lost my sky in skies.

Stain is what stays when stomped by
Ideology;
Turn back, turn back, Jan Bockelsen;[5]
Weeds yawned at Calvary.

Original Sin—call it salt of the earth.
Corruption—call it loam.
My cross's lumber came handy.
Two crossbars to fence you from home.

I dreamed up hives of angels
With never a hairy bee:
Perfection weeded gardens—
Trees reborn through a tree.

By vampire wood clenched closer,
I—peering closer—see
Sahara amok among gardens,
Trees sucked dry by a tree.

A mountain offered me This World.
I shrank, I said "unclean."
. . . I've changed: all's vain but *vanitas*—
Trust no caress that's not obscene.

What slows up sky's
Descending dish?
A sleepy fire
From when you were a fish.

Then, then one stalling flash is
Time, time in reverse:
The last of the terrors, the fourth of the gateways,
The stain that moves the sun and the other stars.

Seed is for vineyards, not crosses.
Eden. Arcady.
. . . Gardens found out about gardens.
Trees hewed to pieces a tree.

(1987–92)

NOTES

1. According to medieval folklore, the cross of the crucifixion was carpentered from the very same applewood as Eden's tree of forbidden knowledge. The two gardens are Eden and Christ's Gethsemane.

2. Yellow star: Nazi star for Jews as well as the star over Bethlehem.

3. At the Nazi death camp of Auschwitz, Jews ended up waiting—like Christ on his Golgotha hill—for water. Neither got it. Christ got vinegar; the death camp got Zyklon-B poison gas, pouring into the "stainless" hygienic shower room.

4. According to thirteenth-century legend, minnesinger Tannhäuser—leaving Venusberg's underground love goddess—was punished by the papacy for this fleshly frailty: no absolution till budding of his barren staff, here imagined to be of the same applewood as Eden's tree and Golgotha's cross.

5. With his slogan of infinite love through infinite terror, Bockelsen here symbolizes all ruthless-righteous saviors, religious or secular, right or left (Torquemada, Calvin, Robespierre, Lenin, Hitler) who crusade for some impossible "stainless" abstraction.

Murdering both aristocrats and Jews, Bockelsen was praised both by the Nazis and the East German Communists. Here is the summary in *The Observer*, London, 1970:

> *King of the New Jerusalem in 1533 in Munster . . . was Jan Bockelsen (John of Leyden). . . . Having announced that the Last Judgment was at hand and that Munster alone would be saved, he declared himself king of the whole world . . . calling on the poor to rise against the world conspiracy of Antichrist, seen in the luxury and avarice of clergy and nobility or Jews . . . A direct line can be traced from the medieval prophets of the millennium to both the Nazi and Leninist movements. . . . Jan Bockelsen imposed a reign of terror proclaiming a rule of love.*

PART V
Walks

Stanzas in Love with Life and August

I.
What can this wind do to these August leaves?
It folds their ears back on the shaggy bough.
Back, back and forward. Rippling weather-vane.
Does this, but nothing worse than this, although
Juggles them like a wave that jumps upon
Seven slower waves to pound apart their foam
In a thousand drops for still more later waves
To squeeze together in one undertow.

Apart, together; apart, together again;
Not once in August shall one leaf blow down.
Let winds be fiddled by the grass they comb;—
What else can winds do to these August leaves?
Green ankles, kick as crazy as you choose,
For none shall tumble until August does.

II.
A pair of slight tennis shoes is hurrying by in August.

III.
Here's life-besotted, writhing rhododendron,
Stretching its sinewy sap in every pore,
Drowsy and fierce, like a great carnivore
Lunging in one green leap upon the sun.
Untamed? Yet all its jungle-grossness fawns
Before two passing slight white cotton socks,
Disheveled perfume, and a burr-starred smock.
For an hour, peace and rage and the music of growth are one.

IV.
Is hurrying by in August.

V.
Inexhaustible waterfalls of green splash up
Crazily, in dark directions lavished,
Rippling through blue veins under cotton blouses

A resonance from flutes beneath the loam.
Down, death; down, dog;
Stop, wind; down, she said.
For one whole hour nobody can harm a leaf.

VI.
Hurrying by in August.

VII.
The winds? Can only harm what's pale and outward;—
How dark and deep the green of August glows!
What can a wind do to an August leaf?
For an hour, kick just as crazy as you choose.
"But if you hear far unseen apples thud?"
What is it to us? Those cannot tug us down,
This being August.
                    August, glow slow, glow long.

VIII.
Hurrying by.

IX.
(Vulnerable August, deaf to all but fountains.)
She paused. Who hoped and touched? She hurries by.
She wears a blouse of cotton summerwhite
—(Is it fountains, listen, or the first torn fruit?)—
And tennis shoes.

X.
Can you see a thud, can you hear green fading?
Glow slowly, holy foliage; apple-red is
Unasked for in this flute-fed, loam-thick hour.
. . . Another thud; closer.
Menace is the name of the small breeze between the leaves.
. . . Closer.

XI.
Turning-point.
A pair of slight tennis shoes hurries by in August.

XII.

How dark, how deep the green of August glows!
Thinks not of all the death it fed upon.
Thinks not of all the life its death will feed.
One hour—O deepening foliage, sweep of lawn,
Heavy green of August—pause before you're gone.
Life-scented, knee-deep-hugging, eerie grass,
Good bluegreen spruce, free unpruned hedge and heath,
Calm moss, wait long. Glow long enough for us,
Petal of the pond-scum, drowner's floating wreath,
Whose bees are frogs in emerald flowers. Slow moss,
Glow long. Deep-breathing, flush-cheeked August, bleed
Your ebb's arterial green in slower tide
Back down into the loam you lean upon.
We pause as long an hour as August does;
Crisscrossed in dark directions overhead,
Hot comets hurt each other as they pass;
Cold moles grub past each other underneath;
All pause as short an hour as August does.
Eyes have met eyes while all that green stood still;
Though it took but one small breeze to burst that spell,—
When eyes pass eyes as dark as August glows,
Eyes shall glance backward after August goes.

A Walk on Moss

I.
Two lovers walking in a lovers' garden,
Dreaming old books with heavy-lidded pages
About two lovers walking in a garden.
They walk as dawdlingly as bark uncurls,
More inwardly than deep green lavishes;
They walk as timelessly as moss spells out
To every step the Braille of "dream forever,"
Where "forever" means an hour's walk on moss.
His eyes that drowse too often, dream illusions:
That worlds—what kind?—exist outside the garden.
Then just in time both dim their eyes—to wake;
And then she sees no grief on earth beyond
The hint of pebbles in a sandal or
A starling lost in rhododendron bushes.

II.
Two lovers, speaking in a garden, spangling
Confetti of tropes. In fun articulating
Extravagant picnics of sound. Let her say: "I am
A mere coiffure of baubles who thank the sun,
'It is your noon that loans us stellar ways.'"

"If head-dress," let him answer, "then Milky Way.
A pompadour of terraced fireflies.
An intricacy of comets at toss of the head,
A disciplined waterfall of well-tuned skies."

Then she: "Disheveler of cosmic primness,
It's you who's orchestrating this electric
Lustre as startlingly as combs in winter."
And he: "Swim, tortoise-shell, on such sweet tides."

So let them speak—like Byzantines of love—
A minute in fun, their courtship having been
In truth least courtierlike of pastorals,
Needing each other as simply as fetching water

From stillness of wells. Two lovers, two true loves:
As inarticulate as bread is shared.

III.
A garden of togethers, waifs of groves,
Two twigs slender as rain, leaning
As tenderly as eyelids almost-meet.
Or else an "ah" and "oh," a pair of breaths
So in, so through, so hoveringly past
Corporeal gates as if two sighs were drifting
Through sultry, gnat-stirred southlands, fluttered at
By dusks of moth-eyed, mild astonishments.
Yet lovers both: branded to the bone with knowledge,
Stifled to the lungs with incense of fulfillment,
Stained with each other's scents like painter's palettes.
Palettes whose perfect white is white and isn't,
Being blended from all colors ever tried.
Dark and pure their thicket of entangling;
Dark and heavy its cloying; darkly white
The gentleness—heavy, heavy—of the gorged lovers.

IV.
From time to time they watch a goldfish circling
Beside white groves. The shade of saplings covers
The pond as chastely as a shadow longs.
White shadow, ceremoniously emblemed
With slow wet rings that fade as sad as gold does.
What have they to do—touching, as they walk,
Only each other's knowing fingertips—
What have they to do, satiated and hungry,
Two lovers in a garden-walk, what else
But watch a rainbow of fins paddle like petals
Across a mirrored indolence of birches?
More real than they themselves are, for an hour
Is not the only solid stuff in dreamland
The slow wet gold reflected from the circlings
Of fish on the reflected white of bark?
Here limbs are air, and contours cannot press.
And only surfaces are deep.
And nothing true except reflectedness.

V.

Here and now, nothing is willed, and nothing touches;
Not even the slowed up air—westering breezelessly—
Ripples the gauze of her shoulders. For an hour,
Luxuriance has grown past wantonness; has grown
Back down into a bud, as darkly pure
As satin, as unfolded as cocoons. . . .
And so two lovers walking in a garden
Became one moon. Clean stain, drained beyond fire,
One moon in empty skies,
Rich beyond clouds and to itself enough.

(1956)

Walks in Rome

A. Stanzas of an Old Unrest

(Viale dei Bambini, Borghese Gardens)

This poem's first draft, 1944, was written in one of the Borghese gardens while the author was soldiering with the American troops in Rome in World War II. Earlier, while the author was stationed in Tunis (cf. "Two Elegies" in Part II, section 2), Americans (including his brother) had landed, under heavy German fire, at the nearby Anzio beachhead. The present new version was written on returning to the same garden in 1991. Poem's place and time: still wartime Rome 1944—except for the abrupt jump to 1991 in the last three lines.

I.
In the garden
Where the cherub statues are,
Pine-north palm-south blend groves; frayed myths
Of childhood peace seem near.
White statues light gentle Viale
Bambini as if there were
No blackouts, no wartime blackouts
In '44.

II.
Chalk warnings, scrawled on black's blank slate,
Bleach every shadow.
The wind tatooing my spine with fear
Can't snuff stone's glow.
Don't tell me, I don't want to know why
Dead heads obsess me so.

III.
Flowering from stone's calyx
With a somehow pleading stare,
The eyes of the children are saddened
(Eyes whiter the darker the air)
By visions of unseen beaches.
They'd be glad if the beaches were far.

IV.
Not far: the marchers, marching
(Their boots and hearts full of sand)
On strands once made for strolling
Hand in hand.
Blurred lanterns of stare, the bambini eyes,
Their stone eroded by rain:
These dimming ghosts in the half-light,
Demanding return.

V.
Because I dim slower and older,
The pudgy phantoms plead
For one spare dawn from my lifetime,
One revenant birth from my seed.
Through cruel Viale Bambini
I flee them row by row.
Their whiteness, bloodred at sunset,
Won't let me go.
Is it their quest I'm fleeing
Or my own unrest?

VI.
Or is it my younger brother, killed
At Anzio beachhead? He
Sends tide birds sends code birds
Inland to me.
Some friends are mourning a friend and some
A war hero's uniform.
I mourn a baby sacrificed
To the Baal of a sundered home.
Inland: gulls healing gulls taunting
Recall me—like sea shells—to sea.

VII.
"The world has a thousand beaches;
Beware.
Exactly one thousand beaches,"
Warns a marble garden child.

"And hands no handclasp reaches
And lovers who pace are there.
And the storms have human voices,
And the voices are tugged by loves.
And the sea birds the tide birds
The code birds are bitter and wild."

VIII.
Beyond the marble arbor
Have I a harbor from storm?
Gardens are inland. There is no inland. None.
Ashes on beaches are cold. Their reach is warm.
Let me go, Anzio ember; remember to let me forget.
For me, storm and harbor are one.

IX.
At last new beaches: tugging
Toward strolling up and down.
Stone's fruit
              shared past
                       shared pain
Now bind me less.
The garden shivers suddenly in every root.
When life distracts and I play Cain
By absent-mindedness,
How now atone?
In answer, gulls taunting gulls healing:
"Life moves. Move on."

X.
"Out of the garden,"
Says the gentlest statue there,
"New eyes her eyes must tug you till
You end where waters are."
. . . Is that (five decades pass) why still
I must keep walking keep walking where
They they the sea gulls talk?

(1944–91)

B. Borghese Gardens, Lago di Esculapio

(rhythms of obsession)

Kind as noon, calm of unfalling petals,
Motionless and recurring creek,
Mild park ambushing the ambler,
Warning the lover: Trespassing Required.

The birds are so light when they land,
Land and hop a little,
So light on the blade of the pond-grass
That it sinks not at all, wings never touch water.

And the blade, the untroubled,
Never even trembling. The pond untingling. The park
Rippled only by the lover, by the rambler saying:

"Always the same." How many times, sometimes with joy,
Has he not said it, and sometimes—"Always the same"—
Desperately? Always only that face.

C. Castel Sant' Angelo

I.

(heavy castle rhythms)

Slow
Stone-walled
Immense
Gate,
Dense
As our own old
Sorrow.
        You! angel up there!,
        Can you conquer
        Sheer weight?
Only love's
Feather
Is heavier.

II.
(light angel rhythms)

Quick
Lightness
Of twig's fall.
Wind's tress
On western wall.
Flick
Of sun's mote.
Grace-note
Music
(Hear the bell
Spill).
      Only love's
      Cruel
      Will
      Is lighter still.

D. Frutta di Stagione

(pacings of completion)

I.

"Fruit of the season" so your menu ends.
"Frutta di stagione," phrase to speak aloud
As slow as branches bend with what they grow.
Then spread the menu out you never wrote;
What gentleness, to flower as slow as seasons,
You of a season, Valerie Sophia.

II.

What sadness also: outlawed from outstaying,
Trust least the closest linkages with boughs.
Juices of the season, of one season only,
Yet altogether that; how goldenly—
These overfilled crescendos of a brim—
They toast the sun round every spoke it slants.
Potion of love . . . and sleep, a wheeling goblet,
A rim of sun around a hub of fruit.
Then, fearless, kiss that brim when offered to you;
Savor it—gulp—twist dripping, drenched at last with
The molten lime-tang of finality.

III.
How many days how far from here there dangled,
Bountiful spendthrifts of themselves, these orbs,
To pile a plate for Valerie Sophia.
Plumaged with twilight, figs swayed ever looser,—
Blue parrots fanned by ever huger ferns.
And nameless southern plants of fiercer nectars
Once basked as secret as suspicions, brewing
Liqueurs like scorpions brooding in the sun;
Not even they outguile their season's halt.
Beside them foam compressions—apricots,
Once free and airy as the genie was
Before his bottling time, now wedged in peel,
Both cheeks hilarious with flush of doom.
An introspectiveness of olives, depth
In smallness, ebbs each bursting rind back; noons
Nudge all rings coreward. But the blackest glow is
The each day wilder density of dates,
As if all history were pressing inward
All sugar globed into a single ache.

IV.
"Last year when I loved Atthis," mourns an echo,
Revolving with an old Ionian year.
Last year when I loved . . . Colors seep away
As melting as the plum-tree's fullest moon.
Receding towards the same invading velvet
That clouds our eyelids two by two by two,
O for the thousand eyes of bees, when death comes,
To savor thousandfold that deepening veil.

V.
Yet simple images compel the more.
"Frutta di stagione," phrase whose slow pride mirrors
Resilient stems when fruits bob shiningly.
And each husk, destined to its own true waning,
Pales vulnerably perfect, Valerie.
Believe the menu, fruits were always so.

Say: "Of the season,"
                    voice as kind as rain;
Believe no branches,
                    eyes as sad as spray.
When destined, tears are seasonable wines.
And each one gentle, Valerie Sophia.

Walks on the Edge

(Rockport, Cape Ann, New England, 1963–67)

A. The Entropy Song

I.
The day is opening like a fan.
The gold is dimming anyhow.
At first the gold looks infinite.
The cold erodes it anyhow.
Above our cliff, below our cliff
Two mirrors bounce back blue for blue.
The dialogue looks infinite
Till sky drinks up the wetter blue.
    The shores that get, the waves that give
    Don't really seesaw endlessly.
    Yet evenings loiter wistfully:—
    World, world, what wreath from soil so thin?
    The roots replenish till the time
    They don't replenish. Many times
    The warmth is gaining. All the time
    The gain is losing anyhow.

II.
Have you heard it, have you heard—
"Just a little, just a little"—
Have you heard the tinkling sound.
Cascading down from leaf to leaf,
The freak is sun. The norm is waste.
We pay to see. The price is night.
Renewed in vain, renewed in vain,
The tinkling sound of light's decline:—
    "Just a little, just a little,"
    Cascading down from fall to fall,
    In vain but paid for anyhow.
    Though thinning down from worlds to world,
    Yet rays can loiter wistfully.
    It isn't much we hanker after,
    Just a little, just a little

Resonance in so much waste.
The race is almost meaningful;
The loss is gaining anyhow.

III.
The day skims many little days
Like porpoises from wave to wave.
Again the peacock spreads its tail
Across the night. Till night spreads too.
One Light resounding—have you heard?—
Relieves frost's weight, renews green's clocks.
Till running down outweighs them all.
Yet evenings loiter wistfully.
> World, world, what tune for so much loss?
> What makes your thin-soiled marshland skim
> A hopeless rose from June to June?
> What keeps feet running to your edge?
> The race is almost meaningful;
> The edge is ebbing anyhow.
> Again, again the peacock tail.
> The stars are cooling anyhow.

B. A Wreath for a Plunge

I.
White forehead on green soarings on black dyings,
Every wave is the youngest wave.
A high, a wreath-demanding forehead,
Balanced between surge and tumble,
Every wave is the youngest wave.
Not green for long, the oldest riddle-solver,
Again, again and always for the first time
A white black grave, the only sure solution,
Every wave is the youngest wave.
Come quick across the wrinkles of the marshland,
You others whom no universal star led;
Come ankle-deep—a prince is born—and garland
The perfect whiteness of his newborn forehead,
Every wave being the youngest wave.

II.

"Welcome your prince"—each wave a new imposter,
Forever newly landing with pomp of foam.
"Call me your king"—no end to Bonnie Charlies,
Retreat and Restoration, ebb and tide.
"Am back, my land, to solve your maze the old way"—
Returning exile who never went away.
Or call it cascade of tsars, each False Dimitri
Returning falser and more noble-browed.
"Weave me a welcome of marsh-vine and berries of marshes,
Roots from thin soil, and feathers to add their fern
To the sparse wreath, and grass blown low on marshes."
So wave after wave, each crest a promise
Steadfast as spray.
                              Prepare what's left of garlands?
We, fading, hail the even faster fader;
Yes, crown with old pale blossoms of the marshes
The brief pale forehead of the youngest wave.

III.

—His empty forehead. Blank-eyed wave, where are
The shared palaver, the taming, all that junked
Reasonableness to steer by? "Children," say
Only the very old, "I can still remember"
(Birds don't need to remember, their berries are always berries)
"Shared truth."

IV.

            (Marsh berries
Don't need to be shared. Seagulls
Don't steer by truth.) Waves brought you merely waves.
Waves are a small perfection, no warm answer.
Walk out and pay for what's not floating in:
The Restoration. But this time facing inward,
This time a full, imperfect forehead, earning
A sparse wreath for a risked plunge:
Man's own restoration of man. (Marsh roses
Are beautiful, very pale, beautiful, scentless, beautiful.)
Wade without foresight or don't wade at all.
Plunge without seeing or you'll never find.

There's only insight. (Gulls read maps, their eyes
Look outward; berries, even winds are solid.
Roses are cold. Even warm roses are cold.)
There's only insight, paid for: not a flashlight,
But night probing night. Walk out alone.

V.
One-way footprints. Crossing the edge
Where orphaned sand is eyed by unthroned waves.
What makes him shamble in his probes of blackness?
If crazed, by what? Is he drunk on abstract echoes
Of angel wing-beats, has an angel scared him
Into his wits? And out of lighted sense?
The lights are fading anyhow; the plunges
Are restorations—why should thirst need angels?
It was the thirst itself led to this edge
Of land and breakers, where two frauds confront:
The pseudo-solid and the empty-eyed.
And whether the upshot is a crown or drowning,
Each in his own way wades unreasonably;—

VI.
Thirst is not reasoned. There is for each own darkness
No general compass. There is earned salt insight.
Only the birds don't earn, their resonance is free.

C. More Wing Than Wings Can Bear

A leaf, a seagull falter.
What sudden warp is here?
Leaf, leaf on the water,
Gull, gull on the air:
Am I your core's decoder
Or all the globe's corroder?
Is even some age-old boulder
Outweighed by one brief stare?

• • •

Fadings on the water.
Driftings on the air.
The inward and the outer,

Will and atom blur,
Shaping a leaf-that-yellows
To Aprils without shadows—
And aimless wings to arrows
That never were.

. . .

It's not just you who falter,
Gull . . . gliding . . . here;
It's more than leaf I alter
With meddling stare.
I, dust, am dust's remolder,
More height than stem can shoulder,
More weight than wings can bear.
Is brow earth's overload?
Do deep-sea fish explode
On reaching air?

. . .

Fleck bob-bobbing on water.
Fluff . . . bouncing . . . on air.
Eyelash's flickering halter
Of gossamer
Tugs—and a whole world's shimmer
Obeys one lash's tremor,
Till sun, black sun, seems dimmer
Than inward flare.

. . .

That symbol-making stare!
More weight than wings can bear.
More wing than wings can bear.
No shell can hold the meaning
That seeming gives to being.
Who is it thirsts while feeding?
The story of man is here.
Is here to fill and alter
The leaf, leaf on the water,
The seagull on the air.

D. Last Walk: Resist

I.
The edge again, honed by a harder year
To rockbottom, harrowing all those low
Heights. Coming to terms with rock, the shadow
That soared shall walk. Enough scope walking. We're

Substance, grounded substance, and surprise
What warmth we can through all our outstretched senses:
Through skin the rub of skin, through ears and eyes
The goldfish-flicker of October branches.

The crayon of the sun pokes down and pencils—
The inkwell of the sea spills up and pens—
A crisscross of auroras on our brain-cells,
Which hurl back boomerangs of golden glance.

The fondling waves of years—for all their sweetness
Of breeze and brine—erode the body's dune.
Yet toward a craggy grace. Each ages toward concreteness.
Merely eternity is out of tune.

Somewhere a scale tilts earthward,
                                    leaves the luring
Desert of spirit. Loam grows with ache and hazard
Our honest rat-death, no transcendent soaring.
And so we wrench a rose free from the desert.

The desert squeezes from a petal's palette
Attar, to hover permanent and pallid.
And leaves us dust to gnaw—I, dust heap, call it
Tang all the sweeter on my own doomed palate.

I, chunky gullet, curse whatever hovers.
My veins block the geometry of highways.
Guerilla of crooked and alluvial byways,
The sentenced heart stokes what palatial hovels.

Out . . . Out . . . An hourglass runs out,
The earth's and mine. A lamp, the sun's, goes out.
I, shivering sand pile, anyhow stretch out
Impossible warmth.
                         So lightning out of cloud.

Eye ear nose mouth and touch, the five surprisers—
For all their warmth—erode each aging face.
Wave after wave of horizontal geysers.
Yet toward a craggy grace.

II.
Waste is the norm and grace the rarity,
One rose-red flicker in a ton of brambles.
I gambled half my life on aimless ambles,
Then stubbed against an aim,
                              this crag by the sea.

What's rock but sand crushed denser?—weight of titans.
What's sand but rock grains?—gritty-souled New England.
Accordion: chron's Year now slacks, now tightens
Its twenty-six-thousand-year squeeze of rock from sand.[1]

New England sandstone: this triassic nettle,
Niched in the shagginess of unkempt earth,
Marking the line where leaf gives way to needle,
Strict sentinel bisecting every north.

Such bulk cleaves more than merely firs from birches.
Sheer chunky substance rolls the past in vengeance
On the thin present. With such landslide lurches,
The ice-age brands across the age of engines

A stony message: that there is no message.
To will what isn't or what is?—no passage
Between two halves of seeing, as if scissored
By nictitations of a thunder lizard.

Still vibrant from the trample of the saurians
Though drowsed of late beneath our pygmy tread,

Stone's layered eons warn the soul's historians
How truthful and how venerable is mud;

And just how brash is soul,
                            not grace of rocks
But flutter-flutter Grace of Golden Treasury "pinions,"
Newfangled bootstrap of the simians,
An interloper meddling forth sermoned brooks:

Upholstering the emptiness of heaven,
Injecting emptiness in tomb and hearse,
The taxidermist of the universe. . . .
A scales reverses. Nothingness is heavy.

III.
Crossroads. My road tilts—where? Evade it? I,
Being both mud and air . . . does choose mean die?
But sullen winds are swelling from the sea.
And if I tilt no scales, the scales tilt me.

Then armed with vocatives shall I call rock "you"?
Invokings force a soul on you, O boulder.
Consciousness, just by being your beholder,
Demotes you to a symbol's retinue.

How many solstices and equinoxes
You've slept through, huddled seed in stolid eras—
Till annexationist man, unlocking boxes,
Walks by. Potentials quicken. Sleepers hear us:—

A droning, a terrible underground droning, the buried
Cicada hunger, dry wings flexing: burrowed
Abstraction, the late-born desert. Here to tame
This lithic balled fist of time.

Solidity hangs by a thread. When all's in deadlock,
Even a mote—by choosing—tips the balance.
Can I still sense, not shape, just sense your bedrock?
Or shall I choose to will with sculptor talons

Timeless mirage and with a sculptor's hatred
(Autumn and ebb and entropy undone)
Force meaning on you and hack unsatiated
Till stoniness is gutted out of stone?

Earth seems to offer us so gold an orchard
But locked in seeds, till hammered forth in torment.
And so with fruits of air, in dream-pods dormant.
Shall it not tempt that all be upward tortured—

By hammer, hammer, hammer—to almost sky?
When all's hallucinated, what's one more lie?
It tempts, it tempts (that symbol-making stare).
RESIST. STAY STONE.
                    Well, we have got this far.

NOTE

1. In triassic New England the characteristic mineral was its undry porous red sand-stone; the characteristic fauna were the dinosaurs, distinguished not only by their size but also by their vertical third eyelid (nictitating membrane of lizards). Their footprints, sur-viving the intervening ice age, are still found on New England sandstone today. The "Year" it takes to condense sandstone from soil is here capitalized as the year of a larger scale than man's, namely the so-called "Great Year" of the planet's 26,000-year equinoctial cycle.

PART VI
Tide and Completions

These three poems complete—respectively—three leitmotifs of the book: the seesaw of ambivalence between Persephone and Dionysus; the merging of Dionysus with Jesus, the Son of Man; and, thirdly, ageing and its doomed last venture.

> *Stroll to the ducklings' pond we once found peaceful.*
> *Kick off your sandals, wade among toy ships.*
> *Lend me the trust I'll forfeit. Fear no evil.*
> *For the first hour we'll just touch fingertips.*
>   —Dionysus to Persephone in "Hacked," p. 17

> *Lightning-prone even in dry skies,*
> *Mind's deserts have big eyes.*
>   —"Counter-Continuities," p. 66

> *Green is red, especially when it isn't. . . .*
> *What if some things are something else?*
>   —"Hut Wait," pp. 115–16

Tide

But such a tide as moving seems asleep,
Too full for sound and foam.

—Tennyson

Why shouldn't two Greek myths (Persephone, Dionysus) be replayed in contemporary America? "Tide" is a feminine-centered counterpoint to the masculine-centered "Dionysus in Old Age."

The woman in the dialogue speaks in quotes and italics, the man in normal print. The woman's speeches are indented. (The occasional and very few interruptions by Pluto are also indented but with no quotes, no italics.)

The man is not only the wine-god Dionysus-Bacchus (or else a traveling-salesman impostor) and not only "Zagreus" (Greek for "torn in pieces," referring to the annual hacking of the god's vine-limbs for future resprouting); he is also Egypt's Osiris—and Others hacked or nailed. He gets scattered each fall, in Osiris's case in fourteen pieces. The Dionysus legends are contradictory. Some call him son of Zeus, some a mere trickster-magician, manipulating his maenads like a modern rock star. A stroller out of Asia, he brought the first grape seed to Greece. Archeology, not legend: wine-making has been traced to the Babylonian valley of the Euphrates River, c. 3500 B.C., thence to Asia Minor and points west.

The female speaker is not only the spring-bringer Persephone-Proserpina-Kora (or else an impostor, a farmer's daughter in a traveling-salesman joke); she is also Isis, Eve, and—via the Nag Hammadi gospels—"Maggie," the Magdalen. Each half-year she alternates between Pluto's cold underground Hades and earth's reblossoming crops. Spring cannot return till the scattered one is regathered by the shuttling one. But suppose, as Pluto's moll, she . . . forgets? As for the mystery of her inconsistencies of diction: if section 4, Part II, doesn't partly surprise the reader, then the author has partly failed.

Part I. Eight of the Nine Waves of Ebb

1. Confronting Her Sleaze Voice
2. Now Suddenly Her Trance Voice
3. Nonstop Fall
4. Bâteau Ivre Strikes Again
5. Dialogue of the Deaf
6. Orpheus on Land's End
7. The Archimage Soliloquy
8. Spring Cleaning

Part II. The Nine Waves of Flow

1. "Sleaze" Re-assessed
2. "Fallible" Re-assessed
3. Chores: The Weights, The Tale
4. Reversals
5. Act Five

Part III. Ninth Ebb

Part I. Eight of the Nine Waves of Ebb

1. *Confronting Her Sleaze Voice*

"Whose tickly-tap step is tap-teasing my stairs?"
A bill collector for tears in arrears.
 "That voice I'd reckernize anywheres:
 It's my lover, Tomdickand—I never had others.
 Their names—I mean yours—I forget, but to show
 I've missed you, my eyes—watch the buckets they spout."
Eyewash, not tears.
 "Then you're here—it's a rip-off—to make me shell out
 To stop your blab-blabbing to Pluto about
 Our once-a-year date in the March Motel
 Of Crocusville."
It's not cash you owe.
 "Then you're here, Tommy-O,
 To purr a bye-bye, O my tomcat boy."
Not only good-bye.
 "Will your Dicky-dick toy play me oo-la-la joy?"
No.
 "Then you've brung—Harry brat, O my hairy pet—
 Your thanks for the heavy honey we et."
Am here to collect—not pay—a debt.
 "When I was meadow and you was plow,
 Crocus was never a no-show.
 But lookit, we've shared what my seaport warms."
Sea is big, port small in storms.
 "Is it true, what they say, you spoke seagull once?"
A dome of scream spans harbor dawns.
 "Was you booze-god once or god-schlemiel?"
Back and forth goes Fortuna's wheel.
 "Are we both on the lam from sea's long hand?"
There is no inland.

"When cave-floors flood, don't drop-outs drown?"
Sleeping bats hang upside-down.
　　"Gulls gods bats? Holed up inside
　　Skull caves?"
　　　　　　　—Flotsam, beached by tide.
　　"Tell tide to pipe down. Are we bossed by its bells?"
Blood in ears hears sea in shells.
　　"Which one's the echo?"
　　　　　　　—Undulance
Ebbs to advance.

2. Now Suddenly Her Trance Voice

　　"Can you live with the news that we gods are dead?"
I fished for the foamborn, I netted a dud:
The you I beached (amid mocking bells)
Prattles.
　　"My selves can burrow too under for surf;
　　You beachcombers beach whichever me you deserve."
Who's under whose spells?
　　"Trance grabs me by the pulse."
And by the vocal cords. That's when they swerve.
That's when you give me gooseflesh, switching voices.
　　"When tide reverses, trance compels.
　　That's when you, gawking skyward, fall in wells."
Can there be terrors only nightmare heals?
　　"What if my half-year stint in hell's
　　Hot ice has made me
　　　　　　　something else?"

　　　　　•　•　•

Are we eerily 'else' to each other, my nightmare your daymare?
My 'else' a counter-terror? Orbits of double star?
　　"When you came to me from the east,
　　You brought (my worst fear's mirror)
　　Not just the grape but power,
　　A more inebriant ware."
I brought you a grape feast and myth feast
But what scary Babylon lore?
　　"The Ishtar gate, the empire lure.
　　You smuggled in your lyre

The half divine, half idiot leer
Of these wing'd bull-gods, id their lair,
Who've never ceased to lour."

The Ishtar gate of Babylon:
This megalomania of gorgeous stone,
Already power's oldest megaton
When Aristotle's pupil died next door.[1]

"Not he but the gate's home talent, Nebuchadnezzar,
Is shorthand for war, gross grandeur galore,
The pseudo-civ gorgeousness victor-barbarians wish for."

The Ishtar arch as domination's wishbone,
A yoke for the nations beneath.

"Stone arch of thighs (they gave not birth but death)
As a Pasiphaë for bull-god stone."

Stone calling stone. Antiphonies of thunder.

"What of stone's terrible thirst
For the first victims of throne?
They, through the arch of the portal,
Poured all their blood for will's parch."

All done now forever, the feeding
Frenzy of idols long gone.

"No bleeding ever gone. Gate still ajar
For each barbarian tempter
From three thousand years before."

Tombed safely far.

"Out of their hatching sepulcher,
Their reach reached here. Too coarse, too near.
I feel it, right through my girdle of 'kulcher' armor,
Like a groping hand in an ill-lit singles bar."

And, of course, you austerely demur.

"I cringe demeaned. No, I rage. No, I might adore
Them, the barbarians at the door—"

(So much for classical décor)

"—Or I might not. Then civ won't fall. Won't fall for
Them. Remember my gender. We're
For real (Tampax, straining at stool, sometimes damp where
Handled) while sharing what counts, the undowned
Dignity—tough, bewildered—of female. Don't
Dare judge our quicksilver.
I zig, I zag, but you—you were

Invasion's chauffeur."
If chauffeur, unaware.
Classic you, classic I, we're less easy to enter
Than a Great Books course. Greek roots are too under
For looters or shrinks. Let invaders beware.
I meant to import wine only; Will was mere fading shimmer,
A harmless stowaway, a faint archaic shiver.
  "Fever, not shiver. Stone bulls stir.
  Their fever strikes quick unless I strike quicker.
  To rescue us both, I whittle—from ice of my winter—
  Affectionately a sliver of silver
  Stake to stick through your heart, my lover."
And so it's come to pass we stalk each other,
Each struck with fear the other is the hunter,
Each stuck with thinking, 'It's I who's the victim, the haunter.'
  "Each sick with will's hunger, a joke without humor.
  Stroke me—I feel like crying—our double star
  Makes us, just when we most seek love, stoke . . . horror."
In the wink of the eye-of-the-storm, the weather is fair.
I sink in a peace that now no furor can hinder.
How mellow a quilt, the stack of the dusk air.
How silk the dewdrops hover.

3. *Nonstop Fall*

  "Dionysus-O, bag of grape-seed-O,
  I once was your planter. Remember me?"
My Isis no more. Re-assembling me,
She re-membered all fourteen strewn members of me;
Later they called her my Maggie.
But they, but they never autumned me.
You, you let me down, my Persephone.
You forgot to re-ember the ashes of me
When March was about to bust out.
  "Is that why the crocus forgot to sprout?
  The seasons don't feel like they used to feel."
Now nonstop fall.
  "Your flesh, your blood wear many a shape."
All grafts from the vine of my Zagreus grape.
  "Osiris? Easter?"
                —My noms-de-plume.

"Old frost-scarred vet of many a tomb,
From grave to grave you're Houdini's escape."
Each time I'm hacked for exit's door,
A wind soughs gently like a nurse
At an old-folks home: 'It never hurts
Much. You've gone through before.'
    "Through! To the bag of the bag-lady whom
    Nature-buffs call earthmom."
You'd sworn to replant me.
                      —*"Got lost in a wood.*
    So I couldn't show up like I said I would."
Is Pluto's bed wood?
              —*"I—er—overslept.*
    Not the end of the world if a date's not kept."
It's the end of O many a world.

4. *Bâteau Ivre Strikes Again*

(After her trance voice of section 2 and her transition voice of 3, her mod-sleaze voice of section 1 now seeps back.)

"Your vine leaves are graying. Or is it your hair?"
I'm capering inches ahead of a plowshare.
"Vines tolling grape-bells. In despair?"
For their frost's plow and their lost vintner.
"Shouldn't they pick (you're a loser) a winner?"
Some seasons are inner.
"Where do crop-ghosts hang out when reapers re-enter?"
Where's Pluto's bar?
"You're a wino he bounced. Or a vine stripped bare?"
Never sure which but am certain of winter.
    "Just because Pluto's my winter vacation,
    You're the alligator of the allegation
    That I'm committing adulteration.
    I'll sue you for liable—lawyers will love it.
    I'm a gracious-type lady—you better believe it:
    I adore genteel grammar like 'whom' and 'thee';
    It's a treat to watch me crook my pinkie;
    Boors who wreck havoc with English disgust me.
    I'm the sinus-cure of all eyes at tea.
    Underarm daintiness! Laciest loungerie!
    Dignity! Pantyhose matching my bra!

I don't wiggle my Parts when I enter a bar.
I've state-of-the-art VCR. I read 'Harpy's Bizarre.'
Elegance warms the cuckolds of my heart.
My salon, to keep its high-class status certain,
Has Venereal blinds instead of a curtain."

     •   •   •

"When I've anxiety ants in my belly,
What sends me is dreaming I'm Jacqueline Grace Kelly,
Trailing long gowns up palace stairs of pink stucco
In ritzy Monaco—
Or sailing a Greek millionaire's yak, full of slurpers
Of bubbly from slippers.
Speaking of boats, I dream I'll get richer and richer
Starring as Joan of the Ark in an epic moom-pitcher
With Prince Charles as Noah—oh wow."

     •   •   •

"In art and et cetera, I opt for highbrow:
'Madame Ovary,' say, by those Nobles Prize fellows,
Or the arms of that smiling Mona Venus de Melos.
That French poet you alla time quoting—Rambo,
I see where he's into tough movies; it just goes to show
Not all artists are fags. As for a genius-musician,
I might could of married one once, except his electric catarrhs
Sounded too noisome for refeened ears.
Just in the neck of time, I cut my umbelly-coil cord
To that cad,
Leaving me in a heart-rendering condition."
Be classic. Like a Persephone painting by Titian.
    "Classy? That's just what I'm tryana be."
I mean, cut out your cheap furbelow-frills.
    "We never shave below, we nature girls.
    Cut out your gropey hints. You're not quite naming
    The ill-bred noun that you're a pain in."
No, no, I'm not hinting at assignations.
    "That noun again. How dare you say 'ass ignitions'?"
My aim's not 'harass'—
               "her what?"—
                             but to make you succeed.
    "I (yuck) always gag when they make me suck seed."

I'm just being brotherly; don't take offense.
> *"There's a name for that: committing incense."*

Stop, or I'll suffer from hypertension.
> *"No news that you suffer from high pretension."*

All I want is 'tendresse.'
> *"To undress? Don't get fresh."*

Don't beat round the bush; quit the blah and grow up.
> *"Beat round my what? Wash your mouth out with soap."*

Meet men who react a wee more maturely.
> *"'Eject prematurely'? That's when they most rile me."*

What's with your—ahem—slightly nympho condition?
> *"Buster, when you're around, it's in remission."*

Be discreet. The New York *Enquirer*
Might photo you with an 'admirer.'
> *"They'd make me a scrapegoat if caught in a clinch*
> *That's 'flagrante-delicious' (poddon my French)."*

Skip trifles, put robes from eternity on.
> *"No way. I don't need a maternity gown.*
> *Plus that's between I and the guy-necrologist X-raying me.*
> *Not that I trust him; they all take that Oath of Hypocrisy."*

All I want is to lie on my Land's End beach
And fight drab lies.
> *"Serves you right—O you men—if you lie on some glad-hand bitch*
> *And have to fight crab lice.*
> *It's the fault of those 'godless permissive sexular humorists.'*
> *I'm anti the pro-verts and pro-nography-ists.*
> *I'm a fan of the yummy Majority Moralists."*

Why wriggle whenever you give them a boost?
> *"They spank sin so it tingles—like being goosed."*

5. *Dialogue of the Deaf*

Urgent: 'heal' earthmom, our very last chance.
> *"Is the ole gal needing new 'heels' to dance?"*

News I brought you arose from mom.
> *"News! You brought me a rose from mom?*
> *What grave did the tightwad steal it from?*
> *Well, 'nature wastes nothing,' not even a bum*
> *Rhyme; she keeps mixing up tomb and womb."*

She's getting a chilly reception from . . . Entropy.
> *"Good grief, shouldn't relatives—never met your Aunt Dopey—*

Be like Supportive? I did meet your father, worse luck,
On his earth safari."
                    —Jupiter?
                              "Stupider

Than ever. That dirty-old-god
Boned up on we natives in Bulfinch's sex guide:
'Take me to your . . . Leader,' sez he with a wink,
Dropping the 'r' and rigged up like an oversize duck."
I'm through with immortals, except for elves and muses.
    "Who-ya-kidn? Elks and mooses,
    Those kinda horny dears, they're ex-stink.
    Earth gods got trashed at 1 A.D."
                              —Vicisti, Galilæe.
    "But earthmom MOVES."
                              —Vicisti, Galileo.²
    "Don't gossip. No gent says 'We-kissed-thee.'"
I'm sick of our deaf dialogue.
(Or pseudo-deaf? Who's pulling whose leg?)
So I'm off to be bard of sea's roller coaster.
    "'Barred'? Why you barred? For indecent exposure?
    Stripped ego? Id unzipped?"
Wines, not just winos, get soused when songs take over.
But bards, being bartenders, stay sober.
    "How can you tell when it's vintage magic?"
My test is the sea-clock's tick.

                ·   ·   ·

Tell it to the Demiurge:
Orpheus and Bacchus merge
For an hour or an age
At—where else?—at the sea's edge.
    "What then?"
                    —Sea shrugs; new cycles rage.
    "If I was Admirable of the navy,
    I'd abolish—you bards done invent it—the sea."

6. Orpheus on Land's End

And sea invents us, us flotsam waifs
Who think we control the web.
I comb my hand through the surf-mane and stroke the waves;

The deeps are the well of my melody,—breakers my wives.
Will their undulance weave into cosy wharves
My cargo of odes—or rend[3] me like wolves?
    "Depends on the catnip a port wafts."
How's your own nippy pheromone?
    "Not moaning for you, what you calling my 'furry moan.'
    Your art stunt (aw, come awff it, Orph)
    Went artsy stale."
                        —My lyre?
    "Is liar. Scan is scam."
                        —My hum?
    "Is ham. Pluto, here I come."
        (She traipses down basement steps, unbuttoning her blouse; then stops midway, hand on
        brow; then trudges back up. And listens.)

7. *The Archimage Soliloquy*

'Lyre' indicted? A cloy-word prop?
    It wasn't for Pindar.
Outdated strings? New strains? No, all's
    One dateless chain.
Full-throated, lofty-themed (as once
    Before song shrank),
Am back as archimage; my stride
    Treads Alps like grapes.
I am disturber, I am restorer,
    Cadence my plow.
Am back to help young rivers molt
    Snake skins of shores.
I send their silver slithering home
    To clouds they rained from.
My stripped red leaves hatch green from masts
    That once were trunks.
Since Thebes,[4] all states are leery of me;
    Being uprooters,
States are arenas; their peoples take turns as
    The martyrs, the lions.
All states, all churches build on rock,
    David's or Peter's;[5]
Ah, had but David used his harp
    To smite Goliath!

Am trying to feel-with; dump me the day I
    Proclaim-at.
Grant me—that day—a bride who'll betray my
    Betrayals.
Am back for my birthright; jubilate,
    Earth-crone. Filch
From hock my bell-capped crown, its lining
Still stained with my three thousand years
Of sweat since first I, Bacchus, baptized
The world with This World's pagan wine.
That day I added Orphic laurel
To my old twine of lover's myrtle
    And tippler's vine.
Since then, all's witchery and wings
    When laurel sings;
In vain the hourglass descends
    When song dissents;
Since then, song stalls with well-wrought sounds
    Time's sands.
Sound-soused, craft-sobered ever since,
    My sons of sons
Belch between hiccups delicate songs,—
            (she interrupting with trance diction of section 2)
        "Sung to the lilts they overheard
        At village walks at village walls
        From daughters balancing on their head
        Water."
                —In urns from ageless wells.
        "Since then, the singers song possessed
        (From dreamless west, from nightmare north)
        Drift forth into my nest-warm south,
        Finding no wellspring for their drouth—"
Except to sing—
            (she clasping his hand)
                "—except to sing."

            •   •   •

        "Almost you persuaded me,
        But your own sea
        Right now explodes our Orphic trance."
Words, aren't words our foolproof fence?

"Sea floats odd meat while you float words."
My lifeguard dolphin, saving bards?[6]
"What gleams like wounds?"
—Refraction's trick?
"Look close and glimpse a bag lady's picnic."
What's there to glimpse but the magic of lyric,
Tuning and taming the sea's swords?
"'Sea spawns,' you said; you didn't say what.
Sea brings what you'd as soon forget."
A Venus whom love's white foam begot?
(she pointing at beached meat)
"A dolphin's red shark-gutted gut."

8. Spring Cleaning

(her section 1 voice)
"I'll paste you together with graveyard mud,
My humping Humpty-Dumpty stud,
O my fourteen-piece jigsaw-puzzle mate."
Too late.
"Then I'll tag-sale your organs. I'll tag every part.
Step up, folks—who'll buy a used prostate or heart?
All fourteen at a discount rate."
Too worn to retread.
"Can't your brain-mush be chow for pet puppies to sup?"
They'd throw up.
"Then I might as well patch you and keep you undead.
So what if I'm flighty and you're a flake?
Ask crone wotta wow of a team we make."
Used to make.
"Don't bellyache, then, if I skip your spring cleaning.
My Community College voted me 'Prom Queen of Spring,'
But I can't clean your vines and make birdies sing
Without I co-opt you."
You stood me up. It figures whose underground stopped you
And what you probably did with him on cold stone.
"I prolly din't; my wrong date of moon.
He's anyways over the age of consent.
Be content I'm not three-timing you. Three's a no-no."
You're a go-go up-and-down shuttle train.
"So's every yoyo of grain."

Part II. The Nine Waves of Flow

1. *Sleaze Re-assessed*

That stomped grain under snow's foot,
Is it your rites renew its root?
    "It's my goofs renew; I'm grass, not Easter lily.
    Hothouse me high and I rot."
And I, I've wronged your secret by setting you right.
    "So 'splain what you calling my secret."
                      —Plucky sleaze.

I've frostbite from universality,
Hypothermia from eternity,—
I needing your grassy low crassness all along.
    "But minus my words, so wrong, so wrong?"
This way, that way, as whim *or* tide decrees,
It's how you tilt, not what your words,
Makes worlds unwilt.
    "So 'splain how I'm moving."
                     —Like Venus Kallipygos.[7]
    "Huh? Venus what? All-hip-she-goes?
    Translate in one-syllables; short words have clout."
It's how you shrug—from throat to butt—
Keeps earth in spin when sage and saint cop out.

      • • •

    "If I wuz a saint, I'd burp you a sermon;
    If I wuz a sage, I'd gab till you yawn;
    If goddess, I'd play hard to get when you summon;
    If salmon, we'd die when we spawn.
    But shucks, I'm no more and no less than a woman."
Witch me no shuckses; I've started to guess
You're a lot more, you're a lot less.

2. *"Fallible" Re-assessed*

    "Raw body needs strain against limit, like river needs shore;
    Even Venus needs hairpins to rassle her hair;
    Dresses are messes without a dressmaker's pattern."
In the gold age of Saturn, my jigsaw chunks
Were a seamless god.
              —*"I'll patch your fourteen meat-hunks*

With my tide-pattern's 'Krazy-Glue.'"
If you get things wrong as you always do,
How can you fix things?
                    —*"Too much unwrongness gets*
    Sterile. Like fixed pets.
    Gods need a swig of what-the-hell,
    A whiff of frail.
    It's on account of I'm fallible
    That you don't fail."
Skip private mess; unfail me a world-class success.
    "Witch glue is local. Don't spread me global-thin."
What's wrong with big numbers.
                    —*"The zeroes they end in."*

3. Chores: The Weights, The Tale

Your voice is too touch. Is that why it changes so much?
    "Your voice is too bookshelf. That's why you dunno
    Your downstairs self."
Down? Since when am I alter-egoed with Pluto?
    "Your fall is his spring, like a bump is a hollow.
    Before seeds pop higher, they need to lie low."
What feeds my green's marrow?
    "His yellow, his yellow."
Did Ma Ceres teach you the farmer-word 'fallow'?
Must I lose you today to nab you tomorrow?
    "Be a reasonable fellow;
    Leave me vacation a half-year downstairs,
    And I'll be your steady for keeps. I mean years.
    I mean six months, not a minute less.
    Of course, being simple and helpless,
    No savvy tough trickster like you,
    I only do what the both of you
    Deep-down want me to."
Of course. . . . Have we inklings, Pluto and I, we duped twins,
As to which of us three really wins?
    "Meaning sneaky ole me? No, the winner is none of us three."
        (back to her trance voice)
    "The winner's the frightening thingamajig each shares,
    The scales of the all. I'm fulcrum. To keep growth straight,
    The all needs your and Pluto's weight,

A balance so steady it holds orbs' orbits together,
A balance so tippy a feather can snafu the stars."
A seesaw making—from Pluto's red—
Green's bed. Leaf's pratfall
Makes grass tall. Year-wheel's low
Makes grow.
  "You butter up Venus, he Mars.
  For me, an equal farce.
  For scales of Libra[8] (tide's nanny),
  An equal whammy.
  But only when you and Pluto are weighed as pair.
  Apart—you salesman, he janitor—
  An equal fake.
  Paired in your duel, earth at stake,
  You ooze real myth with every breath you take.
  Apart, unreal: unpaired, a dud."
Why can't we unreal duds make a deal?
Duels bruise. Suppose both the sprout and the wilt opt out?
  "The stalemate wounds of your no-win war
  Spark the beyonds, bind the rind to the bud,
  The lungfish to land, the brook to the riverbed."
What binds the bind?
  "The handing on of fables (all babies begin
  As apes) makes apeman man. Makes plus. Makes hyphen.
  Generations inherit either tales or tails."
Handing on continuities, is that my chore?
  "Your true chore. More than guzzling all that grape goo.
  That's why it's Dionysus men adore."
They stomp me, they hack me; if that's called 'adore,'
Unwine me, unshrine my shrine.
  "Human's inhuman."
I'm human too. Why am I . . . more than?
  "Kaleidoscope. Less and more."
Why less? Am I just a paper doll? A grotesque?
My weight just a paperweight on the cluttered desk
Of my scribbler inventor?
  "Each other's doll. To be more than human,
  You must first go the human route."
What go is that for my more-yet-less human foot?
  "Drudging through nothingness, on edge's edge;

Hacking through map-lessness, in front, in back;
On stairs twixt two black holes, not those of stars:—
(unconsciously echoing words of Pluto, p. 52)
Footsore and very long is the short human route.
So—in the tale of the three—is the way you must go.
You and Pluto are spokes who think you're the brakes of the wheel.
Stop stalling. Myth chore. Fulfil."
(Dionysus likewise echoing Pluto, pp. 55–56)

Kind dusk. And gentle reverie.
A grandma fabling to children.
This is the ancient tale of the three.
This is the future tale of the trillion.

PLUTO VOICE: (from below, to Persephone)
Quoting me summons me like a séance.
I'm snow in your June, defying your seasons.
It's fun being so unwelcome.
I, janitor of the cellar below,
Warn that a meeting of me with the wino
Goes bang. Like uranium meeting pluto-nium.
Better just you and me bonding together.
My grave-bed's ajar. Be my coffin's significant other.

PERSEPHONE: (to Pluto)
"I'm ebb and flow. Your brief turns come
When fruit-fall pounds your basement home.
My joy: tide's fickle rounds."

PLUTO: If tide is fate and you're its cop
And I and allness are your toy,
I put frost's curse upon your lap
For the injustice of your joy.
Pluto-nium, blow up the globe. I quit.
Sterile frost omnia vincit.

PERSEPHONE: *"I praise your purity of hate*
And rate your cuss a valentine of love
(Though it sounds like the sour grapes of a bedless lover).
You'll reverse it five minutes from now."

DIONYSUS: Our chore begins when our chore is over.
Brooks flow to rivers, and the rivers flow.
Each on its course, according to its core.

PLUTO: (five minutes from "now")

>If we're one river and I part of it,
>I . . . cannot quit.
>We're compelled. My two compellers most of all.

PERSEPHONE: (to both Pluto and Dionysus)

>*"With equal shrugs at the honey, the gall,*
>*Revive the retold, from act five to act one.*
>>(to Dionysus)
>*I've dead masks to shed, you've ax-hacks ahead;*
>*Let the future that's past flow on."*

PLUTO:

>The flows are many, are one.
>Three fakes turn truer than true.
>The tale's of the three who'll be trillion.
>The winner: the frightening scales.
>At stake: the tilt of the all.
>Three, hearing the call of the riverbed,
>Do what each has to do.

>>(End of trialogue. Dionysus-Persephone dialogue resumes.)

4. *Reversals*

You say you'll shed masks. Yours are sound tracks, not faces:
Evie for crossroads, Maggie for Crosses,
Isis for fourteen pieces.
And your quick-change voices, now gum-chew, now priestess,
How can they reverse so abruptly?
>*"It happens my Radcliffe Ph.D.*
>*Was 'PETTY-BOURGEOIS SHOPGIRL DICTION AS CONDESCENDINGLY*
>*IMAGINED BY MALES WITH AN IDENTITY CRISIS.'*
>*Did you relish your haut-bourgeois scorn? Have I mastered*
>*The semantics of faux-naïf,*
>>>>*you smug macho bastard?"*

· · ·

I shrug off—unsmugly—the custard pie you plastered
All over my patriarchy.
>*"And don't think my now-voice (am endlessly older)*
>*Is really me either."*
Pilate should have asked, 'What is reality?'

5. Act Five

In gene's guided missile, we're each a hurtling trapped rat.
>"Trapped man is the missile that tries to change route
>In mid-hurtle. We too (kind of) rate
>As human. The pride of us bipeds is being the pirate
>Who hijacks his own bio-fate."

Jiggled by genes from ant to ape,
Now spawn-explosions choke us. Yet once loam
Slept sealed. Like a childproof bottle top. How come
The very first crocus managed to pop?
>"One meddlesome sunbeam just happened to focus
>On stew a wet juggle just happened to shape."

Lean back your trance to when a moon-rocked wet
Cradle hatched—what?
>"Naked to stars as an offer of booty
>(For eons unfondled, not tickled by corn),
>The globe-lap lay sealed (as potential as putty)
>In plain mud-brown wrappers like photos of porn.
>The wind was a soul on prowl for a body,
>The half-moon a hammock, still sagging forlorn,
>When out of a dawn pool, briny and bloody,
>I—who?—was born."

What broods forth lightning out of cloud?
How first were you twirled on this ball-shaped clod
Of moon-rocked soup and sun-raked sod?
>"Great-grandma was pond scum, amoeba her son."

Escaping the bathtub was crossroads-one?
>"My eggs craved land. The lung gene won."

Then romps on shores?
>"My granny wore furs and fucked on all fours
>And gnawed raw cave-rats on cave-floors."

Like any wholesome out-of-doors
Girlscout with crocodile ancestors—
>"Bearing pacifists because we're carnivores."

Which final crossroads made me me?
>"Cro-Magnons and Neanderthalers
>Dueled to be your progenitors."

Your eggs chose brow, chose me—I'm history!
>"Tough luck you're not a bit browier still."

Enough to invent the wheel.
> *"Mere par for the course. But my own form-flow*
> *Graffiti'd Lascaux."*
I Prometheused light to warm cave's night.

PLUTO VOICE BELOW.
> All. warmth. ebbs. fast.

> *"From ant queen to ape (no other flow climbs uphill)*
> *All eggs are hot arson: against ebb's chill.*
> *Life is a crime (each climb more vast)*
> *That's recidivist."*
Welcome to the slugging match of the century:
A chemical fluke called 'life'
Versus entropy, nicknamed 'Cold Fury.'⁹
> *"Call it self-surpass versus hourglass:*
> *Their daily theater my thousand-century lap.*
> *Who'll win act five?"*

VOICE BELOW. Thermometers drop.

6. *Richly More*

What slows up frost's descending dish?
> *"A sleepy fire from when I was a fish."*
Who stole it from the Pleistocene?
> *"Prometheus was a mutant gene."*
With pelvic seesaw, with fire's wet mix,
Sea rapes both land and laps. Can't both say nix?
> *"The key violation is from within*
> *By a ripe and claustrophobe spore.*
> *Raping the lips of amazed hips,*
> *A bawling head rams them ajar."*
'Politically incorrect' babies? 'Sexual harassment' of mommy?
> *"Too subtle for your crude sarcasm to explore,*
> *All mothers are virgins at some secret core."*
That's why I've loved not much but many,
Learning each time how closed is open door.
How can what half the world has, stay uncanny
Not only to me but to yourselves?

Poor queen bee, knowing all slot machines but the one you are.
> *"The one true cornucopia.*
> *Poor drone, you probe a cranny*
> *No solver solves."*

What bad-taste tropes!
> *"Christian 'good taste' was what uncrowned*
> *Venus, driving her underground."*

She tricks my spores—like bugs—into Venus-flytraps.
> *"Not traps but escape hatch, a two-way traipse.*
> *Spores gain nine-month round-trips."*

And still, with briny troops,
Sea invades land's laps.
> *"Sea lacks*
> *Land's Icarus gamble, the wings*
> *Of youth toward star."*

Tough on youth, tough on wax.
> *"Isn't that why laps have forebodings*
> *. . . And a sad sardonic stare?"*

      • • •

Love's third eye?
> *"Socket of thigh."*

With eyelids four?
> *"The better to cry."*

Tough luck it's blind.
> *"Braille of grind."*

That's all? Just another gene-rigged chore?
> *"But wistful for a something richly more."*

Richly? Low door aspiring high?
A wish on a ladder of pain?
> *"From chain, new rung. From roof, new floor.*
> *We'll scrounge, we jailbirds of DNA-mesh,*
> *Our freedom-crumbs from the garbage at hand:*
> *Gland-spit, nerve-mess, the glob called flesh."*

The insult called 'condition humaine.'
> *"Sardonic and sad, only flesh has said*
> *'Beyond.' Only seed outclimbs seed."*

Short leash: a seesaw chained to a latrine.
> *"And briefly to*
>   *the sun."*

7. Our Second Chance?

(Persephone trance, imagining Ceres-Demeter.)

CERES: Honor the orchards. Honor well-baked bread.
As for your grape god,
Give him—give yourself—one chance more.

PERSEPHONE: Mother, mother!

CERES: As for the apelings, wake them—with nightmare
Pasts—into fresher air.
Though they can't tame mech-tech, they did invent the ode.

PERSEPHONE: Am I their queen of mayhem or of May?

CERES: Balance. Spring dew, winter hail.
Penelope's loom. You heal, you slay.

PERSEPHONE: O wake me early, mother dear, for I'm to be queen of hell.

CERES: Queen of history. Haul
Them through Clio's wringer, downhill
Till they howl and shape up: somehow loftier.
Daughter, honor
Their shaped clay that fetches their thirst quencher.

PERSEPHONE: You keep saying 'honor.' Scorners shout you down.
Even Olympus was never very Olympian.
And now, when a god is an ornament for a yuppie lawn
And even your loftiest human
An elephantiasis of spawned guck,
What can I honor worth a second look?

CERES: You can honor honoring.
Yes, even while ogling man's ending.

(Exit Ceres as Dionysus interrupts:)

Is our ending the end? Can't we grow from the grave?
"Corpse beards may grow till they're needing a shave.
The rest is worm food."

But heritage—history—these can't fade.
"Some pasts men think they've had
Are invented remembrance I plant in their head."

There was never a twentieth century?
"I collaged it from Bosch to warn all you Cro-
Magnons of your Neanderthal undertow."

No Auschwitz Kolyma Hiroshima?
"How could there be?
Think again."

I'm thinking. Some. things. can't. happen.
"By tide-trance of my ancient youth,
I strip the trauma from the truth.

Surprised to still be unblasé
Enough to be surprised,
The twentieth century finds itself . . . exorcised."
You'll stay aboard earth? It's again 1900 today?
You won't take off for . . . outside?
"Each time I've tried to leave (O how often I've tried),
A heartbreak-sweet planet, ashimmer with blue and green,
Yanked me back into human skin.
Each time—out of waters—shadows
Rose: to again begin
The life-churn of surf-sob at Land's End."
And that vile century?
                    —"Unhappened."

                •   •   •

"Nix on unwrinkled gods. I've changed! Right here is my place:
With every single woman whose hair grays.
I wish (but I can't) that I could
Spread my knees wide enough—my immortal brows too—
To enfold in my 'me' every single mortal 'you'
In continual renewal of all who fray."
Some continuities stay?
"Sandaled daughters still carry baked clay
On graceful necks toward ageless wells;
I can't take off; our globe is a
Poet, a trickster; earth compels."

                •   •   •

We reversers, we're still out of sync. This time you my advisor.
"Advice is mush; we honed each other wiser
(Not maudlin slush but diamond cutting diamond)
When love-hate fought-taught. War's the stipend
We paid for wising up."
                          —Although love widened,
Hate ripened; wisdom rasped too strident.
We honed each other into frightened
Dust, poured
Through the heart's arch, from the brow's parch:
For love—hurry hurry—to patch.
"'Heads or tails,' Minerva or Venus: the coin we pitch.
At either end we've paid paid paid."

Yet love—unalone—the mystique of 'shared pad'—
    "We reversers, O what if our lot is to perch
    Lonest when paired?"

      •   •   •

We're both being whirled. To a pit? Or to skies?
    "We're unamused guests on the Ferris Wheel seasons
    Of an Amusement Park star. To rise
    I must fall far."
To rise together?
                  —*"Snow-time aches with treasons.*
    At wheel's deep dip, when pit gapes nearest bone,
    There you'll stand up,
                force doors,
                        fall off alone."

      •   •   •

Why shouldn't we stick together? We've
Merely ruined each other's life.
    "Merely lived each other's ruin. I've
    Got to leave when I have to leave."
Are we each other's Sade and Masoch?
Whose turn to don the leather cassock?
Instead, can't we rescue each other, we drowning pair?
    "Some drown their rescuer."
Go where you must. But before you go,
Say: will we two again—ever at all—?
    "You'll know when you have to know."
When where? Give hints.
    "Who else, the night when you do what they call
    Die, will be clasping your hands?"

      •   •   •

There'll never be lilac if earth-crone's a carcass.
Joined on her mattress, let's bounce forth that crocus.
    "Like a boy's kite in a tree's snare,
    Why are your daydreams snagged in my hair?"
Your mussed hair on your strict brow
Is the sea's shout in the grape's glow.
    "Aw c'mon, I'm just a farm-hick muse
    And you a tout for cheap Greek booze."

Hell no, you're hell-god's hooker now.
   "You, you—I could scratch your eyes out—you
   (When you need me for greening, you swear to be true)
   Were always the stud of Hellas."
My groupie Bacchantes? You were always jealous.
. . . Yet with the others really just us two.
   "I always knew. How can we stay at odds
   When we're the same junkyard of junked ex-gods."
If gods don't exist, not 'so much the worse for gods'
But so much the worse for existence. At least no god's mortal.
   "In your 'Goat Ode' of a while ago
   I already tossed you my bon mot:
   'All. gods. were. immortal.'"
We're on the same debunking roster;
Pater[10] (not Noster) says 'Dreadful Persephone';
'Devouring' is his word for me.
Doubted myth: the only way our names endure.
   "Doubts, when they're lived for life's sake, make myth truer."
Then make. It's your
Turn now; faster; the sprouts get fewer
Each shivery night, your kiss their only cure.
   "Whose fault? Dare you meet my glance?"
Your black-glancing eyes? New hue every trance;
All colors not yet invented:
Bluer than wonder, more dour than dread,
And I their wooer.
               —*"Our second chance?"*
A southful of wings is awaiting a northful of thaws.
   "Outside, the first robin's ahead of the news.
   O what must I tell the grapes you abandoned last winter?"
Tell their gypped sap I'm back, their vintner
Who didn't forget.
               —*"I'll mend the sprigs that splinter.*
   I'll bind the snow-bent twigs."
Alert the birds.
Tell the impatient rawness of grape's buds
I'll make green blue.
               —*"I'll make blue shimmer."*

8. *Cliff-Brink Hour*

"Last fall a pond weed brushed my thighs
Coldly.
This March, a waker under ice
Called me."
I hear ice crunch; no pond crust now delays
Our re-embrace.
"Once in a life—it isn't often—
Comes botched embrace's second chance."
Your second chance comes yearly, mine just once.
"Mine every March when ponds uncoffin,
Thawing your lifeblood as they soften."
I'll be glad to resign from the club of the dead.
(When I fled you, I . . . waited for you.)
"I'm sorry for certain gross insults I said
(Even though they were certainly true)."
No more betrayals, no deadlock. I oar, you oarlock.
"Male-will self-betrays.
But as long as your feet touch Terra's bedrock,
Our trust-warmed handclasp stays."
Why touch her clay as menials touch forelock?
Let's. force. clay's. grace.
"That's just what the progress-creeps try (their disgrace)
With their twelve-lane car park.
They soil her soil, they seal it under tarmac.
Thud of ripe fruit is now a desperate door-knock—
'Mother, we're back'—against a floor block:
'Why can't you let us in? Why did your door lock?'"
What witch or warlock—or wizard from Porlock—[11]
Helps grass assault asphalt, helps plums home to loam?
"Odd goatfoot-marks on tar's paved glaze
Free her from freeways."
Whose foot?
      —*"This god's unknown.*[12]
Were part of him and part of you once one?"
I forget. Who needs him? It's you who's my second chance.
"Re-chance me. And with euphonious resonance."
Lean down till your nipples are brushing my autumn's red easel,
Red heating red till it greens again.

We'll touch as equal touches equal,
As eagle mates in air with eagle,
Tossed on the gusts their wing-beats fan.
> *"Stroll to the ducklings' pond we once found easeful.*
> *Kick off those work boots, wade between toy ships.*
> *Lend me the trust I'll forfeit. Fear no evil.*
> *For the first hour we'll just touch fingertips."*

Without you, I'm lost, a sea gull
Without a beach.
> *"This time no sequel.*
> *Will your overreach*
> *Spoil this renewal, this hour of savor*
> *On cliff-brink of hover?"*

Then hurtling? Each a separate river?
Not separate when love is to itself enough.
> *"My love needs loyalties toward more-than-love.*
> *Your mind needs treasons you're unmindful of."*

But haven't we climbed—as one—this final summit?
What future murk can dim this hour's glimmer?
> *"I wish I didn't know we two must plummet*
> *Direct from spring to fall. With never summer."*

Yet anyhow summer! Forever, forever.
> *"Am ever your anyhow bride:*
> *So long as you cherish—as tide-wave of crops—*
> *The village-green wavelets. Sea's made of small drops.*
> *Only the local is worldwide."*

• • •

(Prose disruption of script: enter a frantic human reader who has just finished reading "Tide.")

READER (to Dionysus): Quit right there. I've read your script and know what's ahead. Hurl the script into the nearest fire.

PERSEPHONE: Illegal to shout "fire" in a theater.

DIONYSUS: What's ahead is a happy ending: traveling salesman wins the farmer's dau—I mean, goddess.

READER: Unhappy lines ahead. Drown your author in white blot-out ink. Hijack his typewriter. Come alive!

DIONYSUS: I can't come alive. I'm being lived. I say not what I want to say but any lines the author makes me say.

PERSEPHONE: Not any lines; not that arbitrary. No outer rottenness in your author's plot without you yourself inwardly willing it.

READER: So who lives whom?

PERSEPHONE: Maybe the author isn't the author. Maybe he's being lived
    by the pathetic power-hunger of a certain overcompensating wimp.
READER. Who dat?
PERSEPHONE. You, the reader.
(Reader vanishes, script resumes.)

9. *Law of Levity*

Now that we're lovers for keeps, I needn't humor
Your coddling of local landmarks any more.
Time to talk Serious.
                    —"Ouch. When I'm stuck
    With that capital 'S' (meaning ego-amok),
    I zoom (saying make-up gone zilch) to the ladies room.
    How else can skirts dodge stuffed shirts?"
Stuffed with—?
                  "—enthused hot air. The Holy Wars
    Of sincerer-than-thou. No bloodbath worse."
Love's bear hug?
    "Worse than tiger's grin."
My world hug?
    "Worse than gangrene.
    Don't kick—when you're thinking in thousands, not twos—
    Landmarks. 'Think big' means stubbed toes."
To green the globe, I'll bulldoze . . . each local village green.
It's roadblocks my kickings aim at.
    "You told me to dump you the day you proclaim-at.
    Today, while proclaiming, you squash underfoot
    An overlooked goat god who alone shields root."
I'm grape god, you're spring god; we seeds from the Zeus groin
Must heal mere lesser grain.
    "A healer's a steam roller; sometimes he heals
    Earth flat. When saviors are loose in my halls,
    I take to the hills.
    . . . You've said I switch selves so fast it gives you a migraine.
    Now you're the switcher—and not for the better—
    While I groan with chagrin."
Unless you stay, my vineyards groan.
    "The past swings round to infect your fate
    With the will-plague you brought from the Ishtar gate.
    I'll stay—if you're letting my land-waves flow

Messy the way the March roots grow.
Try it. Second chance. Love's last bet."
Yes, yes. Agreed, of course. But, but—

Part III. Ninth Ebb

But tide is untidy; so's growth—it's too slow;
Petals too flighty; roots too below.
> *"You're a wino not of what you imagine*
> *Is wine but of word-ferment gin."*
Now that you're back for keeps, we'll adjourn
The tide-farce by forcing unbriefness on June
And briefness on markstones blocking my maps.
> *"Don't—O I'm trying so hard to warn you of traps—*
> *Stub your toe."*
Mere pebbles. I'm striding up into—
> *"Dance—O not strut—over undertow."*
My busy improvements have power to—
> *"Poor pipsqueak Prometheus with a throwback Neanderthal gene,*
> *Turn back before you're too—"*
Too busy to feel-with, I proclaim Serious plans.
> (Unseen behind him, gravediggers prepare his ditch, directed by a slightly officious jani-
> tor from below.)
The best is ahead. With your loyal assistance
I'll straighten the globe—it's too curved—when we join.
> (she leaving for keeps)
> *"Back in a sec. Where's the John?"*
> (Exit goddess, giggling. Curtain.)

(1992–93)

NOTES

1. In 323 B.C. the local priests prophesied correctly that Alexander the Great was doomed if entering Babylon through the gate, ancient already then, of Ishtar. (Among other things, Ishtar had been the monstrous Assyrian war goddess, brandishing sword and fire. Today, near Babylon's site, Hotel Sheraton-Ishtar is brandishing Pepsi Cola.) The gate's stone was admired as "gorgeous" because adorned with so brilliant a colored glaze. This immense triumphal arch was decked with priceless gold and lapis lazuli and was topped by the glaring winged bull-gods. Long before Alexander, antiquity's mightiest conquerors—including Babylon's Nebuchadnezzar (ruling c. 605–562), Persia's Cyrus (when conquering Babylon 539 B.C.)—had "hubrised" through the same Ishtar gate, all three greeted by the chanting Chaldean priests.

2. Julian, Rome's last pagan emperor, 363 A.D.: "Thou hast conquered, O Galilean" ("Vicisti, Galilæe"). Galelei Galileo (1564–1642): "Eppur si muove."

3. *Re* "rend" and Orpheus: this greatest singer in Greek legend could charm the waves, the rocks, the beasts with his lyre. Not the maenads; they tore him to pieces.

4. *Re* the witchcraft of Dionysus-Bacchus against Pentheus, the Theban head of state.

5. Gospel of Matthew, 16:18: ". . . thou art Peter, and upon this rock I will build my church."

6. Cf. the legend of the Orphic poet Arion, saved from drowning by the dolphin he charmed with song. For the dolphin-Venus contrast, cf. end of Rilke's "Geburt der Venus."

7. Kallipygos: from Greek "kalos" (beautiful) and "pyge" (buttocks), as in the famous Venus statue of that name.

8. Four meanings of Libra: Latin for "balance"; major constellation; "scales" sign of zodiak; autumn equinox.

9. *Re* "life" versus the entropy-Fury: cf. *New York Times*, Science Section, December 30, 1986: "Despite the tendency toward entropy, complexity has evolved, leading ultimately to the appearance of life . . . defying the march of entropy."

10. Walter Pater: "Dreadful Persephone, the goddess of destruction and death" and "Dionysus, a chthonian god, . . . sadness . . . hollow and devouring."

11. A mysterious "person from Porlock" interrupted Coleridge's Xanadu poem.

12. *Re* that pagan-Christian synthesis, cf. P. Viereck, *Archer in the Marrow* (Norton, 1987), p. 19: "Just now what goatfoot nicked all village greens?" and p. 211: "Look: goatfoot Jesus on the village green."

Crossbow

> *Son of Zeus, Dionysus was born with goat's horns. He was torn to shreds . . . reconstituted . . . later transformed into a young goat.*
>
> > —*New York Times*, February 3, 1985, section 10, page 21, describing twentieth-century rites at Skyros, where Dionysus is today again worshiped, this time as a goat-footed, Panlike, satyr-like god of spring resurrection.

> *What is it hinting at, that synthesis of God and goat¹ in the satyr? . . . I'd believe only in a god who understood how to dance.*
>
> > —Nietzsche

> *To dance . . . Satyrically, the tragic foot.*
>
> > —William Carlos Williams, *Paterson*

> *The companion of the Savior is Mary Magdalen. But Christ loved her more than all the disciples and used to kiss her often on the mouth. The disciples were offended: . . . "Why do you love her more than all of us."*
>
> > —Gospel (Apocryphal) of Phillip, 63:32–64:5, text in Nag Hammaki Library, New York, 1977.

"Crossbow," 1994, is a much rewritten condensation completing my previous poetry book, *Archer in the Marrow* (W. W. Norton, New York, 1987), to which any interested reader is referred.

FATHER (the old universal thunder god): left-hand margin.
SON (Christ, the Son of Man): indented to right.
YOU: the only voice always in italics and quotes.
APHRODITE (here in amalgam with Eve): sans quotes, sans italics; always labeled.
A dash in a line is for change of speakers.

YOU is a modern American of fluctuating gender and genre. FATHER is the brutality of reality; his the show, his the script. SON, revising the script by now defecting from sky to earth, seeks his lost self, the Asian-Greek Dionysus. But solely mankind, by free choice, can unite the split halves: Hebraic, Hellenic.

> "Crossbow" has four scenes:
> 1. Prologue: Circle or Dot?
> 2. Duel at Land's End
> 3. Showdown
> 4. Epilogue: Prologue to New Spiral

(Stage setting throughout: floor painted as earth, ceiling as sky, with death's meathook dangling from ceiling. Scene 2 and end of scene 3 are on meadow at water's edge.)

1.   Prologue: Circle or Dot?

1.

(son)

Toys don't know they're toys.
If they do, they're not.
At thing or not a thing?
A circle OR a dot?

I.

(father)

When dots are circles, staring back,
And yes affirms them less than no,
When down gets uppity and up swings low,
Not till then can heaven crack.

2.

(son)

My father who looks aside
Assumed blank faces on the toys he tried.
I have learnt different, being sent inside.
In autumn only man is heavy-eyed.

II.

(father)

Your father who takes no side
Faces the eighth day satisfied.
But what if toys look up less blank than lizards?
Next time I'll make man button-eyed.

3.

(son, then you in dialogue)

My father who wrote the play
Assumes a plaything is a thing for play.
"Did he send you as his spy into my pulse-beat?"
I am deserting to the side of clay.
"If a cross is but lumber God borrows
From a tree that's untouchably God's,
If Eve's but an exile God harrows
From the greenest of all the world's woods,

If the foamborn ghost in our marrows
Is but frozen, awaiting spring floods
Can we carve warm applewood arrows to arm
Touchable gods?"

III.
(father to you)

Never. Not till Eve comes strolling back,
Spitting apple pits, new orchards in her wake.
Not till, in Foamborn's wake, your lost sea-home
Gives Lamb goatfeet, gives dust loam.
(father to stagehands, confidently)

Angels, stop lolling on that pin—come quick
And wilt two queens.
(father alone, anxiously)

Just now what goatfoot nicked
All village greens?

2. Duel on Land's End

(Iced marsh; sere meadow. Sign: ALLHALLOWSEVE. Only two voices: father and you. You always in italics. One seagull watching intently.)

I.
(father, then you)

Seaside and bleak; where all last duels are.
"Tunes warmer on winds waywarder—"
Land's End; your lungfish ancestor
Here first slurped air.
"But now—"—You've come a long way,
Ape baby.—*"Now man and you,*
Having. it. out."—And the blue gone gray.
And no shape-changing trickster.—*"Vine always around."*
Kind of late; green gone yellow; no watcher at all—
"Only some gull in the dusk-lull."
Then what are you up to, so chummy with winds?
Picking up feathers to make yourself wings?
"He always—."—No rescue this round.
"Tunes warmer on winds waywarder than others
When from the frozen graves the marshfires glow
Bring me—."—A three-step from your father's fathers,
Kicking warm heels against their jails of snow.
"Waltz-beats? In swamp-churn what avails

Decorum?"—Better not know.
"Some heels look almost shaggy through the ice."
Better not look down, if vertigo—
"It goes right through me—I feel it between my thighs—
That scrape of claws from under their roof of ice."
Their roof: your floor.
"Both lure
Each other. Of course, I'd never dance on ice.
. . . Unless the marshfire guides me safe."—But if
Ignis fatuus also guides a jailbreak, then . . .
"Some graves are made to waltz on."—On,
Or in.—*"Stop: what's that beast-cage whiff*
Of furry copulations just below?"
What's earthmom? Step 2—gap 2—
Takes two.—*"If my birth was step 1—"*
Step 3 is tomb gape: you've tripped on
Your family crypt.—*"Not mine! Each now alone.*
I've shed my dead."
They're back for trick-or-treat. They haven't shed
You.—*"Let me go."*—Their return from ice
Isn't quite birth, but . . . —*"Glow? I hope only marsh glow."*
Allhallows was once not pranks but ghostly flicker.
"Something lower's crawling nearer quicker. Let me go."
If on your grave of many a death ago
You slip on ice—
"I'll waltz with decorum. Let me—"—If from the moat
Your own buried claws—.—*"I feel at my throat*
Hot ice."

> (Interruption: a gull shrieks [the wine-god watcher, the shape-changing trickster from Asia. The watcher cuts man's debacle short by catapulting the "you" safely away into a dialogue with Aprodite].)

3. Showdown

1.
(you, Aphrodite)

"A 'god'—the word is old hat—today means
What?"—A leaping dolphin of delight.
Or leaping electron-quantum. All that shimmers
Uncomputably.—*"A nuisance imp to programs?"*
A bursting grape of spontaneity.
"Spontaneity?—will it blast or heal?"

Heals you of technics. Blasts you, too,
Unless you garden it.
>*"Shedding the chains of programmings, why*
>*Not also of form?*
>*Full speed ahead for the pure of heart, unbound.*
>*Or does 'gardened' mean: no more green?"*
More and sproutier. But green-gone-formless ends as
Youth drugged with truth-
Slogans. Heart's open-road from oh-wow to Sieg Heil.
>*"Are you flesh, you lost gods, or intangible spooks."*
To wraiths we appear as wraiths;
Our bodies, near and disguised,
Are warming you here and now.
God? No, but gods!—who'd strip for mere abstract ones?
Obscenely shrine, piously desecrate us,
Our swelling fruit half terror, half decorum,
Flesh flushed with spilling wine: we touchable gods.
Viewed voyeur,
Have you really looked close at what my opening
Opens? A wound to heal wounds. Salt
To sweeten salt.
A crescent moon of berserk gentleness, parting
A full moon. Shimmer of inner.
. . . I still am I, the mussed-up goddess.
What I've returned to bring is not salvation—
Too much of that too long too many eons—
But choice between God and gods.
Here comes a cypress jury-grove to judge
Your backtalk to the southwind. You have made
The Fig cloacal and the Fountain chemic,
Whereby your sky's first constellation crashed.
For this the courts of Eros sentence you
To health
>and to drum majorettes
>>and to
Street smartness when awkward awe is overdue.
>(Aphrodite now more somber-voiced, then you: *Stabat Mater*)
My oasis was parched by her desert eyes,
By the tug-past-death of Mary's eyes,
Twice beautiful, with birth and then with heartbreak,

TIDE AND COMPLETIONS • PART VI

With a lapful of life and then with world's weightiest death—first
The piety, then the *pietá*—she
Standing there twice with burden in her arms.
For this (though she banned me) I twice kiss the ground
(Though sullenly) where she stood.
    "You, once our bewitcher—"
Now your witch;
My mud crown crueler than his thorns. Don't judge
My Olympus by underground Venusberg.
    "No overground queendom?"
Soon, soon, when my beauty and Mary's
Crisscross with equal pride.
    "Meanwhile your hide-out was—?"
The other Mary.
Till she lost him. Next day I went underground.
      (Aphrodite: *Form,* then you)
I, lowliest now, I scorn your highest who've
No time for time.
Bloom is serene explosion; you blast the slow
Unfold of things.
Impertinence of leaves to root:
Merely the fact that you're so many of you
Is smirk for plague's macabre dance to cure.
From goats that gods in heat have rubbed against,
From noon-struck thickets horned with shaggy hints,
An ancientness of pipings laughs at you.
You geld your satyrs or glut them; twice wrong—attune!
Face, face and hug your formless shivering chaos
Warm into form, Ionia's
                strict wild dance.
Gardening their wishes, terrace over terrace,
Our vineyard children knew: what counts is levels.
Your lusts—don't dare call them lusty—they're inner snigger.
Poison for you: the wine without the wine-god,
Our naked freedom without our
                   formal dance.
    "Form, form—I hate it. How can cramped pond become your
    Foamed ocean?"
Ponds, being form-dense, are bigger than mere oceans.
The foaming I'm born of is wetter than both.

"What made form's pond birth's ocean. Foamborn,
How—why—are you here?"

(Aphrodite huddling against painted ocean backdrop: *The Ripple at Cythera*)[2]

Blue silence. Thickening. Then the long slow ripple.
The waves lobbed one shared language at the headlands.
Who'd guess a girl-child's relevance to harvests?
Yet the nudged beach quivered
A consternation of tiptoe herons;
Though dawn still was pallid,
Wind swayed a wheatfield of wakening nipples.
And from the shorelines up the dunes, a rumor:
'With muffled fins a saboteur has landed.'
But no, not fins; only a calcified Oh,
A nothing, a housed echo. Who'd guess pulse there?
The first boy who pocketed the first
Seashell, knapsack of wounds,
Was smuggling inland the singing birthpangs,
Staining the dry hills with droned foam.
Calamitous blessing,
What sterner sweetness once walked a loveless earth?
Do elms hoard reveries from feverless ages
Before that flabbergasting lilt was born?
No land-sound but was changed forever after,
Rubbing with a new reverberation
The sheens of bloom, the taffetas of wind,—
Riddling the rhythms of the works of man
With added resonance of
Undertow.

(you: mortal's *Invocation to Aphrodite*)

"Undertow,
You other blue,
Tow us to you.
Came sky; in upside-down of sky, there loured
Undertow.
Came Greek year, form held only what a port can
Of undertow.
Came Gothic year and Abelard gored; yet somewhere
Lurked undertow.
Rococo came, pink pudge depilatoried;
Yet undertow.

Queened, demoned, pseudo-tamed, renamed, there always
Was undertow.
Lines of the straighteners, grids of nerves and subways,
Are coming; indestructible below
Is undertow.
Us, goddess, too,
Swerve not too late from where we hurtle to;
Sway up unearned—for us who earn the arson—
The olive too."
        (Aphrodite vanishes. You alone, still partly under her spell.)
"Christ's lips are dry; my sweet wine slakes them wet.
Pan's eyes are dry; my tear-salt aches them wet.
A god can learn from a man;
Half knows only half:
Tears and compassionate pain
Or carousal and passionate laugh."
        (son, entering, then you)
None but your saltsweet earth-race grows
From strict brows
                wild goat-grace.
"Will it storm us the heavenly city?"
When the village below binds fast
A Pan who finds out about pity
And a Jew-god drunk at last.
"Each flawed alone?"—Myself too sober-paced.
"Then why not rites of spring? Fauns giddy-faced?"
In statues grand, in life a bit inane.
"Too frisky?"—Fluffed. No ballast of human-scale pain.
"What makes two rival god-lies true for us?"
Crisscross.

      •   •   •

"I'd said, 'I must duel near water'—
'Water,' I, earthling, called.
I'm yanked to the brink of land's border—
The brine in me yanked by the salt."
The showdown with the Showman must end where the show began:
Land's End again.
"But what can I win there?"—You're now on your own,
My errand done.
"Far sea mist. Thickening nearer. How face Land's End

Without you?"—DON'T RUN. Stand
Where first you landed with fraying fins,
Gasping for breath ever since.
"The blue too gray, the wind too wet."
Just right for showdown at shoreline.
"No gods to the rescue?"—The loving ones chain you with love.
And now good-bye at the edge you were always at.—*"Wait!*
What's left of lamb-goat crisscross if you shake
Me off?"
When the great contraries claim you, take
Over. Twine.

> (Son, hereafter unheard from, vanishes through side curtain. Enter angry father, jarred from sleep and wearing old dressing gown of frayed constellations.)

Earsplitting binge downstairs; some wise-guy
Hollering up—and at this late hour—'old Lizard Eye.'
Is my meddling son inciting the apes again?
What half-assed joke, what half-brained—
"Half-selved. When meddler's lost half gets regained
And he need meddle no more and I'm on my own—"
From a god who's a dartboard, what can you gain?
"The one nailed carpenter made all nails vain."

> (father with arms outstretched toward side curtain)

Sky child, for man's sake traitor, whom I begot:
Sharing all the world's burdens, how could you forget
Mine?—the stern must-it-be-yes-it-must
That gnaws my grin the way my red gnaws green.
Almost I envy dust each groan
It shares between gate and gate.

> (you facing same empty side curtain)

"Was my clown-lamb spirit or gut?
I heard a seashell hum
That it takes a sea queen coming home
To make dust loam, to make lamb goat.
Or was it Eve strolled by my door last week,
Spitting apple pits?—new orchards in her wake.
Jericho falls when—on my grave—I waltz."
Not quite. It's time for our seaside walk.

> (Reversing time to regain control, father now confidently replays the opening "Duel on Land's End." Time: same Allhallows Eve. Place: same bleak seaside meadow. You, then father.)

"Tunes warmer on winds waywarder than others
When from the frozen graves the marshfires glow,
Bring me—."—A three-step from your fathers' fathers.
Against them, you need what I've lent you, your armor of snow.
"Snow round my heart? Snow against rain?"
My winter protects; grow is foe.
"Maybe we two are the foes. Having. It. Out. On
Land's End."—Land's start. Where my million-year showdown with man
Began. . . . Time to end. Your tombed fathers—
"Fathers no more, my faced selves now"—
Are melting your armor—/—"that now I don't need."
Without it, seed grows—/—"already the meadow less yellow"—
Grows amok in the end.
"This time, green's not formless but gardened.
And when, tomorrow, vine's garland—"
These Bacchic spooks you follow, mists they borrow,
Are Rorschach blurs to tease forth selves you bury.
They're Hallowe'en tricksters to harry you; run from the meadow.
"Claws below; breaking through."—RUN; wildness is loose;
Why are you standing?—"Loose? Wildness is freed
To serve
          form's strictest
                    offbeat."
Whose?
"When the hacked joins the nailed, then my arrow—"
My meathooked sky is still your fate.
Green's out of fashion.
"When spring brings back two, not one—"
Don't try to pull two rabbits from old-hat Easter's hat.
"Don't try to distract me by playing a stand-up-comic Mephisto."

(Enter from east a shimmering shape-changing stranger, now satyr, now Pan, now vine. Father and you stare at him through mist.)

Look: who's that dancing . . . kicking dust at sky?
"Here—last time—a gull watched the meadow."
I see . . . odd . . . footprints.—"Yet gestures of my village."
He gibbers odd tongues.—"Yet accents of my village."
Who knows him?—"Known in my marrow."
No dreamscape of classic myth. Look up: real jets.
"Look down: Jerusalem's palms, strewn in homage
Before a leopard-pulled wheelbarrow."³

Cats on a cart. An outer mirage
Your inner mirage begets.
"If I see what I see, the whole world's so narrow
That Land's End is every guy's village."
If it's no ghost, then almost—
"Now two of him, one pale, one noon-tanned—"
Then marrow's bow could almost launch an arrow.
"Two shapes — no, one shape — kicking dust and
Loam at sky."
Warmed lifelike by her who came home, he's only your shadow.
"A shadow who sweats?"
Well, then he's only—/—*"I see—"*
Some wino who swigs—/—*"I see*
Hacked hands; no, pierced—" /—no, mere vine twigs.
"Serene pierced hands . . . bending cross into crossbow.
Look: goatfoot Jesus on the village green."

4. Epilogue: Prologue to New Spiral

(you, casually hanging your cap on ceiling meathook)

> *"Toys don't know they're toys.*
> *Now that we do, we're not.*
> *A thing and not a thing.*
> *A circle AND a Dot."*

(father, turning his back on you and facing audience with bored voice of an old pro)

Somebody had to keep the show on the road.
Am I accountable to stage-props? Tell your lamb
All rounds are simultaneous to sky and
Down. I am that I am.

NOTES

1. Goat: animal associated with the Eros instinct and with satyrs, Pan, and occasionally Dionysus. Even today, Dionysus is celebrated with goat horns and goat feet on the Greek island of Skyros. In the anti-pagan Middle Ages, goats were associated with the devil and with witch orgies.

2. Spawned by the sea from the fallen semen of Zeus, the love goddess first landed—out of a seashell—at Cythera (according to another legend, at Cyprus). "Aphros" is Greek for "foam."

3. Palms were strewn before Christ in Jersualem. Dionysus was drawn by harnessed leopards.

Persephone and Old Poet

(Her "Tide" dialogue was with Dionysus. The present dialogue is with a mortal. Her voice: always in quotes and italics.)

Sections

I heard the footfall of her flowering spring.
> —Sappho, hailing shuttling Persephone as spring-bringer

The ambivalence of Kore [Persephone], promise of salvation or bride of death.
> —Charles Siegal, *Tragedy and Civilization*

I. Prologue

Our three-note prologue: 'out,' 'go,' 'me,'
The same three line-ends, twined throughout
Around your name, Persephone.
　　"A 'rime riche' lilting cargo."
Lilt rising as mist. Mist steamy with god wraith. Ergo
A temple of spring. . . . Or else a projection of me,
A shrine called 'wishful thinking,' my own altered ego.
　　"Your altar-ego."
At least I'm not that wine-god of yours, that go-go
Gigolo. . . . Or does he wear me
As mask? Or I him? Each other inside out.
Who wears whom? It's touch-and-go.
　　"It's back-and-forth. Accept ambiguity; shimmy.
　　Many players. Three rôles only: Pluto and me
　　Plus wine-god. . . . Or plus you? His ventriloquized dummy?"
I can't be a puppet; after all, isn't it me
Who's right now writing this verse-play? Call me
A very mortal geezer with lumbago,

Half trampled leaf, half arrogant hidalgo,
Confronting you head-on. Having it out.
>   *"So many of you poets imagine me*
>   *So many ways. I'm opposites canceling out."*
Your eyes: now gray, now indigo.
>   *"My hair: now green, now red. My lingo:*
>   *Now Anglo, now Greek argot."*
Even your pulse: now petering out,
Now bongo drums à la Congo.
>   *"Even my thoughts: now shrewd, now gaga farrago."*
What happens to crops if you—um, er—go barmy?
>   *"Tough luck for them, not me.*
>   *Oblivion is what they'd undergo."*
While you blubber with Ceres, your mommy.
>   *"You're more manipulative than Iago.*
>   *I'd ban your word-tricks with a stern embargo."*
Where are they now, your clammy
Sycophants, your smarmy
High priests of long ago?
>   *"I time the seasons just by being me."*
Your earth-ball's a rotting mango,
Your flora a bankrupt economy.
'Persephone' means '*per-se*-phoney.'
>   *"I'm not some bogus West Coast swami*
>   *But from Aegean archipelago."*
Hiding what secrets in your hide-out?
>   *"Plenty. But only one I'll now blurt out:*
>   *Your younger hands, the time they fondled me*
>   *(It wasn't long, and it was long ago),*
>   *Woke spring too soon. By driving winter out*
>   *In winter, you gave my calendar vertigo.*
>   *I balance earth's income and outgo.*
>   *Wrong rhythm freaks her out."*
It was December. That month is my personal enemy.
April/virgo. December/virago.
>   *"The wheel relentless and the tempo largo."*
Your wheel-clock pieties are cockamamie;
I wilt; the sandglass sandbagged me.
Yet I'll re-sculpt you, statuesque Persephone.
>   *"Your hands, your hands, I wish they'd fondled me*

To death. But death's a trip we gods forgo."
Pout in some Parthenon, some marble cop-out.
Only we dust-heaps thaw out.
    "Brief lives love warmer; 'fadeless' is my logo;
    I need you faders to unstatue me.
    I've used up lots of frogs without
    Kissing forth a prince. None ever, ever thawed me."
Gross bullfrogs croak your name as 'Pussy-phone-me.'
    "Though godly and though biped, I'm no jingo
    For gods or men. Wise plants—vines, grass—entice me.
    At bedtime, flower beds suffice me.
    The way gold's shipped by Brinks and by Wells Fargo,
    I transport pollen—in transports of joy, June's epitome."
Are bees your rôle-model 'imago'?
Swat them, and join my stately old-age tango.
    "Unstately! Age is a spastic fandango
    (Flayed of all dignity) towards your Penelope,
    Your waiting grave-hole. Tell her 'Open Sesame.'"
Persephone, here's what you share with me:
Inedible both, you marbly, I soon wormy.
    "I hate you—O you did thaw me,
    My prince, my prince, but in the wrong season—get out."

II. Calendar

Kaleidoscoped by snow's, lawn's, mud's
Collage, you're the chameleon of their moods.
    "I serve the wheel. Blame it, not me for seasons."
Guilty of innocence.
    "I'm freeze, I'm thaw, I'm many everythings at once.
    Drown me for sorcery? My dyings nourish me.
    Or shrine my nursery? I couldn't care less."
Dizzy with circlings: the dervishing goddess.
Your future, being an elastic cord
Umbilic to prehistory, snaps backward.
Where to? Your past I can't foresee.
    "Snows bloom hot rosebuds at my toes.
    I tread ripe roses into snows.
    The tenth muse hymned my footprints.[1]
    My feet, foot-fetished ever since,

Caress the dust you've been, the dust you'll be."
You take too much. Not just my life. Your spring
Steals even my dying.
　　"I take, I bring."

　　　　　• • •

You have a small, sadly complicated smile.
It hurts my Adam's apple painlessly. While
You walk Cerberus down Main Street, colors deepen.
Where you go jogging, pear trees ripen.
Your kidnapping at Enna[2] is a three-hankie sitcom.
Then why, gentlest daughter of earthmom,
Why do they call you 'deadly Persephone,' 'the maiden
Whose name may not be spoken'?[3]
Why do you—why do tropics—alarm me?
　　"I'm the menacing vibes of sprout. I untame
　　The plants from which the animals came. My name
　　Is spoken when the southwind speaks."
No pillow except the river-loam has such soft cheeks.
Hold tight my animal paw and pillow me home.

　　　　　• • •

　　"I sow to reap. I reap you to resow.
　　Reaping, I feel a sweet murderous sorrow.
　　I mean, unmurderous, making growth grow.
　　Sun giddies my earth park
　　With light packed so dense it's dark."
I'm not your goatboy. I'm your outdated lyre.
　　"I'm not your free god of Greek lore.
　　The frost I jail is my jailer.
　　Yours too. For all your valor,
　　You feel the lure of Pluto's lair.
　　Disguised in April's color,
　　The cross-dressed 'Indian' summer
　　Of fall has scalped both you and me."
It's you who invented November.
　　"Not alone. Complicitous we."

III. Hex

"All you leaves rotate like ducks in a shooting gallery.
Each round you pop back merrily."
My atoms do. Not my me. Are you really
The voltage called 'life'? Say!
"Not that dead cliché."
Then what's reality anyway?
"It's what, when you don't believe in it, won't go away."
Then just who are you?
"When you pin down
Quicksilver, guess what's gone."
Your 'what' is gone most far right here.
"In fall you'll feel my absence all too . . . near."
What sign rewarms the waning year?
"Moon's other tide,
The girl-tide males can't know.
An ancient Thracian puberty rite
Scrawls lap's red signature on snow.
In the calendar of harvest, year's hormone
Of thaw and month's Etna are one."
That's hex. Hex isn't so.
"Your un-so is my so.
It takes a cycle to hex a cycle,
A flow to reverse a flow."
Some lava flows backward; Act One is Five's sequel.
Nine coffins munch,[4] nine newborns suckle.
The hand that rocks the cradle, swings fall's sickle.
Nine straight lines bend full circle.
"The way Olympus's voluptuaries
Chase woodnymph quarries, I chase death-chasing-birth
And balance both.
Faster. The chase can't stop for breath.
In twigs, in veins: my sap, my broth.
Pluto I kick out of bedroom's berth.
Red leaves I give a green bath."
For humans, what gift from your topside booth?
"A verb with two meanings (for pelvis, for shoulder):
'Bear.'"

IV. Mending

You tyrant giantess, the globe your footstool,
Are tyrannized by the small, the rule
Of fern, azalea, feather, toadstool.
> *"Yes, motes most finite rule my rôle:*
> *Starlings, not stars. Birds know they fall.*
> *Not stars: these twitching fireflies,*
> *Strung on the spider web of skies.*
> *My shuttle's not stellar, it's local.*
> *Stars are a moron infinity.*
> *There's just one orb where pain's hot coal*
> *Becomes—by knowing—musical.*
> *Where leaf rhymes brief. Where grief is lyrical.*
> *Where the first red leaf makes you brieflings exalt yet recoil—*
> *And makes me yearn to feel woundable, not godly.*
> *The invulnerable can see—but not make—beauty.*
> *Music is something I cannot make but can be.*
> *Your wounds I can't feel, but the music I am makes them vocal.*
> *'Mend us,' I hear you lifelings call and call."*
The music you are is my death-row musicale.
> *"The row where sour notes are protocol.*
> *The condemned man ate a hearty gall."*
I feed on leftovers when white hairs shackle.
> *"Young lion, old jackal."*
I'm yanked by ebb's receding crackle.
> *"That's only half my chronicle.*
> *I cull the garden to garden it, not kill.*
> *The frond gone frayed, the hearth gone cool*
> *I mend. For a while."*
> > Then what?
> *"The last note is peace. Except that it's not."*

V. Chore

What I can't excuse: good earth made gushy by 'earthy'
('Ah nest, ah nurse'): art parodied by arty.
'Earthy' is litcrit earth, not Mater, not even pater,
But Walter Pater.
> *"Peccavi, Pater, but I've no time for*

Earth gush, only for earth chore.
My eons pass quicker than hours."
My hours, your eons, an equally brief midge-dance,
Compared to these star spans:
The wing span of Ouranos[5] over the light-years of Chronos.
"Because no other globe makes motes aware,
Earth remains the pre-Copernican center.
On earth one hand-squeeze outspans galaxies."
Your 'earth chores'? Trifles! While stars spin round and round
At miracle-speeds with too many zeroes to count.
"But meanwhile nipples, frail as wings of moths,
Scrawl vaster miracles on newborn mouths."
But after 'ah nest, ah nurse,' you've icy aftermaths:
Like the heads they shrink on the Amazon,
A wizened sun squints wan.
"Downed leaves fall up. Downed seeds rebound.
My mother Ceres—"
                                        —couldn't stop his rape; all moms
Cry 'April, April' during Pluto's months.
Tears can't make wheels less round.
"'Trifles' of earth loom larger later:
From the first pond-froths of life to sidereal behemoths."
Whiz-kid astronomers or Magna mater:
Two myths that measure rival maths.
"Astros? They're bratsy voyeurs—they poke at stars
With horny stares as if at her apertures.
Yes, brats. With pathetic taut organs called telescopes. Comic,
Not cosmic. Pure sci isn't pure."
Nor's Mater. To nudge renewing,
To make rebirth recur:
No manicure of T. L. Care,
Only the mess of growing.
Outwitting Pluto, death's epicure,
With 'April!' her *cri de coeur*,
She plops—replaying Act One—
A mutt on a butt-wiggling cur:
A ray-spurting yellow-furred sun
On a bitch-in-heat called 'spring.'
"You talk so dainty—be my Valentine."

Sarcastic sugar (my darling Clementine)
Won't solve our clash of myths.
>   *"Merge clashing monoliths: one juggernaut cart*
>   *Rolled irresistably.*
>   *Then days of magic, even to me a mystery,*
>   *Start. Days of fact depart."*
Turning point. Which turn brings cure?
>   *"How. probe. tide's. core?"*

VI. Medusa

How will it feel (what onrush of joy-scare,
In trumpet-blare what craze of hush?)
On the day you unwrap your blaze?
O Persephone, O Persephone, I know we then won't hear
Have-a-nice-day from food marts; there'll rear
Angels and eagles from food carts, there'll roar
Wolf cubs we taught to coo. Be
Your inmost self. Don't be so slow to be.
>   *"I've run through gamuts, and the gamuts stay.*
>   *All veils are different pasts. The pasts all stay.*
>   *My veils became skin-grafts—they're me.*
>   *Isn't that why there isn't a me?*
>   *I'm all the shadows the campfires kept at bay."*
You're a game of connect-the-dots. When I connect will I see,
As I freeze into icy stone, Medusa-Persephone?
>   *"Don't you already? Don't you go numb*
>   *Each autumn?"*
Like you, like you, I melt snow.
Not with your blood but my ink-talk.
Whatever I rhyme, I desecrate—into
Rekindled ember; this petal, that stalk,
The brittle glow of white birch bent double by winter.
(Sweet grandeur-delusions, don't let these lines, this wonder
Be writ-in-water.)
>   *"You're one with the light on birch bark;*
>   *I've many an elsewhere to wander.*
>   *I rotate freeze/swelter. You bee-line whence/whither.*
>   *I'm whirler, you're walker."*
You living pendulum, you piroutte of weather,

Your wheatfields rippled by gusty air,
Your ivies trailing like racer's hair,
Your belly-dance wobbling your hills in landscape's welter.
  "Wheel being law, I'm wheel's wheeler."
Wheel back till I meet not corrupt Medusa-Persephone
But young you: before you went two-timing summer and winter.
  "Corrupt gods are wiser. We falling gods rebuke
  Heights. My dirty street-smarts bake
  Buds out of deserts, a cornucopian wafer,
  A lizard trick of limb-regrowing comeback."
Again be Enna's unspoilt flower-wreather.
In these myth-debunk days, you're a has-been in a book.
Mortals die fast, immortals die faster. Who's worthier?
  "I know who's wordier."
Goddess and bard are each a lasting watcher.
Who outlasts whom, there's the wager.
  "Your hubris bloats weirder. I'm wider, you're waner.
  A shuttler's no wilter. You wither."
I wither. Into music. Though you balk,
Are not these very lines (which magic is winner?)
My Perseus mirror against your Gorgon gawk?

VII. Epilogue: My Future Prologue

I start a fresh new life today.
  "Fresh for a day."
I now trust only the fumblers, the shabby, the unsure,—
My lungfish great grandpa who first (out of sheer
Absent-mindedness) fumbled to shore.
  "Being so human-scale mortal, so mortally human,
  You cheer just a half-cheer for man."
Like you, I now trust the stained biology-tree
(With branching veins we're each a walking tree),
Not stainless-steel geometry.
  "A straight line is the longest distance between two points."
And the bloodiest. Progress disappoints.
Fear perfect system.
  "So seven decades taught you one thing new,
  What my flukey weather always knew:
  Systemlessness as system."

With preference for outdated deep foundations,
Dark seedbeds that the sterile light of day shuns.
    "Like Ovid among Dacians,[6]
    The old are exiled from the wine called warmth.
    Last leaves droop.
    For what are you waiting before you go drop?"
For the unlikely chance of unexplainable warmth.

       •   •   •

All my unlikely trek from From to To,
Rung over rung as eons sped,
The Bang I squirreled my atoms from,
The rogue amoeba that split in two,
The green gang whose oxygen-drug I got high with
(Speeding me faster than 'speed'),[7]
The soup I just happened to chin myself from,
The brow-bulge baby I Darwined to
(Through hips that I browbeat to widen their width),[8]
Even my Homer-Shakespeare-etc. occident:
All's accident.
Right now my accidental new start starts.

       •   •   •

    "Though hooked fish twitch, ends—ends!—aren't starts.
    No more Chronos coins in your till."
Before frost's subpoena, I've Unda Marina—
The foamborn's arena—to till.
    "Always another last 'last' voyage. Until."
I'll pay the piper, but I'll write the tune.
I'll reach—through storms of Neptune—
Love's island. Port or scam?
Or is it the silent cypress island,
The one port that never is sham?
    "Still always cypress against Cyprian."[9]
The singer topples, but his songs still scan.
    "Which lodestar guides you west, what siren-chants?"
I've no guides at all. Only unrest and chance.
    "That's like shooting rapids by rowboat.
    Going 'west' means not only Hesperides, but."
Isn't that what 'chance' is about?
    "How come a few of you neo-lungfish rebut

The odds and live to reach
That accident-beach? With highbrow apes as heirs."
Maybe some accidents are less accidental than others.

• • •

"What resource remains from our past?"
Remorse. Two groped and passed.
"One fell. What cure can befall
Humpty Dumpty?"
—A deeper fall.
"What cures your crashed head's headache?"
A warm fall into heartbreak.
"Take care: you might fall into lit—
As grist for nitwit litcrit."
Enough (out there, there's frostbite) of smart art.
I won't let down my heliotropic heart.
For Attis and his knife, no antidote.
"It took you a whole botched lifetime to indict
Your heart's starvation diet."
Unexplainable warmth is now my blind date.
"On your daft trip to your last redoubt,
Take half my blessing along—and all my doubt.
Because I dote on you so, I'd stay for a quickie duet
If, if.
The wheel won't let me do it."

• • •

Ordained by no genes, ordained by no stars
(What causes causation?), my voyage starts.
"I can't listen longer, must mend a bruised starling,
But I'll hear—far off—your sadness when you're sad."
What most needs saying is said
Never. . . . Now winds overhead
Call me. Abysses are staring.
These are sly codes I must heed.
"Your voice shows (I know you) you're writing some startling
New play. Who is starring?"
Fluke, needed fluke, is my argonaut, steering
To where new mess, new growingness is stirring.
"Launchings need power; your power's worn out.
You've not the spare parts of a robot."

My knack of fumbling empowers both heart and head.
   "I almost believe in you. But."
My riskiest launching—full speed ahead!—
(Well, half speed) is starting, is starting.
   "Brief humans, my eons still can't figure you out."

(1995)

NOTES

1. Cf. the opening Sappho epigraph about footfall.

2. Persephone, daughter of the crop goddess Ceres, was a young virgin picking flowers in the field of Enna when Pluto dragged her below to become his half-year winter bride.

3. W. Pater: "Dreadful Persephone, the goddess of destruction and death." E. Hamilton: "Persephone was the radiant maiden of spring . . . But after the lord of the dark world carried her away, there was something strange and awesome about her . . . said to be 'the maiden whose name may not be spoken.'"

4. In Greek, sarcophagus literally means flesh eater.

5. Ouranos (accent on first syllable): the sky god. Chronos: time.

6. Exiled by Augustus from Rome to cold Dacia (today Rumania), Ovid complained bitterly of the lack of drinkable wines.

7. "Speed": street slang for the very energizing drug amphetamine, often peddled illegally. The photosynthesis of early green plants, such as algae, speeded up earth's oxygen and hence evolution.

8. Natural selection widened women's hips to accommodate the wider gray matter of the brow-bulge baby. The thin-hipped died in childbirth. Brains cost dear.

9. Böcklin's painting of funereal cypresses, entitled "Toteninsel" (Isle of the Dead), was much admired by Nietzsche and Stefan George. Here it is contrasted with unfunereal Cyprus, the island in some legends (Cythera in others) of Aphrodite-Aphrogeneia, Greek for foamborn. Already in Homer, she is Kypris ("Cyprian," later misused for prostitute).

Select Bibliography

Prose Books

Meta-Politics: From the Romantics to Hitler. Hardcover (out of print with Knopf), New York, 1941.

Meta-Politics: The Roots of the Nazi Mind. G. Putnam Sons, Capricorn paperback, New York, 1965. Out of print.

Conservatism Revisited: The Revolt against Revolt. British hardcover edition, Preface by Sir Duff Cooper, London, 1950, out of print (available only from author).

Conservatism Revisited and the New Conservatism: What Went Wrong? Macmillan Free Press Paperback, New York, 1956, out of print. Reprinted in hardcover by Greenwood Press, 88 Post Road West, Westport, Connecticut 06881, 1978.

Dream and Responsibility: Test Cases of the Tension between Poetry and Society. Hardcover and paperback, University Press of Washington, D.C., 1953, Library of Congress card number 53-12584. Out of print.

Shame and Glory of the Intellectuals: Babbitt Jr. Versus the Rediscovery of Values. G. Putnam Sons, Capricorn paperback, New York, 1965, out of print; reprinted by Greenwood, 1978, with supplement on "The Radical Right: From McCarthy to Goldwater."

Conservatism from John Adams to Churchill: A History and Anthology. Greenwood Press, 1978, hardcover reprint of the out-of-print 1956 Van Nostrand edition.

The Unadjusted Man: Reflections on the Distinction between Conserving and Conforming. Hardcover reprint of 1956 Beacon Press edition. Greenwood Press, Westport, Connecticut, 1973.

"Conservatism." A long historical monograph in the 15th edition, 1979–1986, of the *Encyclopedia Britannica.*

Strict Wildness: Prose about Poetry. Publisher to be announced, 1996.

Poetry Books

Terror and Decorum. Awarded Pulitzer Prize for poetry. Hardcover, Greenwood Press, Westport, Connecticut, 1972 reprint of out-of-print 1948 Scribner's edition.

Strike through the Mask: New Lyrical Poems. Hardcover, Greenwood Press, 1972 reprint of out-of-print 1950 Scribner's edition.

The First Morning. Hardcover, Greenwood Press, 1972 reprint of out-of-print 1952 Scribner's edition.

The Persimmon Tree: New Lyrics and Pastorals. Hardcover, University Microfilms, Ann Arbor, Michigan. Reprint of out-of-print 1956 Scribner's edition.

New and Selected Poems, 1932–1967. Hardcover, selections from five books with frontispiece by the Spanish painter Fernando Zobel, 1967 first edition, Bobbs-Merrill, New York, out of print. 1980 reprint available from University

Microfilms, 300 North Zeeb Road, Ann Arbor, Michigan 48106 or 30 Mortimer Street, London, England WIN 7RA.

Archer in the Marrow: The Applewood Cycles of 1967–1987. Hardcover $14.55, Paper $6.95; W.W. Norton Company, New York, New York, 1987.

Tide and Continuities: Last and First Poems, 1995–1938, with a preface in verse by Joseph Brodsky. University of Arkansas Press, Fayetteville, Arkansas, 1995.

Transplantings: Stefan George and Georg Heym, Englished and Analyzed: With Reflections on Modern Germany, on Poetry, and on the Craft of Translation. Work in progress for 1996.

Verse Drama

The Tree Witch. Staged 1961 by the Poets Theater at Harvard University's Loeb Theater. Hardcover, verse drama, Greenwood Press, Westport, Connecticut, 1973, a reprint of out-of-print 1961 Scribner's edition.

OpComp. A modern medieval miracle play, work in progress for 1996.

Book about Peter Viereck

Peter Viereck, Historian and Poet. Marie Henault. Hardcover, Twayne Press, New York, 1969; Paperback, College and University Press, New Haven, Connecticut, 1971. Both out of print.